NoSQL Essentials: Navigating the World of Non-Relational Databases

Kameron Hussain and Frahaan Hussain

Published by Sonar Publishing, 2024.

NOSQL ESSENTIALS: NAVIGATING THE WORLD OF NON-RELATIONAL DATABASES

First edition. January 29, 2024.

ISBN: 979-8223209027

Written by Kameron Hussain and Frahaan Hussain.

Table of Contents

Chapter 1: Introduction to NoSQL

1.1 Understanding the Basics of NoSQL

The Need for NoSQL

Categories of NoSQL Databases

Conclusion

1.2 The Evolution of Database Technology: From SQL to NoSQL

The SQL Era

The Rise of NoSQL

The NoSQL Revolution

1.3 Key Characteristics of NoSQL Databases

1. Schema Flexibility

2. NoSQL Data Models

3. Horizontal Scalability

4. NoSQL Querying

5. CAP Theorem

6. Scalability Challenges

7. Use Cases

1.4 Types of NoSQL Databases: An Overview

1. Document-Oriented Databases

2. Key-Value Stores

3. Column-Family Stores

4. Graph Databases

5. Multi-Model Databases

6. Time-Series Databases

7. In-Memory Databases

1.5 Advantages and Use Cases of NoSQL

Advantages of NoSQL Databases

Use Cases of NoSQL Databases

Chapter 2: NoSQL Database Types

2.1 Document-Oriented Databases Explained

Key Features of Document-Oriented Databases

Advantages of Document-Oriented Databases

Common Use Cases

Document-Oriented Database Examples

2.2 Key-Value Stores: Concepts and Applications

Key Features of Key-Value Stores

Advantages of Key-Value Stores

Common Use Cases

Key-Value Store Examples

2.3 Column-Family Stores: Structure and Utility

Key Features of Column-Family Stores

Advantages of Column-Family Stores

Common Use Cases

Column-Family Store Examples

2.4 Graph Databases: Understanding Relationships

Key Features of Graph Databases

Advantages of Graph Databases

Common Use Cases

Graph Database Examples

2.5 Choosing the Right Type of NoSQL Database

Factors to Consider When Choosing a NoSQL Database

Common NoSQL Database Selection Scenarios

Evaluating NoSQL Database Solutions

Chapter 3: Core Concepts in NoSQL

3.1 Data Modeling in NoSQL

Understanding Data Modeling

Key Considerations in NoSQL Data Modeling

Data Modeling in Different NoSQL Database Types

Practical Tips

3.2 Understanding NoSQL Schemas

Traditional Relational Database Schemas

NoSQL Database Schema Flexibility

Advantages of NoSQL Schema Flexibility

Considerations with NoSQL Schemas

3.3 Indexing in NoSQL Databases

Understanding Indexing

Indexing in Traditional Relational Databases

Indexing in NoSQL Databases

Importance of Indexing in NoSQL Databases

3.4 CAP Theorem and NoSQL

CAP Theorem Basics

CAP Theorem Trade-offs

Implications for NoSQL Databases

Practical Considerations

3.5 Consistency, Availability, and Partition Tolerance

Consistency (C)

Availability (A)

Partition Tolerance (P)

CAP Trade-offs in NoSQL Databases

Configurable Consistency Levels

Monitoring and Tuning

Chapter 4: Implementing NoSQL Solutions

4.1 Setting Up a NoSQL Database

Choose the Right NoSQL Database

Installation and Deployment

Configuration and Initialization

Data Modeling and Schema Design

Data Ingestion

Testing and Optimization

Backups and Disaster Recovery

Monitoring and Maintenance

4.2 CRUD Operations in NoSQL

Create (Insert) Operations

Read Operations

Update Operations

Delete Operations

Consistency Considerations

4.3 Querying in NoSQL Databases

Document-Oriented Databases

Key-Value Stores

Column-Family Stores

Graph Databases

Consistency and Query Performance

Indexing

Distributed Querying

Query Optimization

4.4 Data Migration to NoSQL

Why Data Migration?

Data Modeling

Data Transformation

Data Extraction

Data Loading

Data Validation

Testing and Rollback

Monitoring and Optimization

Data Synchronization

Challenges and Considerations

4.5 Best Practices in NoSQL Implementation

1. Understand Your Data and Use Case

2. Plan Your Data Model Carefully

3. Normalize or Denormalize as Appropriate

4. Optimize Queries

5. Implement Security Measures

6. Backup and Disaster Recovery

7. Monitor Performance

8. Scaling Strategies

9. Consider Data Consistency Levels

10. Data Compression and Caching

11. Regular Updates and Maintenance

12. Data Migration Strategies

13. Documentation and Training

14. Plan for Failures

15. Consider the Cloud

16. Compliance and Regulations

17. Regularly Review and Optimize

Chapter 5: NoSQL and Big Data

5.1 The Role of NoSQL in Big Data

Characteristics of Big Data

Challenges of Traditional Databases

How NoSQL Addresses Big Data Challenges

Use Cases of NoSQL in Big Data

NoSQL and Big Data Technologies

5.2 Handling Large Scale Data with NoSQL

Distributed Architecture

Data Partitioning

CAP Theorem and Trade-Offs

Caching and In-Memory Databases

Parallel Processing and MapReduce

Compression and Data Serialization

Monitoring and Auto-Scaling

5.3 NoSQL for Real-Time Analytics

Characteristics of Real-Time Analytics

NoSQL Databases for Real-Time Analytics

Use Cases of NoSQL in Real-Time Analytics

Components of Real-Time Analytics Systems

Real-Time Analytics with NoSQL Example

5.4 Integration with Big Data Technologies

Big Data Ecosystem

Benefits of Integrating NoSQL with Big Data

Integration Strategies

Example of Integration

5.5 Case Studies: NoSQL in Big Data Applications

1. Airbnb: Scaling with Apache Cassandra

2. Netflix: Real-Time Analytics with Apache Kafka and Cassandra

3. Uber: Managing Geospatial Data with Redis

4. Twitter: Analyzing Social Media Trends with HBase

5. Facebook: Handling Graph Data with Apache TinkerPop and Gremlin

Chapter 6: NoSQL and Scalability

6.1 Understanding Scalability in NoSQL

What is Scalability?

Types of Scalability

Challenges in Scalability

6.2 Horizontal vs. Vertical Scaling

Horizontal Scaling

Vertical Scaling

Choosing Between Horizontal and Vertical Scaling

6.3 Auto-Scaling Capabilities in NoSQL

What is Auto-Scaling?

Benefits of Auto-Scaling in NoSQL Databases:

How Auto-Scaling Works in NoSQL Databases:

Considerations for Implementing Auto-Scaling:

6.4 Scalability Challenges in NoSQL

1. Data Distribution and Sharding:

2. Data Consistency:

3. Query Optimization:

4. Network Latency:

5. Load Balancing:

6. Data Backups and Recovery:

7. Resource Management:

8. Schema Evolution:

9. Security:

6.5 Case Studies: Scalability Solutions

1. Netflix: Managing Massive Streaming Data

2. Uber: Handling Real-Time Geospatial Data

3. Instagram: Supporting Rapid Growth

4. Amazon Web Services (AWS): Scaling for Cloud Services

5. Twitter: Handling Real-Time Tweets

Chapter 7: NoSQL and Security

7.1 Security Challenges in NoSQL Databases

1. Authentication and Authorization:

2. Data Encryption:

3. Injection Attacks:

4. Data Exposure:

5. Denial of Service (DoS) Attacks:

6. Auditing and Compliance:

7. Secure Configuration:

8. Third-Party Dependencies:

9. Backup and Disaster Recovery:

7.2 Implementing Data Encryption

1. Encryption at Rest:

2. Encryption in Transit:

3. Application-Level Encryption:

4. Key Management:

5. Data Masking:

7.3 Access Control in NoSQL

1. Authentication:

2. Authorization:

3. Access Tokens and API Keys:

4. IP Whitelisting and Firewall Rules:

5. Audit Trails:

6. Encryption and Secure Channels:

7.4 Auditing and Compliance

1. Importance of Auditing:

2. Compliance Requirements:

3. Auditing Features:

4. Audit Trail Analysis:

5. Data Retention Policies:

6. Access Control for Audit Logs:

7. Regular Auditing and Testing:

8. Documentation and Reporting:

9. Continuous Improvement:

7.5 Best Practices for NoSQL Security

1. Role-Based Access Control (RBAC):

2. Data Encryption:

3. Authentication Mechanisms:

4. Network Security:

5. Regular Patching and Updates:

6. Backup and Disaster Recovery:

7. Audit Logging:

8. Data Minimization:

9. Incident Response Plan:

10. Security Awareness Training:

11. Third-Party Integrations:

Chapter 8: Performance Tuning in NoSQL

8.1 Analyzing NoSQL Performance

Monitoring and Metrics:

Profiling Queries:

Load Testing:

Query Optimization:

Scaling:

Caching:

Regular Maintenance:

Connection Pooling:

Distributed Database Considerations:

8.2 Optimization Techniques

Data Modeling:

Indexing:

Query Optimization:

Sharding:

Load Balancing:

Caching:

Connection Pooling:

Compression:

Parallel Processing:

Regular Maintenance:

8.3 Caching Mechanisms

The Significance of Caching:

Types of Caching:

Strategies for Effective Caching:

Caching Tools:

Sample Code (Using Redis in Python):

8.4 Balancing Read and Write Speeds

The Read-Write Trade-off:

Strategies for Balancing Read and Write Speeds:

Sample Code (Python with MongoDB):

8.5 Monitoring and Maintenance

Monitoring NoSQL Databases:

Maintenance Best Practices:

Sample Code (MongoDB Maintenance in Shell):

Chapter 9: NoSQL in the Cloud

9.1 Cloud-Based NoSQL Services

Understanding Cloud-Based NoSQL Services:

Advantages of Cloud-Based NoSQL Services:

Sample Code (Amazon DynamoDB - AWS SDK for Python):

9.2 Benefits of NoSQL in the Cloud

1. Scalability and Flexibility:

2. Cost-Efficiency:

3. Global Availability:

4. High Availability and Disaster Recovery:

5. Security and Compliance:

6. Automatic Updates and Maintenance:

7. DevOps Integration:

8. Data Analytics and Machine Learning:

9.3 Choosing a Cloud Provider for NoSQL

1. Database Compatibility:

2. Service Offerings:

3. Pricing:

4. Performance and Scalability:

5. Geographic Reach:

6. Security and Compliance:

7. Data Migration and Integration:

8. Vendor Lock-In:

9. Support and Documentation:

10. Ecosystem and Services:

11. Community and User Feedback:

12. Trial and Testing:

9.4 Migration Strategies to Cloud NoSQL

1. Assessment and Planning:

2. Data Modeling and Schema Design:

3. Backup and Disaster Recovery:

4. Data Migration Tools:

5. Gradual Migration:

6. Data Transformation and Validation:

7. Testing and Validation:

8. Rollback Plan:

9. Monitoring and Optimization:

10. Data Synchronization:

11. Security and Compliance:

12. Documentation:

13. Training and Knowledge Transfer:

14. Post-Migration Optimization:

15. Continuous Improvement:

9.5 Managing NoSQL in Cloud Environments

1. Cloud Provider Selection:

2. Service Models:

3. NoSQL Database as a Service:

4. Scalability:

5. Backup and Recovery:

6. High Availability:

7. Security:

8. Compliance:

9. Cost Optimization:

10. Performance Monitoring:

11. Automation:

12. Disaster Recovery:

13. Data Lifecycle Management:

14. Training and Skill Development:

15. Performance Optimization:

16. Cost Visibility:

17. Vendor Lock-In:

Chapter 10: NoSQL for Mobile and Web Applications

10.1 NoSQL in Mobile App Development

1. Data Synchronization:

2. Flexibility in Schema:

3. Offline Data Access:

4. Real-Time Data:

5. Scalability:

6. Performance:

7. Cross-Platform Development:

8. Use Cases:

9. Security:

10. Best Practices:

10.2 Building Scalable Web Applications with NoSQL

1. Data Distribution and Sharding:

2. Horizontal Scaling:

3. Load Balancing:

4. Caching:

5. Asynchronous Processing:

6. Event-Driven Architectures:

7. Microservices:

8. Serverless Computing:

9. Auto-Scaling:

10. Best Practices:

10.3 Real-Time Data Sync in NoSQL

1. Change Streams:

2. WebSockets:

3. Publish-Subscribe (Pub/Sub) Patterns:

4. Webhooks:

5. Event-Driven Architectures:

6. Conflict Resolution:

7. Scalability Considerations:

10.4 Offline Data Handling

1. Offline Data Storage:

2. Conflict Resolution:

3. Offline-First Architectures:

4. Data Synchronization Strategies:

5. Conflict-Free Replicated Data Types (CRDTs):

6. Progressive Web Apps (PWAs):

10.5 Case Studies: Successful NoSQL Implementations

1. E-commerce: Amazon DynamoDB

2. Social Media: Instagram's Cassandra

3. Financial Services: Goldman Sachs' ScyllaDB

4. Healthcare: UnitedHealth Group's MongoDB

5. Gaming: Riot Games' Redis

6. IoT: General Electric's InfluxDB

7. Content Management: Adobe Experience Manager's MongoDB

Chapter 11: Advanced Querying in NoSQL

Section 11.1: Complex Queries in NoSQL

Section 11.2: Aggregation Frameworks

Key Concepts

Example

Use Cases

Section 11.3: MapReduce in NoSQL

Key Concepts

Example

Use Cases

Section 11.4: Query Optimization Techniques

Indexing

Denormalization

Query Projection

Caching

Query Planning and Profiling

Sharding

Compression and Data Encoding

Section 11.5: Working with Unstructured Data

What is Unstructured Data?

NoSQL Databases and Unstructured Data

Use Cases for Unstructured Data

Handling Unstructured Data in NoSQL Databases

Chapter 12: NoSQL Data Replication and Distribution

Section 12.1: Principles of Data Replication

What is Data Replication?

Types of Data Replication

Data Consistency and Replication

Implementation in NoSQL Databases

Section 12.2: Data Distribution Strategies

1. Key-Range Partitioning

2. Hash-Based Partitioning

3. Directory-Based Partitioning

4. Consistent Hashing

5. Geographical Data Distribution

Section 12.3: Handling Data Consistency

1. Eventual Consistency

2. Strong Consistency

3. Causal Consistency

4. Read-Your-Write Consistency

5. Tunable Consistency Levels

Section 12.4: Conflict Resolution in Distributed Databases

1. Last-Write-Wins (LWW)

2. Vector Clocks

3. Dotted Version Vectors

4. Custom Conflict Resolution Logic

5. Automatic Conflict Resolution Policies

Section 12.5: Geo-Distributed NoSQL Deployments

1. Benefits of Geo-Distributed Deployments

2. Challenges of Geo-Distributed Deployments

3. Strategies for Geo-Distributed NoSQL Deployments

4. Use Cases for Geo-Distributed Deployments

Chapter 13: Transitioning from SQL to NoSQL

Section 13.1: Comparing SQL and NoSQL

1. Data Models

2. Schema

3. Query Language

4. Scalability

5. Consistency

6. Use Cases

7. Flexibility and Agility

8. Cost

Section 13.2: Decision Factors for Migrating

1. Data Model Compatibility

2. Scalability Requirements

3. Data Complexity and Structure

4. Querying and Performance

5. Consistency and Transactions

6. Development Flexibility

7. Cost Considerations

8. Existing Expertise

9. Use Case Suitability

10. Migration Planning

Section 13.3: Migration Planning and Execution

1. Assessment and Inventory

2. Selecting the NoSQL Database

3. Data Mapping and Schema Transformation

4. ETL (Extract, Transform, Load) Process

5. Query and Application Code Refactoring

6. Testing and Validation

7. Performance Tuning

8. Backup and Rollback Strategy

9. Data Synchronization and Downtime Planning

10. Training and Skill Development

11. Monitoring and Post-Migration Support

12. Documentation

13. User Communication

14. Execution and Validation

15. Continuous Improvement

Section 13.4: Handling Data Conversion Challenges

1. Data Type Mismatch

2. Data Volume and Scale

3. Data Consistency and Integrity

4. Complex Data Structures

5. Data Cleansing and Transformation Rules

6. Error Handling and Logging

7. Testing and Validation

8. Data Mapping Documentation

Section 13.5: Post-Migration Evaluation

1. Data Consistency and Completeness

2. Query Performance

3. Scalability

4. Data Validation

5. Security and Access Control

6. Error Monitoring and Logging

7. Backup and Recovery

8. Documentation and Training

9. Feedback and Optimization

10. Future Planning

Chapter 14: NoSQL in Enterprise Applications

Section 14.1: Enterprise Needs and NoSQL Solutions

1. Scalability

2. Flexibility and Schema-less Data Models

3. High Throughput and Low Latency

4. Availability and Fault Tolerance

5. Support for Unstructured and Semi-structured Data

6. Real-time Analytics and Insights

7. Cost-Efficiency

8. Integration with Modern Technologies

9. Multi-model Databases

Section 14.2: Integrating NoSQL with Existing Systems

1. Assessment and Planning

2. Data Migration

3. APIs and Connectors

4. Data Synchronization

5. Security and Access Control

6. Testing and Validation

7. Monitoring and Maintenance

8. Documentation and Training

9. Scalability and Future-Proofing

10. Performance Optimization

Section 14.3: NoSQL for Data Warehousing

1. Challenges in Traditional Data Warehousing

2. NoSQL's Role in Data Warehousing

3. Data Modeling in NoSQL Data Warehousing

4. Data Ingestion and ETL

5. Querying and Analytics

6. Data Security and Compliance

7. Performance Optimization

8. Scalability and Future-Proofing

9. Monitoring and Maintenance

10. Use Cases and Case Studies

Section 14.4: Handling Transactional Data

1. Transactional Data in NoSQL

2. Consistency in Transactional Data

3. ACID Transactions

4. Implementing Transactions in NoSQL

5. Distributed Transactional Data

6. Use Cases for Transactional Data in NoSQL

7. Considerations for NoSQL Transactional Data

Section 14.5: Case Studies: Enterprise Success with NoSQL

1. Netflix: Personalized Content Recommendation

2. Uber: Real-Time Data Analysis

3. Airbnb: Search and Booking Optimization

4. Cassandra at Apple: Scalable Time-Series Data

5. Walmart: Inventory Management

6. LinkedIn: Graph Data Processing

7. NASA: Data Storage for Space Missions

8. Financial Institutions: Fraud Detection

Chapter 15: NoSQL and the Internet of Things (IoT)

Section 15.1: IoT Data and NoSQL

Challenges in Handling IoT Data

Why NoSQL for IoT

Use Cases for NoSQL in IoT

Choosing the Right NoSQL Database

Section 15.2: Real-Time Data Processing in IoT

The Need for Real-Time Data Processing

Challenges in Real-Time Processing

How NoSQL Databases Enable Real-Time Processing

Real-Time IoT Use Cases with NoSQL

Section 15.3: NoSQL for Device Management and Monitoring in IoT

Challenges in IoT Device Management and Monitoring

How NoSQL Databases Address Device Management and Monitoring Challenges

Device Management and Monitoring Use Cases

Example of Device State Monitoring with NoSQL

Section 15.4: Data Storage and Retrieval Challenges in IoT

Challenges in IoT Data Storage and Retrieval

Strategies for IoT Data Storage and Retrieval

Example of Efficient Data Retrieval in IoT

Section 15.5: Case Studies: IoT Implementations Using NoSQL

Case Study 1: Smart Home Automation

Case Study 2: Industrial IoT (IIoT) Monitoring

Case Study 3: Environmental Monitoring in Agriculture

Chapter 16: Open Source NoSQL Databases

Section 16.1: Exploring Open Source Options

MongoDB

Apache Cassandra

Redis

Apache CouchDB

Apache HBase

Section 16.2: Community Support and Development

Community Support

Active Development

Section 16.3: Customization and Extensibility

Custom Data Models

Extensible Querying

Plug-ins and Add-ons

Community Contributions

Section 16.4: Pros and Cons of Open Source NoSQL Databases

Pros:

Cons:

Section 16.5: Popular Open Source NoSQL Databases

1. MongoDB:

2. Cassandra:

3. Couchbase:

4. Redis:

5. Neo4j:

6. Elasticsearch:

7. HBase:

Chapter 17: NoSQL and Artificial Intelligence

Section 17.1: AI Applications in NoSQL

1. Machine Learning Data Management:

2. Predictive Analytics with NoSQL:

3. Real-Time Decision Making:

4. Integrating AI Algorithms with NoSQL:

5. Natural Language Processing (NLP):

Section 17.2: Machine Learning Data Management

1. Data Collection and Storage:

2. Data Preprocessing:

3. Data Versioning:

4. Data Labeling and Annotation:

5. Scalability and Performance:

Section 17.3: Predictive Analytics with NoSQL

1. Data Storage for Predictive Models:

2. Real-Time Data Ingestion:

3. Scalable Model Training:

4. Integration with Machine Learning Frameworks:

5. Real-Time Predictions:

6. Handling Unstructured Data:

Section 17.4: Real-Time Decision Making

1. Low Latency Data Access:

2. Event-Driven Architectures:

3. Complex Event Processing:

4. Real-Time Alerts and Notifications:

5. Personalization and Recommendations:

6. Internet of Things (IoT) Applications:

Section 17.5: Integrating AI Algorithms with NoSQL

1. AI-Driven Data Processing:

2. Personalized Recommendations:

3. Predictive Analytics:

4. Real-Time Decision Making:

5. Streamlining Data Management:

6. Advanced Search and Recommendations:

Chapter 18: NoSQL Database Administration

Section 18.1: Roles and Responsibilities of a NoSQL DBA

1. Database Deployment and Configuration:

2. Monitoring and Performance Tuning:

3. Backup and Recovery Strategies:

4. Security and Access Control:

5. Scaling and Clustering Management:

6. Disaster Recovery Planning:

7. Patch Management and Upgrades:

8. Documentation and Training:

Section 18.2: Backup and Recovery Strategies

1. Regular Backups:

2. Snapshot Backups:

3. Commit Logs:

4. Off-Site Backups:

5. Automated Backup Scheduling:

6. Restore Testing:

7. Versioning Backups:

8. Monitoring and Alerts:

9. Backup Encryption:

10. Retention Policies:

11. Backup Metadata and Catalogs:

Section 18.3: Performance Monitoring and Tuning

1. Real-Time Monitoring:

2. Query Analysis:

3. Indexing Strategies:

4. Query Caching:

5. Load Balancing:

6. Scaling Strategies:

7. Compaction and Cleanup:

8. Monitoring Queries:

9. Resource Allocation:

10. Replication Lag Monitoring:

11. Disaster Recovery Planning:

12. Query Throttling and Rate Limiting:

13. Regular Maintenance:

14. Benchmarking and Testing:

Section 18.4: Scaling and Clustering Management

1. Horizontal Scaling:

2. Vertical Scaling:

3. Data Sharding:

4. Automatic Sharding:

5. Load Balancing:

6. Replication and Failover:

7. Monitoring and Alerts:

8. Capacity Planning:

9. Disaster Recovery Planning:

10. Performance Testing:

11. Balancing Resources:

12. Rolling Upgrades:

Section 18.5: Disaster Recovery Planning

1. Backup and Restore:

2. Offsite Backups:

3. Redundancy and High Availability:

4. Disaster Recovery Testing:

5. Data Archiving and Retention Policies:

6. Service Level Agreements (SLAs):

7. Geographical Distribution:

8. Disaster Recovery as a Service (DRaaS):

9. Documentation and Runbooks:

10. Communication Plan:

11. Regular Audits and Reviews:

Chapter 19: Future Trends in NoSQL

Section 19.1: Emerging Technologies in NoSQL

Section 19.2: NoSQL and Blockchain

Section 19.3: New Challenges and Opportunities

Section 19.4: Predictions for the Future of NoSQL

Section 19.5: Preparing for the Next Wave in Database Technology

Chapter 20: Conclusion and Further Resources

Section 20.1: Summarizing NoSQL Essentials

Chapter 1: Introduction to NoSQL

Chapter 2: NoSQL Database Types

Chapter 3: Core Concepts in NoSQL

Chapter 4: Implementing NoSQL Solutions

Chapter 5: NoSQL and Big Data

Chapter 6: NoSQL and Scalability

Chapter 7: NoSQL and Security

Chapter 8: Performance Tuning in NoSQL

Chapter 9: NoSQL in the Cloud

Chapter 10: NoSQL for Mobile and Web Applications

Chapter 11: Advanced Querying in NoSQL

Chapter 12: NoSQL Data Replication and Distribution

Chapter 13: Transitioning from SQL to NoSQL

Chapter 14: NoSQL in Enterprise Applications

Chapter 15: NoSQL and the Internet of Things (IoT)

Chapter 16: Open Source NoSQL Databases

Chapter 17: NoSQL and Artificial Intelligence

Chapter 18: NoSQL Database Administration

Chapter 19: Future Trends in NoSQL

Section 20.2: Lessons Learned and Key Takeaways

Section 20.3: Further Reading and Resources

Section 20.4: The Future Landscape of Databases

Section 20.5: Final Thoughts and Encouragement for Continued Learning

Section 20.2: Lessons Learned and Key Takeaways

1. Flexibility and Scalability

2. Choosing the Right NoSQL Database

3. Data Modeling and Indexing

4. NoSQL in Big Data and IoT

5. Security and Compliance

6. Continuous Learning

7. Open Source Options

Section 20.3: Further Reading and Resources

1. Books

2. Online Courses

3. Documentation and Official Websites

4. Community and Forums

5. Blogs and Websites

6. Conferences and Meetups

7. Online Communities

Section 20.4: Predictions for the Future of NoSQL

1. Multi-Model Databases

2. Serverless and Managed Services

3. Real-Time Data Processing

4. Advanced Analytics and Machine Learning Integration

5. Security and Compliance

6. Blockchain and NoSQL

7. Graph Databases for Complex Relationships

8. Polyglot Persistence

9. Containerization and Orchestration

10. Edge Computing and NoSQL

Section 20.5: Final Thoughts and Encouragement for Continued Learning

Embracing Flexibility

Diversity of Use Cases

Continuous Learning

Experimentation and Innovation

Integration with Other Technologies

Data Privacy and Security

Scalability and Performance

Community and Collaboration

Diverse Career Opportunities

Inspiration from Success Stories

Chapter 1: Introduction to NoSQL

1.1 Understanding the Basics of NoSQL

In this section, we will delve into the fundamental concepts of NoSQL databases. NoSQL, which stands for "Not Only SQL," represents a diverse group of database management systems designed to address various challenges posed by modern data processing needs. Unlike traditional relational databases, NoSQL databases are schema-less, meaning they don't enforce a rigid structure for data storage. Instead, they offer flexibility and scalability for handling various types of data, from structured to semi-structured and unstructured data.

The Need for NoSQL

The rise of web applications, social media, IoT devices, and big data has generated vast amounts of data that traditional relational databases struggle to handle efficiently. NoSQL databases emerged to fill this gap, offering a range of data models and storage mechanisms optimized for specific use cases. Let's explore some key reasons why organizations turn to NoSQL databases:

1. **Flexible Data Models**: NoSQL databases can store and manage data in various formats, including JSON, XML, key-value pairs, and more. This flexibility allows organizations to adapt to changing data requirements without altering their database schema.
2. **Scalability**: NoSQL databases are inherently designed for horizontal scalability. They can handle high volumes of data and traffic by distributing data across multiple nodes or clusters, ensuring that performance remains consistent

as the load increases.

3. **High Availability**: Many NoSQL databases provide built-in mechanisms for ensuring high availability, even in the face of hardware failures or network issues. This is critical for mission-critical applications that require constant uptime.
4. **Real-Time Processing**: NoSQL databases excel at real-time data processing and analytics. They are well-suited for applications that need to make rapid decisions based on incoming data, such as recommendation engines and fraud detection systems.
5. **Simplified Development**: With NoSQL databases, developers can work with data in its natural format, reducing the need for complex data transformation. This simplifies application development and speeds up time-to-market.

Categories of NoSQL Databases

NoSQL databases are categorized into four main types, each with its own strengths and use cases:

1. **Document-Oriented Databases**: These databases store data in documents, often in JSON or XML format. They are suitable for content management systems, catalogs, and user profiles, where data structures can vary.
2. **Key-Value Stores**: Key-value stores are simple and efficient. They associate data with unique keys and are commonly used for caching and session management in web applications.
3. **Column-Family Stores**: Column-family databases are optimized for write-heavy workloads and can handle large volumes of data. They are commonly used in time-series

data, event logging, and analytics.

4. **Graph Databases**: Graph databases are designed for storing and querying data with complex relationships, making them ideal for social networks, recommendation engines, and fraud detection.

Conclusion

In this introductory section, we've covered the need for NoSQL databases and explored the various categories they fall into. As you proceed through this book, you'll gain a deeper understanding of NoSQL concepts, their applications, and how to choose the right NoSQL database for your specific use case.

1.2 The Evolution of Database Technology: From SQL to NoSQL

Over the years, the landscape of database technology has undergone significant evolution, leading to the emergence of NoSQL databases as a viable alternative to traditional SQL databases. In this section, we will explore this evolution, understanding how we transitioned from the SQL era to the era of NoSQL databases.

The SQL Era

SQL databases, also known as relational databases, have been the dominant database technology for several decades. They are characterized by structured data with predefined schemas, enforced data integrity through relationships, and ACID (Atomicity, Consistency, Isolation, Durability) transaction properties. SQL databases like Oracle, MySQL, and PostgreSQL have played a pivotal role in managing data for various applications, from finance to e-commerce.

However, as the digital age advanced, SQL databases faced several challenges:

1. **Rigid Schemas**: SQL databases require a fixed schema, making it challenging to adapt to evolving data structures. This rigidity can slow down development and hinder flexibility.
2. **Scalability Challenges**: Scaling SQL databases vertically (by adding more resources to a single server) has limitations. Horizontal scaling (distributing data across multiple servers) is complex and often results in performance bottlenecks.
3. **Complex Joins**: Queries involving multiple tables with complex joins can lead to performance degradation, especially with large datasets.
4. **High Availability**: Ensuring high availability and fault tolerance in SQL databases requires complex setups, such as master-slave replication and clustering.

The Rise of NoSQL

The shortcomings of SQL databases paved the way for NoSQL databases, which offer a fresh approach to data management. Here's how NoSQL databases address the limitations of SQL databases:

1. **Flexible Schema**: NoSQL databases are schema-less or schema-flexible, allowing organizations to store data in various formats without predefined schemas. This flexibility is well-suited for applications with changing data requirements.
2. **Horizontal Scalability**: NoSQL databases are designed for horizontal scaling. They can distribute data across multiple nodes or clusters, accommodating high volumes

of data and traffic.

3. **Performance Optimization**: NoSQL databases optimize read and write operations for specific use cases. For example, key-value stores excel in read-heavy workloads, while column-family stores are efficient for write-heavy workloads.
4. **High Availability**: Many NoSQL databases offer built-in features for ensuring high availability, making them suitable for applications that require constant uptime.

The NoSQL Revolution

The rise of NoSQL databases represents a revolution in data management. Organizations now have a broader range of database options to choose from, allowing them to select the most suitable database technology for their specific use cases. NoSQL databases have found applications in web and mobile development, IoT, big data analytics, and more.

As we delve deeper into this book, you'll gain a comprehensive understanding of NoSQL databases, their various types, core concepts, implementation strategies, and real-world use cases. This knowledge will empower you to make informed decisions about when and how to leverage NoSQL databases in your own projects.

1.3 Key Characteristics of NoSQL Databases

NoSQL databases share several key characteristics that distinguish them from traditional SQL (relational) databases. In this section, we will explore these fundamental features that define the nature of NoSQL databases.

1. Schema Flexibility

One of the defining characteristics of NoSQL databases is their schema flexibility. Unlike SQL databases, which require a predefined and rigid schema, NoSQL databases allow you to work with data in a more flexible manner. Data can be stored without a fixed schema, making it easier to adapt to changing data requirements. This flexibility is particularly beneficial in scenarios where the data structure evolves over time, such as in agile development environments.

// Example of schema-less data in a document-oriented NoSQL database

```
{
"name": "John Doe",
"age": 30,
"email": "john@example.com"
}
```

2. NoSQL Data Models

NoSQL databases offer a variety of data models to cater to different use cases. The main types of NoSQL data models include:

- **Document-Oriented**: Documents, often in JSON or XML format, are used to store data. This model is suitable for scenarios where data varies in structure.
- **Key-Value**: Data is stored as key-value pairs, making it efficient for simple read and write operations.

- **Column-Family**: Organizes data into column families, optimized for write-heavy workloads and large volumes of data.

- **Graph**: Focuses on relationships between data entities, making it ideal for applications involving complex data relationships.

3. Horizontal Scalability

NoSQL databases are designed for horizontal scalability, allowing you to distribute data across multiple servers or nodes. This scalability is achieved through sharding, partitioning, or replication. As your data and traffic grow, you can easily add more servers to your NoSQL cluster to handle increased load, ensuring that performance remains consistent.

4. NoSQL Querying

Querying in NoSQL databases differs from SQL databases. While SQL databases use SQL (Structured Query Language) for querying, NoSQL databases often provide their own query languages or APIs tailored to their data models. This can include methods for filtering, sorting, and retrieving data based on the database's unique structure.

```
// Example of a query in a document-oriented NoSQL database

db.collection("users").find({ age: { $gte: 25 } });
```

5. CAP Theorem

The CAP theorem is a fundamental concept in NoSQL databases. It states that in a distributed system, you can have at most two of the following three properties: Consistency, Availability, and Partition Tolerance. NoSQL databases are categorized based on their adherence to the CAP theorem. Some prioritize consistency (CA), while others prioritize availability (AP) and partition tolerance (P).

6. Scalability Challenges

While NoSQL databases offer horizontal scalability, they also come with challenges, such as managing distributed data, handling data consistency in distributed environments, and addressing performance bottlenecks that can arise in complex architectures. NoSQL databases often require careful planning and architectural considerations to ensure they scale effectively.

7. Use Cases

NoSQL databases are well-suited for various use cases, including:

- Real-time data analytics
- Content management systems
- IoT data storage and processing
- Social media platforms
- Mobile app backends
- E-commerce applications

Understanding these key characteristics of NoSQL databases is essential as you explore their different types and consider their applicability to your specific project requirements. In the following chapters, we will delve deeper into each type of NoSQL database and provide practical guidance on how to use them effectively.

1.4 Types of NoSQL Databases: An Overview

NoSQL databases encompass a diverse range of database management systems, each tailored to specific use cases and data models. In this section, we will provide an overview of the main types of NoSQL databases and their characteristics.

1. Document-Oriented Databases

Document-oriented databases store data in documents, often using formats like JSON or XML. Each document can have a unique structure, allowing for flexibility in data modeling. These databases are ideal for scenarios where data structures may change over time, such as content management systems and user profiles.

Popular Document-Oriented Databases:

- MongoDB
- Couchbase
- RavenDB

2. Key-Value Stores

Key-value stores are simple and efficient databases that associate data with unique keys. They are optimized for rapid read and write operations and are commonly used for caching, session management, and real-time analytics. Key-value stores excel in scenarios where data retrieval speed is critical.

Popular Key-Value Stores:

- Redis
- Amazon DynamoDB

- Riak

3. Column-Family Stores

Column-family stores organize data into column families, similar to tables in SQL databases. They are well-suited for write-heavy workloads and can handle large volumes of data efficiently. Column-family stores are commonly used in time-series data, event logging, and analytics applications.

Popular Column-Family Stores:

- Apache Cassandra
- HBase
- ScyllaDB

4. Graph Databases

Graph databases focus on representing and querying complex relationships between data entities. They are designed for scenarios where the relationships between data elements are as important as the data itself. Graph databases excel in social networks, recommendation engines, and fraud detection systems.

Popular Graph Databases:

- Neo4j
- Amazon Neptune
- OrientDB

5. Multi-Model Databases

Some NoSQL databases offer support for multiple data models within a single database system. These multi-model databases provide greater flexibility and can adapt to various data structures and use cases within the same database.

Popular Multi-Model Databases:

- ArangoDB
- MarkLogic
- CouchDB

6. Time-Series Databases

Time-series databases specialize in handling time-stamped data points. They are optimized for storing and querying time-series data, making them ideal for applications that involve monitoring, sensor data, and IoT devices.

Popular Time-Series Databases:

- InfluxDB
- OpenTSDB
- TimescaleDB

7. In-Memory Databases

In-memory databases store data entirely in RAM, enabling lightning-fast read and write operations. They are commonly used for real-time data analytics, caching, and applications requiring low-latency access to data.

Popular In-Memory Databases:

- Redis (also a key-value store)
- Memcached
- VoltDB

Understanding the types of NoSQL databases and their characteristics is crucial for selecting the right database solution for your specific application needs. Each type has its strengths and weaknesses, and choosing the appropriate one can significantly impact the performance and scalability of your system. In the following chapters, we will dive deeper into each type of NoSQL database, providing insights into their usage and best practices.

1.5 Advantages and Use Cases of NoSQL

NoSQL databases offer numerous advantages and find applications in a wide range of use cases. In this section, we will explore the key advantages of NoSQL databases and provide insights into where they are most commonly used.

Advantages of NoSQL Databases

1. **Schema Flexibility**: NoSQL databases allow for flexible data modeling, accommodating changing data structures without the need for rigid schemas. This flexibility is especially valuable in dynamic environments where data requirements evolve over time.
2. **Scalability**: NoSQL databases are designed for horizontal scalability, making them capable of handling high volumes of data and traffic. As your application grows, you can add more servers or nodes to scale your database system.

3. **High Performance**: NoSQL databases are optimized for specific use cases, resulting in high-performance read and write operations. Key-value stores, for example, offer rapid data retrieval, while column-family stores excel in write-heavy scenarios.
4. **NoSQL Data Models**: Different NoSQL data models cater to diverse use cases. Document-oriented databases are well-suited for content management, while graph databases excel in applications involving complex relationships.
5. **Real-Time Data Processing**: NoSQL databases are ideal for real-time data processing and analytics. They enable applications to make rapid decisions based on incoming data, making them valuable in scenarios like recommendation engines and fraud detection systems.
6. **High Availability**: Many NoSQL databases provide built-in features for ensuring high availability, even in the presence of hardware failures or network issues. This is critical for applications that require constant uptime.
7. **Simplified Development**: NoSQL databases often allow developers to work with data in its natural format, reducing the need for complex data transformations. This simplifies application development and accelerates time-to-market.
8. **Multi-Model Support**: Some NoSQL databases offer support for multiple data models within a single system, providing greater flexibility for diverse use cases.

Use Cases of NoSQL Databases

1. **Web and Mobile Applications**: NoSQL databases are commonly used as backend data stores for web and mobile applications. They provide the flexibility to handle varied data types and high concurrent user loads.

2. **IoT Data Management**: Internet of Things (IoT) applications generate massive volumes of time-stamped data. NoSQL databases, especially time-series databases, are well-suited for efficiently storing and analyzing IoT data.
3. **Real-Time Analytics**: NoSQL databases are instrumental in real-time analytics, enabling businesses to make immediate decisions based on incoming data. They find applications in monitoring, dashboards, and data visualization.
4. **Content Management Systems (CMS)**: Document-oriented NoSQL databases are a popular choice for CMS platforms, where content structures can vary widely.
5. **E-commerce**: E-commerce platforms often employ NoSQL databases to manage product catalogs, user profiles, and shopping cart data. The ability to handle varying product attributes is crucial in this domain.
6. **Social Media**: Social media platforms benefit from graph databases, which model complex relationships between users, posts, and interactions. These databases help deliver personalized content and recommendations.
7. **Big Data**: NoSQL databases play a significant role in big data analytics by storing and processing vast amounts of unstructured and semi-structured data.
8. **Caching and Session Management**: Key-value stores, such as Redis, are frequently used for caching frequently accessed data and managing user sessions in web applications.
9. **Time-Series Data**: Time-series databases are essential for applications that involve tracking and analyzing data over time, including sensor data, financial market data, and monitoring systems.

10. **IoT Device Management**: NoSQL databases help manage IoT devices, tracking their status, configurations, and telemetry data in real-time.
11. **Recommendation Engines**: Graph databases are instrumental in building recommendation engines that analyze user preferences and connections to suggest relevant content or products.
12. **Log and Event Data**: Column-family stores are suitable for storing log and event data, which often involves a high volume of write operations.

Understanding the advantages and use cases of NoSQL databases allows organizations to make informed decisions about adopting NoSQL technology to meet their specific needs. As we proceed through this book, we will delve deeper into each type of NoSQL database and provide practical guidance on how to implement them effectively in various scenarios.

Chapter 2: NoSQL Database Types

2.1 Document-Oriented Databases Explained

Document-oriented databases are a prominent type of NoSQL database that stores data in documents, typically using formats like JSON or XML. In this section, we will explore the characteristics of document-oriented databases, their advantages, and common use cases.

Key Features of Document-Oriented Databases

1. **Flexible Schema**: Document-oriented databases embrace a schema-less or schema-flexible approach. Each document can have a different structure, allowing you to store data with varying attributes. This flexibility is particularly valuable in applications where data structures evolve over time.
2. **Documents as the Unit of Storage**: Data is stored as documents, which are self-contained and can represent a single entity or record. These documents are often represented in JSON format, making it easy to work with semi-structured data.
3. **Rich Querying**: Document-oriented databases typically provide rich querying capabilities. You can query data using various criteria, including field values, ranges, and nested attributes. This flexibility in querying enables you to retrieve specific subsets of data efficiently.

Advantages of Document-Oriented Databases

1. **Schema Flexibility**: The schema-less nature of document-

oriented databases allows developers to adapt to changing data requirements without modifying the database structure. This agility is essential in dynamic application environments.

2. **Complex Data Structures**: Document-oriented databases are well-suited for storing complex and nested data structures. This makes them ideal for applications with hierarchical or nested data, such as e-commerce product catalogs or user profiles.
3. **High Performance**: Document-oriented databases optimize read and write operations for document retrieval. This makes them perform well in scenarios where quick data access is crucial.
4. **Horizontal Scalability**: Document-oriented databases are designed for horizontal scalability. You can distribute documents across multiple nodes or servers, ensuring that your database can handle high traffic and data volumes.

Common Use Cases

1. **Content Management Systems (CMS)**: Document-oriented databases are often used in CMS platforms, where content can have varying structures and attributes. This flexibility simplifies content storage and retrieval.
2. **User Profiles**: Storing user profiles, which may have different attributes for each user, is a common use case for document-oriented databases.
3. **Catalogs and Product Management**: E-commerce platforms utilize document-oriented databases to manage product catalogs with diverse attributes and variations.
4. **Real-Time Analytics**: Document-oriented databases are suitable for real-time analytics, allowing applications to analyze and display data in real-time, such as tracking user

interactions on a website.

Document-Oriented Database Examples

Popular document-oriented databases include:

- **MongoDB**: MongoDB is one of the most widely used document-oriented databases. It provides robust querying capabilities, horizontal scalability, and support for large-scale applications.

- **CouchDB**: CouchDB is known for its built-in multi-master replication, which enables data synchronization across distributed systems. It offers high availability and schema flexibility.

- **RavenDB**: RavenDB is a document-oriented database designed for .NET applications. It provides strong consistency and supports ACID transactions.

Understanding document-oriented databases and their capabilities is essential when choosing a database solution for projects that involve dynamic or nested data structures. In the following sections, we will explore other types of NoSQL databases, each tailored to different data modeling needs.

2.2 Key-Value Stores: Concepts and Applications

Key-value stores are a fundamental type of NoSQL database that excel in simplicity and efficiency. In this section, we will delve into the characteristics of key-value stores, their advantages, and common use cases.

Key Features of Key-Value Stores

1. **Simplicity**: Key-value stores are among the simplest types of databases. They store data as pairs of keys and associated values. Each value is associated with a unique key, allowing for quick retrieval.
2. **Efficiency**: Key-value stores are highly efficient for basic operations. Retrieving a value by its key is typically done in constant time, making them ideal for scenarios where read and write speed is critical.
3. **No Schema**: Key-value stores do not enforce a predefined schema. Each key-value pair can have a different structure or content type, providing flexibility in data storage.

Advantages of Key-Value Stores

1. **High Performance**: Key-value stores are optimized for rapid data retrieval, making them suitable for caching, session management, and scenarios where low-latency access to data is essential.
2. **Scalability**: Key-value stores are horizontally scalable, allowing you to distribute data across multiple servers or nodes. As your application grows, you can add more nodes to maintain performance.
3. **Simplified Data Model**: The simplicity of key-value stores simplifies data modeling. They are particularly well-suited for scenarios where data is naturally represented as simple key-value pairs.

Common Use Cases

1. **Caching**: Key-value stores are frequently used for caching frequently accessed data to reduce the load on primary data

stores. Popular caching solutions like Redis leverage key-value stores.

2. **Session Management**: Web applications often use key-value stores to manage user sessions. Storing session data as key-value pairs allows for quick retrieval and expiration.
3. **User Preferences**: Key-value stores are useful for storing user preferences or settings, where each preference can be associated with a unique key.
4. **Real-Time Analytics**: Key-value stores are employed in real-time analytics scenarios where quick access to aggregated or summarized data is required.

Key-Value Store Examples

Several key-value store databases are widely used:

- **Redis**: Redis is an in-memory key-value store known for its blazing-fast performance. It supports advanced data structures like lists, sets, and sorted sets, making it versatile for various use cases.

- **Amazon DynamoDB**: DynamoDB is a managed key-value store service provided by Amazon Web Services (AWS). It offers scalability, high availability, and automatic data replication.

- **Riak**: Riak is a distributed key-value store known for its fault-tolerance and availability. It is designed for use cases requiring high availability and resilience.

Understanding key-value stores and their characteristics is essential when designing applications that require efficient data retrieval, caching, or session management. In the following sections, we will explore other types of NoSQL databases, each catering to distinct data modeling needs and use cases.

2.3 Column-Family Stores: Structure and Utility

Column-family stores are a type of NoSQL database that organizes data into column families, providing efficiency in managing large volumes of data. In this section, we will explore the characteristics of column-family stores, their advantages, and common use cases.

Key Features of Column-Family Stores

1. **Column-Family Organization**: Column-family stores organize data into column families, which act as containers for related data. Each column family can have a unique schema, allowing for varied data structures within the same database.
2. **Wide-Column Storage**: Column-family stores use a wide-column storage model, which means data is stored in rows and columns, similar to a table in a relational database. However, unlike relational databases, the columns within a column family can vary for each row.
3. **Scalability**: Column-family stores are designed for horizontal scalability, allowing you to add more servers or nodes to accommodate growing data volumes. This scalability is particularly valuable for write-heavy workloads.

Advantages of Column-Family Stores

1. **Write-Optimized**: Column-family stores are optimized for write-heavy workloads. They excel in scenarios where

data is frequently updated or appended.

2. **Scalability**: The horizontal scalability of column-family stores makes them suitable for applications that need to handle large volumes of data, such as time-series data, event logs, and analytics.
3. **High Availability**: Many column-family stores provide mechanisms for ensuring high availability, making them resilient to hardware failures and network issues.
4. **Schema Flexibility**: Within a column family, you can have different columns for each row, allowing for flexibility in data modeling. This flexibility is valuable when dealing with heterogeneous data.

Common Use Cases

1. **Time-Series Data**: Column-family stores are well-suited for storing time-series data, where each data point is associated with a timestamp. Examples include sensor data, log files, and financial market data.
2. **Event Logging**: Applications that generate extensive event logs often use column-family stores to efficiently store and query log data.
3. **Analytics**: Column-family stores are employed in analytics platforms to manage large datasets and perform complex data analysis.
4. **Content Management**: In content management systems, column-family stores can be used to manage content and metadata efficiently.

Column-Family Store Examples

Some well-known column-family stores include:

- **Apache Cassandra**: Cassandra is a highly scalable and distributed column-family store known for its fault tolerance. It is widely used in applications requiring high availability and write-intensive workloads.

- **HBase**: HBase is an open-source, distributed column-family store designed to work with the Hadoop ecosystem. It offers scalability and integrates well with big data processing frameworks.

- **ScyllaDB**: ScyllaDB is a high-performance, distributed column-family store designed as a drop-in replacement for Apache Cassandra. It offers improved performance and resource efficiency.

Understanding column-family stores and their capabilities is essential when considering databases for applications that involve managing large volumes of data with diverse structures. In the following sections, we will explore other types of NoSQL databases, each tailored to specific data modeling needs and use cases.

2.4 Graph Databases: Understanding Relationships

Graph databases are a specialized type of NoSQL database designed to efficiently model and query complex relationships between data entities. In this section, we will explore the characteristics of graph databases, their advantages, and common use cases.

Key Features of Graph Databases

1. **Graph Data Model**: Graph databases use a graph data model to represent data entities and the relationships

between them. In this model, data is stored as nodes (entities) and edges (relationships), allowing for rich and interconnected data structures.

2. **Property Graphs**: In graph databases, nodes and edges can have associated properties or attributes. These properties can store additional information about the nodes and edges, making the data model expressive and versatile.
3. **Traversals**: Graph databases excel in traversing relationships between nodes. They provide efficient mechanisms for navigating complex graph structures, allowing for queries like finding connections, shortest paths, and pattern matching.

Advantages of Graph Databases

1. **Efficient Relationship Queries**: Graph databases are designed for efficient querying of relationships. They are ideal for applications where understanding and analyzing the connections between data entities is essential.
2. **Schema Flexibility**: Graph databases offer schema flexibility, allowing you to add nodes, edges, and properties as needed. This adaptability is valuable in scenarios where data structures evolve.
3. **Complex Data Models**: Graph databases are suitable for modeling and querying complex data structures, making them ideal for applications involving social networks, recommendation engines, and fraud detection.

Common Use Cases

1. **Social Networks**: Graph databases are frequently used to model and analyze social networks. They can efficiently represent connections between users, posts, comments, and

other social elements.

2. **Recommendation Engines**: Recommender systems benefit from graph databases to model user preferences, content, and relationships, enabling accurate content recommendations.
3. **Fraud Detection**: Graph databases are valuable in fraud detection systems, where they help identify suspicious patterns and connections between entities.
4. **Network and IT Operations**: Graph databases are used in network management and IT operations to model and analyze network topologies, dependencies, and incident resolution.

Graph Database Examples

Some notable graph databases include:

- **Neo4j**: Neo4j is a popular and mature graph database known for its expressive query language (Cypher) and high-performance graph traversal capabilities. It is widely used in various industries.

- **Amazon Neptune**: Neptune is a fully managed graph database service provided by AWS. It supports both property graph and RDF graph models and is suitable for highly available and scalable applications.

- **OrientDB**: OrientDB is a multi-model database that supports graph database capabilities. It provides ACID transactions and can work as both a document-oriented and graph database.

Understanding graph databases and their capabilities is essential when dealing with data that involves complex relationships. In the following sections, we will explore other types of NoSQL databases, each tailored to different data modeling needs and use cases.

2.5 Choosing the Right Type of NoSQL Database

Selecting the appropriate type of NoSQL database for your project is a crucial decision that significantly impacts the performance, scalability, and flexibility of your application. In this section, we will discuss the factors and considerations to help you make an informed choice.

Factors to Consider When Choosing a NoSQL Database

1. **Data Model**: The nature of your data and how it should be structured are fundamental considerations. Different NoSQL databases are optimized for specific data models, such as documents, key-value pairs, columns, or graphs. Choose a database that aligns with your data modeling requirements.
2. **Querying Requirements**: Assess your querying needs. Some NoSQL databases offer SQL-like querying languages, while others have their own query languages or APIs. Consider whether your application requires complex querying or can benefit from simpler, key-based retrieval.
3. **Scalability**: Determine whether your application is expected to scale horizontally to handle increased data and traffic. NoSQL databases are designed with various scalability options, including sharding, partitioning, and replication. Choose a database that can accommodate your scalability needs.
4. **Consistency vs. Availability**: Understand the trade-off

between consistency, availability, and partition tolerance (as per the CAP theorem). Some NoSQL databases prioritize consistency, ensuring that all nodes return the same data, while others prioritize availability, ensuring that nodes remain responsive even in the presence of network partitions.

5. **Use Case and Application**: Consider the specific use case and requirements of your application. Each NoSQL database type has strengths and weaknesses that make it suitable for certain scenarios. For example, document-oriented databases are well-suited for content management, while graph databases excel in relationship-heavy applications.
6. **Data Volume and Throughput**: Estimate the expected data volume and transaction throughput of your application. Some NoSQL databases are optimized for handling large volumes of data and high write loads, while others focus on read-intensive workloads or real-time analytics.
7. **Schema Flexibility**: Evaluate the level of schema flexibility your application needs. NoSQL databases vary in their schema enforcement, ranging from schema-less (flexible) to schema-defined (rigid). Choose a database that aligns with your evolving data requirements.
8. **Data Consistency Requirements**: Determine the level of data consistency required by your application. NoSQL databases offer varying levels of consistency, including strong consistency, eventual consistency, and tunable consistency models. Consider which consistency model best suits your application's needs.

Common NoSQL Database Selection Scenarios

1. **Document-Oriented Database Selection**: Choose a document-oriented database like MongoDB or Couchbase when your application deals with semi-structured data, content management, or evolving data schemas. These databases provide flexibility and rich querying.
2. **Key-Value Store Selection**: Opt for a key-value store like Redis or Amazon DynamoDB when your application requires fast data retrieval, caching, session management, or real-time analytics. Key-value stores excel in read and write performance.
3. **Column-Family Store Selection**: Select a column-family store like Apache Cassandra or HBase for write-intensive workloads, time-series data, or applications with large data volumes. These databases provide horizontal scalability and efficient write operations.
4. **Graph Database Selection**: Consider a graph database like Neo4j or Amazon Neptune if your application relies on complex relationships, social networks, recommendation engines, or fraud detection. Graph databases excel in traversing and querying graph structures.

Evaluating NoSQL Database Solutions

Before finalizing your choice, it's essential to evaluate and test NoSQL database solutions that fit your criteria. Consider factors like ease of setup, documentation, community support, and compatibility with your development stack. Prototype and benchmark the database with your application to ensure it meets your performance and scalability expectations.

Choosing the right NoSQL database is a critical step in building a successful application. Each type of NoSQL database has its strengths, and selecting the one that aligns with your project's requirements can lead to improved performance and a more efficient development process. In the following chapters, we will explore various aspects of each NoSQL database type in more detail, providing you with the knowledge needed to make an informed decision.

Chapter 3: Core Concepts in NoSQL

3.1 Data Modeling in NoSQL

Data modeling is a fundamental aspect of database design, and it plays a crucial role in the effectiveness of your NoSQL database. In this section, we will explore the principles and practices of data modeling in the context of NoSQL databases.

Understanding Data Modeling

Data modeling involves defining the structure and relationships of your data in a database. In the NoSQL world, data modeling differs from the traditional relational database modeling due to the flexibility and varied data models supported by NoSQL databases. Here are some key considerations:

1. **Schema Flexibility**: NoSQL databases often offer schema-less or schema-flexible data modeling, allowing you to store data with different structures in the same database. This flexibility is advantageous in scenarios where data evolves over time.
2. **Data Abstraction**: NoSQL databases abstract data into different formats, such as documents, key-value pairs, columns, or graph nodes and edges. The choice of data abstraction depends on your data's nature and relationships.
3. **Denormalization**: Unlike traditional relational databases, where normalization is a common practice, NoSQL databases often promote denormalization. Denormalization means storing redundant data to optimize query performance, as joins are typically avoided

or limited in NoSQL databases.

Key Considerations in NoSQL Data Modeling

When modeling data for a NoSQL database, consider the following factors:

1. **Use Case**: Start by understanding your application's specific use case and data access patterns. This knowledge will guide your data modeling decisions.
2. **Data Relationships**: Identify relationships between different pieces of data. Depending on your chosen NoSQL database type (document, key-value, column-family, or graph), represent these relationships accordingly.
3. **Query Patterns**: Analyze the types of queries your application will execute. Design your data model to optimize these queries, ensuring that data retrieval is efficient.
4. **Scalability**: Keep scalability in mind, as NoSQL databases are often used for large-scale applications. Design your data model to scale horizontally by distributing data across multiple nodes or servers.

Data Modeling in Different NoSQL Database Types

Each NoSQL database type has its own approach to data modeling:

- **Document-Oriented Databases**: In document-oriented databases like MongoDB, data is stored as documents. You should design your data model around the structure of these documents. Nested documents or arrays can be used to represent relationships.

- **Key-Value Stores**: Key-value stores like Redis focus on simple data storage and retrieval. Consider how to structure keys and values to optimize your access patterns. Keys often represent entities, while values hold the associated data.

- **Column-Family Stores**: Column-family stores like Apache Cassandra use wide-column storage. Data is organized into column families, where each row can have different columns. Think about how to structure column families and rows to support your queries.

- **Graph Databases**: Graph databases like Neo4j are designed for modeling relationships. Nodes represent entities, and edges represent relationships. Define node and edge types to capture the semantics of your data.

Practical Tips

- Start with a clear understanding of your application's requirements and data access patterns before designing your data model.

- Avoid over-normalization in NoSQL data modeling. Denormalize when necessary to optimize query performance.

- Be mindful of data consistency and choose an appropriate consistency model for your use case.

- Test and iterate your data model as your application evolves and scales.

Data modeling in NoSQL databases requires a deep understanding of your application's needs and the database's capabilities. By carefully designing your data model, you can harness the full potential of your NoSQL database to build efficient and scalable applications. In the following sections, we will explore more aspects of NoSQL databases, including schema management, indexing, and consistency.

3.2 Understanding NoSQL Schemas

In the world of NoSQL databases, the concept of a schema differs significantly from traditional relational databases. NoSQL databases offer more flexibility in handling data schemas, and in some cases, they embrace a schema-less approach. In this section, we will explore the concept of NoSQL schemas and how they differ from traditional relational database schemas.

Traditional Relational Database Schemas

In a traditional relational database, a schema defines the structure of the data, including tables, columns, data types, relationships, constraints, and indexes. The schema is typically defined before data is inserted, and it enforces a strict structure that all data must adhere to. Any deviation from the schema results in an error.

For example, consider a relational database schema for a library application:

CREATE TABLE Books (

ISBN VARCHAR(13) **PRIMARY KEY**,

Title VARCHAR(255),

Author VARCHAR(100),

PublishedDate DATE

);

CREATE TABLE Users (

UserID INT **PRIMARY KEY**,

Username VARCHAR(50) **UNIQUE**,

Email VARCHAR(100),

RegistrationDate DATE

);

In this schema, we have two tables: Books and Users, each with predefined columns and data types. Any attempt to insert data that doesn't conform to this schema will be rejected.

NoSQL Database Schema Flexibility

In contrast, NoSQL databases offer varying levels of schema flexibility:

1. **Schema-less**: Some NoSQL databases, like document-oriented databases, are schema-less. They allow you to insert data without a predefined schema, and each document can have a different structure. For example, in MongoDB, you can insert documents with different sets of fields:

// **Document 1**

{

"title": "NoSQL for Beginners",

"author": "John Doe"

}

// **Document 2**

{

"title": "Data Modeling in NoSQL",

"publishedDate": "2022-02-15"

}

Here, the two documents have different structures, and MongoDB doesn't enforce a fixed schema.

1. **Flexible Schema**: Other NoSQL databases offer schema flexibility within predefined data types. For instance, in a key-value store like Redis, you can store various data types (strings, lists, sets, etc.) under different keys, but you must adhere to the data type's rules.

SET user:1 "{ 'name': 'Alice', 'age': 30 }"

LPUSH friends:1 "Bob"

SADD interests:1 "Reading" "Travel"

In this example, we store user data, a list of friends, and a set of interests, all under different keys, but each data type has specific constraints.

1. **Schema-Defined**: Some NoSQL databases, especially column-family stores, offer a schema-defined approach.

You define the column families and their structures, but the columns within a column family can vary between rows. For example, in Apache Cassandra, you can define column families and insert rows with different columns:

```
CREATE TABLE UserProfiles (

UserID UUID PRIMARY KEY,

FirstName TEXT,

LastName TEXT

);

INSERT INTO UserProfiles (UserID, FirstName, LastName, Email)

VALUES (uuid(), 'Alice', 'Smith', 'alice@example.com');
```

In this case, the schema defines the column families and their types, but you can insert rows with varying columns.

Advantages of NoSQL Schema Flexibility

The flexibility of NoSQL schemas offers several advantages:

- **Agility**: You can adapt to changing data requirements without altering the database schema. This is valuable in agile development environments.

- **Efficiency**: Schema-less or flexible schemas can reduce development time and effort by allowing data insertion without strict validation.

- **Diverse Data**: NoSQL databases can handle diverse data structures within the same database, making them suitable for applications with evolving or heterogeneous data.

Considerations with NoSQL Schemas

While NoSQL schema flexibility can be advantageous, it also requires careful consideration:

- **Data Quality**: With flexible schemas, data quality and validation may need to be handled at the application level. You must ensure data consistency and integrity.

- **Querying Challenges**: Schema-less data can pose challenges when querying. Complex queries may require handling missing or varying fields.

- **Documentation**: Clear documentation of data structures and expectations becomes crucial when dealing with flexible schemas to maintain data integrity and understand data semantics.

In summary, NoSQL databases offer varying degrees of schema flexibility, allowing you to choose the level that best fits your application's needs. Understanding the trade-offs and implications of schema flexibility is essential when designing and working with NoSQL databases.

3.3 Indexing in NoSQL Databases

Indexing is a fundamental concept in database systems, including NoSQL databases. It plays a crucial role in improving query performance by enabling efficient data retrieval. In this section, we will explore indexing in NoSQL databases, its significance, and how it differs from indexing in traditional relational databases.

Understanding Indexing

An index in a database is a data structure that provides a quick and efficient way to look up records based on specific columns or fields. Instead of scanning the entire dataset to find matching records, an index allows the database system to directly access the relevant data, reducing query response times.

Indexing in Traditional Relational Databases

In traditional relational databases, indexing is a well-established concept. It involves creating one or more indexes on specific columns of tables to speed up query execution. These indexes are typically implemented as B-tree or hash data structures.

For example, consider an SQL query to retrieve all books published by a particular author:

SELECT * **FROM** Books **WHERE** Author = 'John Doe';

In a relational database, an index on the Author column would significantly improve the query's performance by quickly identifying the relevant rows without scanning the entire Books table.

Indexing in NoSQL Databases

Indexing in NoSQL databases shares the same core concept of improving query performance, but it can take different forms depending on the type of NoSQL database and its data model:

1. **Document-Oriented Databases**: In document-oriented databases like MongoDB, indexing is essential for efficient

queries. You can create indexes on specific fields within documents. For example, indexing the Author field allows you to quickly find all documents authored by a specific author.

```
db.books.createIndex({ Author: 1 });
```

1. **Key-Value Stores**: In key-value stores like Redis, indexing is often less explicit compared to relational databases. The choice of keys and their organization can be considered a form of indexing. You create keys that allow you to retrieve values efficiently based on your access patterns.

```
SET user:alice "{ 'name': 'Alice', 'age': 30 }"
```

1. **Column-Family Stores**: In column-family stores like Apache Cassandra, indexing is achieved through the definition of secondary indexes. Secondary indexes allow you to query data based on columns other than the primary key columns. For example, you can create a secondary index on the Email column in a UserProfiles column family.

```
CREATE TABLE UserProfiles (

UserID UUID PRIMARY KEY,

FirstName TEXT,

LastName TEXT,

Email TEXT

);
```

CREATE INDEX ON UserProfiles (Email);

1. **Graph Databases**: In graph databases like Neo4j, indexing plays a vital role in optimizing graph traversal. Indexes are used to quickly locate nodes or relationships that match specific criteria, such as a node's property value or label.

MATCH (user:User { Username: 'alice' }) RETURN user;

Importance of Indexing in NoSQL Databases

Efficient indexing is critical in NoSQL databases for several reasons:

- **Query Performance**: Indexes significantly improve query performance by reducing the amount of data that needs to be scanned or traversed.

- **Scalability**: Well-designed indexes can scale with the data, ensuring that query performance remains acceptable as the dataset grows.

- **Flexibility**: NoSQL databases often handle schema-less or schema-flexible data, making indexing an essential tool for querying data with varying structures.

- **Data Retrieval**: Indexes enable quick and precise data retrieval, which is crucial in applications that require real-time or low-latency responses.

- **Complex Queries**: For databases that support complex queries, indexes facilitate efficient execution of these queries by reducing the number of operations required.

In summary, indexing in NoSQL databases serves the same fundamental purpose as in traditional relational databases: improving query performance. However, the implementation and considerations may differ based on the NoSQL database type and its data model. Understanding how indexing works in your chosen NoSQL database is essential for building efficient and responsive applications.

3.4 CAP Theorem and NoSQL

The CAP theorem, also known as Brewer's theorem, is a fundamental concept in distributed database systems and is highly relevant to NoSQL databases. It articulates the trade-offs that exist between three essential properties of a distributed system: Consistency, Availability, and Partition Tolerance. In this section, we will explore the CAP theorem and its implications for NoSQL databases.

CAP Theorem Basics

- **Consistency (C)**: This property implies that all nodes in a distributed system see the same data at the same time. In other words, if a write operation is successful, all subsequent read operations will return the written value. Achieving strong consistency can be challenging in distributed systems.

- **Availability (A)**: Availability means that every request to the distributed system, whether read or write, receives a response without guaranteeing that it returns the most recent data. High availability implies that the system is always responsive to requests.

- **Partition Tolerance (P)**: Partition tolerance refers to a system's ability to continue functioning even in the presence of network partitions or communication failures between nodes. Distributed systems must be partition-tolerant to ensure fault tolerance.

CAP Theorem Trade-offs

The CAP theorem asserts that in a distributed database system, you can only guarantee two out of the three properties simultaneously. This means that when facing network partitions or failures, you must make trade-offs between consistency and availability. Here are the classic trade-off scenarios:

1. **CA**: If you prioritize Consistency (C) and Availability (A), your system may not be Partition Tolerant (P). In this case, the system ensures strong consistency and high availability but may become unavailable when network partitions occur.
2. **CP**: If you prioritize Consistency (C) and Partition Tolerance (P), availability during network partitions may be compromised. In this scenario, the system remains consistent and can handle network partitions but may not always be available.
3. **AP**: If you prioritize Availability (A) and Partition Tolerance (P), you may need to sacrifice strong Consistency (C). In this case, the system remains available and can tolerate network partitions but may provide eventually consistent data.

Implications for NoSQL Databases

The CAP theorem has significant implications for NoSQL databases, as they are often used in distributed and highly available architectures. Here's how it relates to NoSQL databases:

1. **Consistency Models**: NoSQL databases offer different consistency models to address the CAP theorem trade-offs. Some databases provide strong consistency, while others offer eventual consistency. Developers must choose the appropriate consistency level based on their application's requirements.
2. **Database Types**: Different NoSQL database types prioritize different aspects of the CAP theorem. For example, some document-oriented databases prioritize Consistency and Partition Tolerance (CA), while some key-value stores prioritize Availability and Partition Tolerance (AP).
3. **Tunable Consistency**: Many NoSQL databases allow developers to tune the consistency level on a per-query or per-operation basis. This flexibility enables applications to strike a balance between strong consistency and high availability according to specific use cases.

Practical Considerations

When working with NoSQL databases in distributed systems, consider the following practical aspects related to the CAP theorem:

- **Understand Application Requirements**: Clearly define your application's requirements for consistency, availability, and fault tolerance. The choice of a NoSQL database and its configuration should align with these requirements.

- **Test for Failure Scenarios**: Conduct thorough testing to ensure that your chosen NoSQL database behaves as expected during network partitions or other failure scenarios. Understand how the database handles data in these situations.

- **Use Multi-Datacenter Deployments**: Some NoSQL databases support multi-datacenter deployments, which can improve both availability and partition tolerance. Consider leveraging such features for critical applications.

- **Monitoring and Alerting**: Implement monitoring and alerting systems to detect and respond to issues related to consistency, availability, and network partitions. Quick response to failures is crucial for maintaining system reliability.

In conclusion, the CAP theorem is a fundamental concept that impacts the design and operation of distributed systems, including NoSQL databases. Understanding the trade-offs between Consistency, Availability, and Partition Tolerance is essential for making informed decisions when choosing and configuring NoSQL databases in distributed applications.

3.5 Consistency, Availability, and Partition Tolerance

In the previous section, we discussed the CAP theorem and the trade-offs it presents in distributed systems, including NoSQL databases. Now, let's delve deeper into the concepts of Consistency, Availability, and Partition Tolerance (often abbreviated as CAP) and their implications for NoSQL databases.

Consistency (C)

Consistency in the context of the CAP theorem refers to the requirement that all nodes in a distributed system see the same data at the same time. When consistency is prioritized, it means that after a write operation is successful, any subsequent read operation will return the written value.

In NoSQL databases, consistency levels vary based on the database type and configuration. Some databases offer strong consistency, ensuring that all nodes return the most recent data, while others provide eventual consistency, where data may temporarily diverge but eventually converges to a consistent state.

For example, in a strongly consistent NoSQL database, if you perform a write operation and then immediately perform a read operation, you are guaranteed to see the written data. In an eventually consistent database, you may see the previous value for a short time until the system converges to the updated value.

Availability (A)

Availability means that every request to a distributed system, whether read or write, receives a response. High availability implies that the system is always responsive to requests, even in the presence of failures or network issues. Achieving high availability is essential for critical applications where downtime is unacceptable.

NoSQL databases, especially when used in distributed architectures, often prioritize availability. They are designed to handle faults, recover from failures, and remain operational even during network partitions or hardware issues. This focus on availability makes them suitable for applications that require constant uptime.

Partition Tolerance (P)

Partition tolerance is the ability of a distributed system to continue functioning despite network partitions or communication failures between nodes. In real-world scenarios, network partitions can occur due to various reasons, such as network congestion or hardware failures.

NoSQL databases must be partition-tolerant to ensure fault tolerance and data availability. When network partitions happen, a partition-tolerant database can continue to operate, although it may make trade-offs between consistency and availability, as discussed in the CAP theorem.

CAP Trade-offs in NoSQL Databases

NoSQL databases face the challenge of striking a balance between the three CAP properties. The CAP theorem suggests that in a distributed system, you can optimize for at most two of these properties simultaneously. Here are some common trade-offs in NoSQL databases:

1. **CA (Consistency and Availability)**: Some NoSQL databases prioritize both consistency and availability, sacrificing partition tolerance. They ensure that all nodes return the same data and remain available as long as there are no network partitions. However, they may become unavailable during network partitions.
2. **CP (Consistency and Partition Tolerance)**: Other NoSQL databases prioritize both consistency and partition tolerance, but availability during network partitions may be compromised. These databases aim to maintain strong consistency and tolerate network partitions but may not always be available.

3. **AP (Availability and Partition Tolerance)**: Many NoSQL databases, especially those used in highly available and distributed systems, prioritize availability and partition tolerance. They focus on remaining responsive even during network partitions but may provide eventual consistency instead of strong consistency.

Configurable Consistency Levels

NoSQL databases often allow developers to configure the consistency level on a per-query or per-operation basis. This configurability is crucial because it enables applications to make trade-offs based on specific use cases. Developers can choose the appropriate consistency level depending on the importance of consistency, availability, and partition tolerance for a particular operation.

For example, a financial application may require strong consistency for transactions to maintain data integrity, while a social media platform may prioritize availability during high traffic periods, accepting temporary inconsistency in exchange for responsiveness.

Monitoring and Tuning

To effectively manage consistency, availability, and partition tolerance in NoSQL databases, it's essential to implement monitoring and tuning mechanisms. Monitoring tools can help detect and respond to issues related to CAP properties, ensuring that the database operates within the desired parameters.

Tuning database configurations, consistency levels, and replication strategies can optimize the performance and behavior of NoSQL databases based on the application's requirements and the expected workload.

In conclusion, understanding and managing Consistency, Availability, and Partition Tolerance (CAP) is essential when working with NoSQL databases in distributed systems. NoSQL databases offer various options for configuring these properties, allowing developers to tailor their choices to specific application needs. Striking the right balance between these properties is a critical aspect of building robust and responsive distributed applications.

Chapter 4: Implementing NoSQL Solutions

4.1 Setting Up a NoSQL Database

Setting up a NoSQL database is the first step in implementing NoSQL solutions for your applications. In this section, we will explore the process of setting up a NoSQL database, including the necessary steps and considerations.

Choose the Right NoSQL Database

Before setting up a NoSQL database, it's crucial to choose the right database type that aligns with your application's requirements. As discussed in previous chapters, there are several types of NoSQL databases, including document-oriented, key-value stores, column-family stores, and graph databases. Each type has its strengths and weaknesses, so make an informed choice based on your use case.

Installation and Deployment

Once you've selected the NoSQL database type, the next step is to install and deploy the database. Here are some common installation and deployment methods for various NoSQL databases:

Document-Oriented Databases

- **MongoDB**: MongoDB provides official installation packages for various platforms. You can download and install MongoDB Community Server for free.

Additionally, cloud-based MongoDB services are available for easy deployment.

 # Install MongoDB on Ubuntu

sudo apt-get install -y mongodb

• **Couchbase**: Couchbase offers installation packages and container images for different platforms. You can download and install Couchbase Server or use containerization tools like Docker.

 # Pull and run Couchbase Server in a Docker container

docker run -d—name couchbase -p 8091-8094:8091-8094 -p 11210:11210 couchbase:latest

Key-Value Stores

• **Redis**: Redis provides installation packages and container images. You can easily set up a Redis server on various operating systems or use Docker for containerization.

 # Pull and run Redis in a Docker container

docker run -d—name redis -p 6379:6379 redis:latest

Column-Family Stores

• **Apache Cassandra**: Cassandra offers installation packages and Docker images. You can install Cassandra on your servers or use containerization for testing and development.

 # Pull and run Apache Cassandra in a Docker container

docker run -d—name cassandra -p 9042:9042 cassandra:latest

Graph Databases

- **Neo4j**: Neo4j provides installation packages and Docker images. You can set up Neo4j on your system or use Docker for quick deployment.

 # Pull and run Neo4j in a Docker container

docker run -d—name neo4j -p 7474:7474 -p 7687:7687 neo4j:latest

Configuration and Initialization

After installation, you'll need to configure and initialize the NoSQL database. Configuration settings may include network settings, authentication, data directory locations, and more. Refer to the database's official documentation for detailed configuration instructions.

For some NoSQL databases, you may need to initialize the database by creating keyspaces, tables, or collections. This step involves defining the data structures and schemas required for your application.

Data Modeling and Schema Design

Data modeling is a critical aspect of setting up a NoSQL database. Depending on the database type, you may need to design document structures, define column families, or create graph schemas.

Carefully plan and implement your data model to align with your application's requirements and access patterns.

Data Ingestion

Once the database is set up and configured, you can begin ingesting data. This involves inserting or importing data into the NoSQL database. The method of data ingestion may vary based on the database type and your application's needs. NoSQL databases often support various data formats, making it easier to work with different data sources.

Testing and Optimization

After data ingestion, it's essential to conduct thorough testing to ensure that the NoSQL database behaves as expected. Test the database's performance, scalability, and fault tolerance under different conditions. Identify and address any bottlenecks or issues.

Optimization is an ongoing process. You may need to fine-tune database configurations, indexes, and query patterns to achieve the desired performance and scalability for your application.

Backups and Disaster Recovery

Implement a backup and disaster recovery strategy for your NoSQL database to safeguard your data. Regularly back up the database and ensure that backups are stored securely. Create a plan for recovering data in case of unexpected failures or data loss.

Monitoring and Maintenance

Set up monitoring tools to keep an eye on the database's health and performance. Monitoring can help detect issues early and allow for proactive maintenance. Regularly apply updates, patches, and security fixes to keep the database secure and up to date.

In summary, setting up a NoSQL database involves choosing the right database type, installing and deploying the database, configuring and initializing it, designing the data model, ingesting data, testing, optimizing, implementing backups and disaster recovery plans, and setting up monitoring and maintenance procedures. Careful planning and execution at each step are

4.2 CRUD Operations in NoSQL

CRUD (Create, Read, Update, Delete) operations are fundamental when working with NoSQL databases, just as they are in traditional relational databases. In this section, we will explore how CRUD operations are performed in NoSQL databases, emphasizing the differences and similarities with SQL databases.

Create (Insert) Operations

Document-Oriented Databases

In document-oriented databases like MongoDB, creating a new document is straightforward. You insert a JSON or BSON document into a collection.

```
// Insert a new document into the "users" collection

db.users.insert({

name: "Alice",

age: 30,

email: "alice@example.com"
```

})

Key-Value Stores

In key-value stores like Redis, you set a key with an associated value.

```
# Set a key "user:1" with a JSON value
SET user:1 "{ 'name': 'Alice', 'age': 30 }"
```

Column-Family Stores

In column-family stores like Apache Cassandra, creating a new row involves specifying the keyspace, table, and values for columns.

```
—Insert a new row into the "user_profiles" table
INSERT INTO user_profiles (user_id, first_name, last_name, email)
VALUES (1, 'Alice', 'Smith', 'alice@example.com');
```

Graph Databases

In graph databases like Neo4j, creating nodes and relationships is the primary operation for data creation.

```
// Create a new user node
CREATE (user:User { name: 'Alice', age: 30 })
// Create a friendship relationship
MATCH (alice:User { name: 'Alice' }), (bob:User { name: 'Bob' })
CREATE (alice)-[:FRIENDS]->(bob)
```

Read Operations

Document-Oriented Databases

Reading documents in MongoDB is done using the find() method.

// Find all documents in the "users" collection

db.users.find()

Key-Value Stores

In Redis, you can read the value associated with a key.

 # Get the value associated with the key "user:1"

GET user:1

Column-Family Stores

Reading data in Cassandra involves executing queries, such as SELECT statements.

—Retrieve user profile data by user ID

SELECT * FROM user_profiles WHERE user_id = 1;

Graph Databases

Neo4j uses the Cypher query language to retrieve data based on patterns.

// Find all users

MATCH (user:User)

```
RETURN user;

// Find friends of Alice

MATCH (alice:User { name: 'Alice' })-[:FRIENDS]->(friend)

RETURN friend;
```

Update Operations

Document-Oriented Databases

To update documents in MongoDB, you can use the update() or updateOne() method.

```
// Update Alice's age

db.users.update({ name: "Alice" }, { $set: { age: 31 } })
```

Key-Value Stores

Redis allows you to update the value associated with a key.

```
# Update Alice's age

SET user:1 "{ 'name': 'Alice', 'age': 31 }"
```

Column-Family Stores

In Cassandra, updates can be performed using UPDATE statements.

```
—Update Alice's email address

UPDATE user_profiles SET email = 'alice.new@example.com' WHERE user_id = 1;
```

Graph Databases

Neo4j allows you to update properties of nodes or relationships.

```
// Update Alice's age
MATCH (user:User { name: 'Alice' })
SET user.age = 31;
```

Delete Operations

Document-Oriented Databases

Deleting documents in MongoDB can be done using the remove() method.

```
// Delete all documents with age greater than 30
db.users.remove({ age: { $gt: 30 } })
```

Key-Value Stores

In Redis, you can delete a key and its associated value.

```
# Delete the key "user:1"
DEL user:1
```

Column-Family Stores

Deletion in Cassandra is performed using DELETE statements.

```
—Delete a user's profile by user ID
DELETE FROM user_profiles WHERE user_id = 1;
```

Graph Databases

In Neo4j, you can delete nodes, relationships, or properties as needed.

```
// Delete Alice and her relationships

MATCH (user:User { name: 'Alice' })-[r]-()

DELETE user, r;
```

Consistency Considerations

One of the key differences between NoSQL and SQL databases is the consistency model. NoSQL databases often provide tunable consistency, allowing you to choose between strong or eventual consistency for different operations. It's essential to understand and configure the consistency level that suits your application's requirements when working with NoSQL databases.

In conclusion, CRUD operations in NoSQL databases involve creating, reading, updating, and deleting data. The specific syntax and methods vary depending on the type of NoSQL database you are using. Additionally, NoSQL databases offer flexibility in terms of data modeling and consistency, allowing you to tailor your approach to your application's needs.

4.3 Querying in NoSQL Databases

Querying data is a fundamental aspect of working with databases, including NoSQL databases. In this section, we will explore how querying works in various types of NoSQL databases and the different approaches you can take to retrieve and manipulate data.

Document-Oriented Databases

In document-oriented databases like MongoDB, querying is typically performed using the database's query language. MongoDB uses a flexible and powerful query language that allows you to search for documents based on criteria, filter fields, and project specific fields in the results.

Here's an example of a MongoDB query to find all users with an age greater than 25:

```
// Find users with age greater than 25

db.users.find({ age: { $gt: 25 } })
```

You can also perform complex queries, including logical operators, sorting, and aggregation operations.

Key-Value Stores

Key-value stores like Redis primarily rely on key-based lookups. To query data, you need to know the key associated with the value you want to retrieve. Key-value stores are highly efficient for simple read operations by key.

```
# Get the value associated with the key "user:1"

GET user:1
```

However, querying by attributes within the values is not a primary feature of key-value stores, and complex queries are typically not supported.

Column-Family Stores

Column-family stores, such as Apache Cassandra, use a query language to retrieve data. Cassandra's query language (CQL) allows you to define queries based on specific column values or ranges.

Here's an example CQL query to find user profiles with a specific email address:

```
—Find user profiles by email

SELECT * FROM user_profiles WHERE email = 'alice@example.com';
```

Cassandra's querying capabilities are suitable for a wide range of data retrieval scenarios.

Graph Databases

Graph databases, like Neo4j, are designed for querying complex relationships between data points. These databases use query languages specifically tailored to traverse and analyze graph structures.

Here's an example Cypher query in Neo4j to find friends of a user named Alice:

```
// Find friends of Alice

MATCH (alice:User { name: 'Alice' })-[:FRIENDS]->(friend)

RETURN friend;
```

Cypher allows you to express intricate patterns in the graph, making it well-suited for applications involving complex relationships.

Consistency and Query Performance

When querying data in NoSQL databases, it's essential to consider the consistency level you want for your queries. Some NoSQL databases offer tunable consistency, allowing you to choose between strong consistency and eventual consistency based on your application's requirements.

Query performance can vary depending on the size of the dataset, the complexity of the query, and the database's indexing and optimization capabilities. NoSQL databases often provide tools and features to optimize query performance, such as secondary indexes, caching mechanisms, and query optimization.

Indexing

Indexing plays a crucial role in optimizing query performance in NoSQL databases. By creating indexes on specific fields, you can speed up data retrieval for queries that filter or sort based on those fields.

For example, in MongoDB, you can create an index on the "age" field to improve the performance of queries that filter by age:

```
// Create an index on the "age" field

db.users.createIndex({ age: 1 })
```

Similarly, in Cassandra, you can create secondary indexes to enable efficient querying of non-primary key columns.

Distributed Querying

In distributed NoSQL databases, querying may involve multiple nodes or partitions. Distributed querying presents challenges related to data consistency and coordination across nodes. Most distributed

NoSQL databases handle these aspects internally, but developers should be aware of the underlying mechanisms to design efficient queries.

Query Optimization

Query optimization is an ongoing process in NoSQL databases. As your dataset grows and query patterns change, you may need to review and adjust your queries to maintain optimal performance. Some NoSQL databases provide query profiling and performance analysis tools to help identify bottlenecks and areas for improvement.

In summary, querying in NoSQL databases varies depending on the database type, and each type offers specific features and capabilities. Understanding the query language and indexing options for your chosen NoSQL database is essential for effectively retrieving and manipulating data. Additionally, considering consistency, query performance, and optimization strategies is crucial to building robust and efficient applications with NoSQL databases.

4.4 Data Migration to NoSQL

Data migration is a critical aspect of implementing NoSQL solutions, especially when transitioning from traditional relational databases (SQL) to NoSQL databases. In this section, we will explore the considerations, challenges, and strategies involved in migrating data to NoSQL databases.

Why Data Migration?

Data migration is necessary for various reasons, including:

1. **Application Requirements**: If your application's data

model evolves, you may need to migrate data to accommodate new structures or relationships.
2. **Scaling Needs**: As your application grows, you may need to migrate data to a more scalable NoSQL database to handle increased data volume and traffic.
3. **Performance Improvement**: NoSQL databases are designed for specific use cases and can offer better performance for certain types of queries and workloads.
4. **Cost Efficiency**: NoSQL databases often provide cost advantages for massive datasets compared to traditional SQL databases.

Data Modeling

Before migrating data, it's essential to design the data model in the NoSQL database to match your application's needs. This may involve defining collections, key spaces, column families, or graph schemas. Ensuring that the data model aligns with your application requirements is crucial for a successful migration.

Data Transformation

Data may need to be transformed from its original format to fit the data model of the NoSQL database. This can include restructuring JSON documents, splitting data into multiple collections or tables, or aggregating data for efficient querying.

Here's an example of transforming SQL data into a format suitable for a document-oriented NoSQL database:

—SQL Table

CREATE TABLE users (

id INT **PRIMARY KEY**,

```
name VARCHAR(255),
age INT
);
```

—Document-Oriented NoSQL Format

```
{
_id: 1,
name: "Alice",
age: 30
}
```

Data Extraction

To migrate data, you need to extract it from the source database. This may involve writing scripts or using ETL (Extract, Transform, Load) tools to export data from SQL databases, CSV files, or other sources into a format compatible with the NoSQL database.

Here's a simplified example of extracting data from a CSV file and inserting it into a MongoDB collection using Python:

```
import csv
from pymongo import MongoClient
# Connect to MongoDB
client = MongoClient('mongodb://localhost:27017/')
db = client['mydb']
collection = db['users']
```

```
# Extract data from CSV and insert into MongoDB
with open('data.csv', 'r') as file:
reader = csv.DictReader(file)
for row in reader:
collection.insert_one(row)
```

Data Loading

Once data is extracted and transformed, it needs to be loaded into the NoSQL database. This can involve bulk insertion or batch loading, depending on the size of the dataset.

Data Validation

Data migration should include validation steps to ensure data integrity. Verify that the migrated data matches the original data in terms of structure, content, and relationships.

Testing and Rollback

Before deploying the migrated data in a production environment, it's essential to thoroughly test it in a staging or development environment. Testing helps identify any issues or discrepancies that may have occurred during the migration process.

Additionally, having a rollback plan is crucial in case the migration encounters unexpected problems or errors during testing. Being able to revert to the previous state ensures minimal disruption to your application.

Monitoring and Optimization

After migrating data, monitor the performance of your NoSQL database and make any necessary optimizations. Adjust indexing, query patterns, and configurations to ensure optimal query performance and resource utilization.

Data Synchronization

In some scenarios, data migration is not a one-time event but an ongoing process. Implement mechanisms for data synchronization between your SQL and NoSQL databases to keep them up-to-date as your application continues to evolve.

Challenges and Considerations

Data migration to NoSQL databases can present several challenges, including:

- Handling data consistency during migration.
- Dealing with data that spans multiple tables or collections in SQL databases.
- Ensuring data security and access control in the NoSQL environment.
- Addressing differences in data types and structures between SQL and NoSQL databases.
- Managing large volumes of data efficiently during the migration process.

In conclusion, data migration to NoSQL databases is a critical step when transitioning from SQL databases or when accommodating changing application needs. Proper planning, data modeling, extraction, transformation, and validation are essential to ensure a successful and efficient migration. Regular monitoring and optimization are also crucial to maintaining data integrity and performance in the NoSQL environment.

4.5 Best Practices in NoSQL Implementation

Implementing NoSQL solutions effectively requires adherence to best practices that ensure optimal performance, scalability, security, and maintainability. In this section, we will explore a set of best practices to consider when working with NoSQL databases.

1. Understand Your Data and Use Case

Before choosing a NoSQL database and designing your data model, thoroughly understand your data and application use case. Different types of NoSQL databases are better suited for specific scenarios, so choose the one that aligns with your requirements.

2. Plan Your Data Model Carefully

Design your data model to match your application's query patterns. In document-oriented databases, this involves structuring your documents to optimize retrieval. In graph databases, define node and relationship types that reflect your data's relationships.

3. Normalize or Denormalize as Appropriate

Decide whether to normalize or denormalize your data. Normalization reduces data redundancy and updates but may require more complex queries. Denormalization simplifies queries but can result in data redundancy. Strike a balance based on your application's needs.

4. Optimize Queries

NoSQL databases offer various query options, so choose the appropriate query method and index your data effectively. Understand the query language and capabilities of your chosen NoSQL database to create efficient queries.

5. Implement Security Measures

Implement robust security measures, including authentication and authorization mechanisms, to protect your NoSQL database. Ensure that sensitive data is encrypted, and access control is well-defined and enforced.

6. Backup and Disaster Recovery

Set up regular backups and establish a disaster recovery plan. NoSQL databases can also benefit from replication and sharding for data redundancy and high availability.

7. Monitor Performance

Use monitoring tools to track your NoSQL database's performance. Identify and address performance bottlenecks, resource utilization issues, and slow queries promptly.

8. Scaling Strategies

Plan for scalability from the beginning. Understand whether your NoSQL database supports horizontal scaling and design your application to take advantage of it. Implement auto-scaling solutions where possible to handle increased workloads.

9. Consider Data Consistency Levels

Understand the consistency models offered by your NoSQL database. Choose the appropriate consistency level for your use case, balancing between strong consistency and high availability.

10. Data Compression and Caching

Implement data compression techniques to reduce storage costs and improve data transfer efficiency. Use caching mechanisms to reduce the load on your NoSQL database and improve query response times.

11. Regular Updates and Maintenance

Stay up to date with the latest releases and updates of your NoSQL database. Apply security patches and performance enhancements regularly to keep your system secure and efficient.

12. Data Migration Strategies

Have a well-defined data migration strategy in place, especially if you plan to transition from a SQL to a NoSQL database. Test data migration thoroughly in a non-production environment before executing it in production.

13. Documentation and Training

Document your database schema, data models, and configurations comprehensively. Ensure that your team is well-trained in using the chosen NoSQL database effectively.

14. Plan for Failures

Anticipate failures and implement strategies for failover and recovery. Test failover scenarios to ensure minimal downtime in case of node or network failures.

15. Consider the Cloud

Evaluate the benefits of cloud-based NoSQL solutions, which can simplify infrastructure management, scaling, and disaster recovery. Choose a cloud provider that aligns with your requirements.

16. Compliance and Regulations

If your application handles sensitive or regulated data, ensure that your NoSQL implementation complies with relevant data protection and privacy regulations.

17. Regularly Review and Optimize

Periodically review your NoSQL implementation to identify areas for optimization. The needs of your application may change over time, so adapt your database accordingly.

By following these best practices, you can maximize the benefits of NoSQL databases while minimizing potential pitfalls. Effective NoSQL implementation is essential for building robust and scalable applications that can handle the demands of modern data-driven environments.

Chapter 5: NoSQL and Big Data

5.1 The Role of NoSQL in Big Data

Big data has become a critical aspect of modern business and technology landscapes. It refers to the vast amounts of structured and unstructured data generated at high velocity and requiring sophisticated tools and technologies for storage, processing, and analysis. NoSQL databases play a significant role in managing and harnessing the power of big data. In this section, we will explore the role of NoSQL in handling big data challenges.

Characteristics of Big Data

Big data is characterized by the "Three Vs":

1. **Volume**: The sheer amount of data generated, often in terabytes, petabytes, or even exabytes, exceeds the capacity of traditional relational databases.
2. **Velocity**: Data is generated and updated at an unprecedented rate, making real-time processing and analysis crucial.
3. **Variety**: Big data encompasses various data types, including structured, semi-structured, and unstructured data, such as text, images, videos, and social media content.

Challenges of Traditional Databases

Traditional SQL databases face limitations when dealing with big data:

• Scalability: SQL databases struggle to scale horizontally to accommodate the volume and velocity of big data.

• Schema Rigidity: Fixed schemas in SQL databases can hinder the storage of diverse data types.

• High Latency: Complex joins and transactions may result in high latency, affecting real-time data processing.

• Cost: Scaling vertically to handle big data often incurs substantial hardware and licensing costs.

How NoSQL Addresses Big Data Challenges

NoSQL databases are well-suited for big data scenarios due to their flexible data models, horizontal scalability, and real-time processing capabilities:

1. **Flexible Schema**: NoSQL databases, especially document-oriented and key-value stores, allow you to store and query data without rigid schemas. This flexibility accommodates the variety of data encountered in big data applications.
2. **Horizontal Scalability**: NoSQL databases can distribute data across multiple nodes, enabling them to handle large volumes of data and high velocity. This scalability ensures that systems can grow as data grows.
3. **Real-time Processing**: Many NoSQL databases are designed for low-latency read and write operations, making them suitable for real-time analytics and processing of streaming data.
4. **Distributed Architectures**: NoSQL databases are often built on distributed architectures, providing fault tolerance and high availability. This is crucial for ensuring data integrity in big data environments.
5. **Cost-Effective**: NoSQL databases can be more cost-effective for storing and processing massive datasets

compared to traditional SQL databases, thanks to their horizontal scaling capabilities.

Use Cases of NoSQL in Big Data

NoSQL databases find applications in various big data use cases:

- **Internet of Things (IoT)**: NoSQL databases can handle the massive volumes of data generated by IoT devices, storing sensor data, telemetry data, and event logs for analysis.

- **Social Media Analytics**: NoSQL databases are used to store and analyze social media data, including user-generated content, sentiment analysis, and trending topics.

- **Log and Event Data**: NoSQL databases are ideal for storing log files, event data, and clickstream data, which are generated at high velocity and require real-time analysis.

- **Recommendation Systems**: NoSQL databases are used to build recommendation engines by storing and processing user behavior data to suggest products, services, or content.

- **Fraud Detection**: NoSQL databases help detect fraudulent activities by processing large datasets in real-time and identifying anomalous patterns.

NoSQL and Big Data Technologies

NoSQL databases often work in tandem with other big data technologies, such as Hadoop, Spark, and Kafka. These ecosystems provide tools for data processing, batch and stream processing, and data ingestion, while NoSQL databases store and serve the processed data.

In summary, NoSQL databases have become integral to managing and extracting insights from big data. Their flexibility, scalability, and real-time capabilities make them well-suited for addressing the challenges posed by the volume, velocity, and variety of data in the big data landscape. Organizations can harness the power of big data by leveraging NoSQL databases in their data architectures and analytics pipelines.

5.2 Handling Large Scale Data with NoSQL

Handling large-scale data is a central aspect of big data applications, and NoSQL databases excel in managing vast volumes of data efficiently. In this section, we will explore how NoSQL databases address the challenges of handling large-scale data and the strategies and features they offer for scalability and performance.

Distributed Architecture

One of the primary reasons NoSQL databases are suitable for large-scale data is their distributed architecture. NoSQL databases are designed to operate across multiple nodes or servers, allowing data to be distributed and partitioned across the cluster. This architecture provides several advantages:

- **Scalability**: NoSQL databases can scale horizontally by adding more nodes to the cluster. This horizontal scaling enables them to handle growing data volumes and traffic loads effortlessly.

- **Fault Tolerance**: Distributed NoSQL databases are fault-tolerant, meaning they can continue functioning even if individual nodes or servers fail. Data redundancy and replication mechanisms ensure data integrity.

- **Load Balancing**: Requests are evenly distributed across nodes, preventing overloading of any single server and ensuring consistent performance, even under heavy loads.

Data Partitioning

Data partitioning is a key technique used in NoSQL databases to manage large datasets efficiently. Partitioning involves splitting the data into smaller subsets and distributing them across nodes. There are various partitioning strategies, including:

- **Range Partitioning**: Data is partitioned based on a specific range of values, such as date ranges or numerical ranges. This strategy is effective for time-series data.

- **Hash Partitioning**: Data is partitioned based on a hash of a unique key or identifier. Hash partitioning evenly distributes data and helps with load balancing.

- **Sharding**: Sharding involves dividing the data into shards, where each shard is a self-contained subset of data with its own nodes. This strategy is common in document-oriented and column-family databases.

CAP Theorem and Trade-Offs

NoSQL databases often adhere to the principles of the CAP theorem (Consistency, Availability, Partition Tolerance). According to the CAP theorem, a distributed system can provide at most two of the following three guarantees:

- **Consistency**: All nodes in the system see the same data simultaneously.
- **Availability**: Every request to the system receives a response, without guaranteeing that it contains the most recent data.
- **Partition Tolerance**: The system continues to operate even in the presence of network partitions or communication failures.

NoSQL databases make trade-offs between these guarantees based on their use cases. For example, some prioritize availability and partition tolerance, while others prioritize consistency. Understanding the trade-offs is crucial when selecting a NoSQL database for handling large-scale data.

Caching and In-Memory Databases

Caching is another strategy for optimizing the performance of NoSQL databases when dealing with large-scale data. Caching involves storing frequently accessed data in memory, reducing the need to retrieve it from disk, which is slower. In-memory databases, such as Redis, specialize in fast data retrieval by keeping data entirely in RAM.

Caching can significantly reduce latency for read-heavy workloads, making it suitable for applications that require real-time access to data. However, it may require careful management to ensure that cached data remains consistent with the underlying database.

Parallel Processing and MapReduce

Some NoSQL databases support parallel processing and MapReduce, a programming model for processing large datasets in parallel across a distributed cluster. MapReduce allows developers to perform complex data transformations and analytics on large-scale data efficiently.

For example, Hadoop, a popular big data framework, uses MapReduce for batch processing of vast datasets. NoSQL databases like MongoDB also offer MapReduce capabilities for data analysis tasks.

Compression and Data Serialization

Efficient storage and transmission of data are crucial when dealing with large-scale data. NoSQL databases often provide features for data compression and serialization. Compression reduces the storage space required for data, while serialization ensures data can be efficiently transmitted over the network.

By using these features, NoSQL databases can minimize the storage costs and network bandwidth required to handle large-scale data effectively.

Monitoring and Auto-Scaling

To manage large-scale data effectively, NoSQL databases often provide monitoring and auto-scaling capabilities. Monitoring tools help administrators track database performance, identify bottlenecks, and optimize resource utilization.

Auto-scaling allows the database to dynamically allocate additional resources as needed to handle spikes in traffic or data growth. This ensures that the system remains responsive and available during periods of high demand.

In conclusion, NoSQL databases are well-suited for handling large-scale data due to their distributed architecture, partitioning strategies, and various optimization techniques. When working with large-scale data, it's essential to choose the right NoSQL database, implement effective partitioning and caching strategies, and consider trade-offs related to consistency and availability. Additionally, monitoring and auto-scaling play crucial roles in ensuring that the database can adapt to the demands of large-scale data processing and storage.

5.3 NoSQL for Real-Time Analytics

Real-time analytics is a critical component of many modern applications and businesses. It involves the continuous analysis of data as it is generated or ingested, providing insights and actionable information instantly. NoSQL databases are well-suited for real-time analytics due to their ability to handle high-velocity data streams and flexible data models. In this section, we will explore how NoSQL databases are used in real-time analytics scenarios.

Characteristics of Real-Time Analytics

Real-time analytics is characterized by the following key features:

- **High Velocity**: Data is generated, ingested, and analyzed in near-real-time, often at sub-second or millisecond intervals. This requires databases that can keep up with the data's rapid pace.

- **Streaming Data**: Data arrives in a continuous stream, such as log data, sensor data, social media updates, or financial transactions. Real-time analytics systems process and analyze data as it arrives.

- **Low Latency**: The speed of data processing is crucial. Users expect minimal delay between data generation and the availability of insights or responses.

- **Complex Queries**: Real-time analytics often involves complex queries, aggregations, and transformations to derive meaningful insights from the data.

NoSQL Databases for Real-Time Analytics

Several types of NoSQL databases are commonly used in real-time analytics:

1. **Key-Value Stores**: Key-value stores like Redis are well-suited for caching and real-time data lookups. They provide fast read and write operations, making them ideal for serving frequently accessed data.
2. **Document-Oriented Databases**: Document-oriented databases like MongoDB and Couchbase can store and query semi-structured data, making them suitable for real-time analytics where data structures may evolve rapidly.
3. **Column-Family Stores**: Column-family stores like Apache Cassandra excel in handling high write and read throughput. They are used in applications where data is ingested rapidly and queried frequently.
4. **In-Memory Databases**: In-memory databases like Apache Ignite and Redis are optimized for storing and querying data entirely in RAM, offering ultra-low latency for real-

time analytics.

5. **Time-Series Databases**: Time-series databases like InfluxDB and TimescaleDB are specialized for storing and analyzing time-series data, making them ideal for applications that require real-time monitoring and analytics of time-stamped data.

Use Cases of NoSQL in Real-Time Analytics

Real-time analytics powered by NoSQL databases find applications in various domains:

- **E-commerce**: Real-time product recommendations, inventory management, and fraud detection in online transactions.

- **IoT**: Monitoring and analyzing data from IoT devices for predictive maintenance, anomaly detection, and real-time decision-making.

- **Social Media**: Analyzing social media streams for sentiment analysis, trending topics, and user engagement insights.

- **Financial Services**: Detecting fraudulent transactions, real-time risk assessment, and algorithmic trading.

- **Healthcare**: Real-time monitoring of patient data, medical equipment, and drug interactions for patient care and research.

Components of Real-Time Analytics Systems

Building a real-time analytics system with NoSQL databases involves several key components:

1. **Data Ingestion**: Data from various sources, such as sensors, logs, or user interactions, is ingested into the system in real-time. Streaming platforms like Apache Kafka and Apache Flink are often used for data ingestion.
2. **Data Processing**: Data is processed as it arrives, including filtering, enrichment, aggregation, and transformation. Stream processing frameworks like Apache Kafka Streams and Apache Spark Streaming are commonly used.
3. **NoSQL Database**: The NoSQL database stores and serves the processed data, enabling real-time querying and analysis. Data models and indexing play a crucial role in optimizing query performance.
4. **Query Engine**: A query engine or analytics tool allows users to interact with the data in real-time, running ad-hoc queries and generating reports or visualizations.
5. **Monitoring and Alerting**: Real-time analytics systems typically include monitoring and alerting mechanisms to detect anomalies, issues, or performance bottlenecks.

Real-Time Analytics with NoSQL Example

Let's consider a simplified example of real-time analytics using Apache Kafka for data ingestion, Apache Spark for data processing, and Apache Cassandra as the NoSQL database. In this scenario, we are analyzing website traffic data in real-time to identify popular pages:

```
# Python code for Apache Kafka data ingestion
```

```
from kafka import KafkaProducer

producer = KafkaProducer(bootstrap_servers='kafka-server:9092')

producer.send('web-traffic', value='{"page": "/homepage", "timestamp": "2023-01-15T10:30:00"}')

# Apache Spark Streaming for data processing

from pyspark.streaming import StreamingContext

from pyspark.streaming.kafka import KafkaUtils

ssc = StreamingContext(sparkContext, 1)

kafkaStream = KafkaUtils.createStream(ssc, 'localhost:2181', 'web-traffic', {'web-traffic': 1})

# Real-time analytics using Apache Cassandra

from cassandra.cluster import Cluster

cluster = Cluster(['cassandra-node1', 'cassandra-node2'])

session = cluster.connect('web_analytics')

# Process incoming data and store in Cassandra

def process_data(rdd):

# Perform analytics and store data in Cassandra

rdd.foreach(lambda record: session.execute("INSERT INTO popular_pages (page, timestamp) VALUES (?, ?)",

(record['page'], record['timestamp'])))

# Define the data processing pipeline
```

```
kafkaStream.map(lambda record: json.loads(record[1])).foreachRDD(process_data)

ssc.start()

ssc.awaitTermination()
```

In this example, data is ingested from a Kafka topic, processed in real-time using Spark Streaming, and stored in Cassandra for querying and analytics.

In summary, NoSQL databases are instrumental in enabling real-time analytics by efficiently handling high-velocity data streams and offering flexible data models. They find applications in various domains, from e-commerce to IoT and social media analytics. Building real-time analytics systems with NoSQL databases involves a combination of data ingestion, processing, storage, and query components,

5.4 Integration with Big Data Technologies

Integrating NoSQL databases with other big data technologies is a common practice to build robust and scalable data processing pipelines. This integration enables organizations to leverage the strengths of both NoSQL and big data tools for various data-driven applications. In this section, we will explore how NoSQL databases are integrated with big data technologies and the benefits of such combinations.

Big Data Ecosystem

The big data ecosystem consists of a wide range of tools and frameworks designed for different aspects of data processing, storage, and analysis. Some of the prominent components of the big data ecosystem include:

- **Hadoop**: An open-source framework for distributed storage (HDFS) and batch processing (MapReduce) of large datasets.

- **Apache Spark**: A powerful and versatile data processing framework that supports batch processing, real-time streaming, machine learning, and graph processing.

- **Apache Kafka**: A distributed event streaming platform used for real-time data ingestion and streaming analytics.

- **Apache Flink**: A stream processing framework that offers low-latency processing of data streams and complex event processing.

- **Apache Hive**: A data warehousing and SQL-like query language for querying and analyzing large datasets stored in Hadoop.

- **Apache HBase**: A distributed, scalable, and NoSQL database designed to provide real-time read/write access to large datasets.

- **Apache Cassandra**: A highly scalable, distributed NoSQL database for handling large volumes of data across multiple nodes.

Benefits of Integrating NoSQL with Big Data

Integrating NoSQL databases with big data technologies offers several advantages:

1. **Scalability**: Big data tools provide horizontal scalability, allowing NoSQL databases to handle massive datasets and growing workloads. This scalability is essential for applications with fluctuating data volumes.
2. **Real-Time Processing**: Combining NoSQL with real-time data processing frameworks like Apache Kafka and Apache Flink enables organizations to perform real-time analytics and make data-driven decisions instantly.
3. **Diverse Data Types**: NoSQL databases excel in handling diverse data types, such as semi-structured and unstructured data. They can store and serve data from sources like social media, IoT devices, and log files, which can be processed by big data tools.
4. **Complex Queries**: Big data frameworks like Apache Hive and Apache Spark allow users to run complex queries on vast datasets. When integrated with NoSQL, they can leverage the database's fast read capabilities.
5. **Machine Learning**: Big data and NoSQL databases can be integrated to support machine learning workflows. Large datasets stored in NoSQL databases can be processed and analyzed using big data frameworks to train machine learning models.

Integration Strategies

There are various strategies for integrating NoSQL databases with big data technologies:

1. **Batch Processing**: NoSQL databases can be used as data sources or sinks for batch processing frameworks like Hadoop and Spark. Data is extracted from the database, processed in batches, and results are stored back in the database.

2. **Real-Time Streaming**: NoSQL databases can ingest and store data from real-time streams processed by platforms like Apache Kafka or Apache Flink. This approach enables real-time analytics and decision-making.
3. **Polyglot Persistence**: Organizations can adopt a polyglot persistence approach, where different data storage technologies are used for specific use cases. NoSQL databases are chosen when data needs to be accessed and modified quickly, while big data tools are used for complex analytics.
4. **Data Warehousing**: NoSQL databases can feed data into data warehousing systems like Apache Hive for SQL-based querying and reporting. This approach combines the strengths of NoSQL for data storage and big data tools for analysis.

Example of Integration

Let's consider an example of integrating Apache Cassandra, a NoSQL database, with Apache Spark, a big data processing framework, for real-time analytics:

```
import org.apache.spark.{SparkConf, SparkContext}

import org.apache.spark.streaming.{Seconds, StreamingContext}

import com.datastax.spark.connector._

// Create a SparkConf and SparkContext

val conf = new SparkConf().setAppName("CassandraIntegration")

val sc = new SparkContext(conf)

// Create a Cassandra connector and specify the keyspace and table
```

```
val cassandraConnector = CassandraConnector(sc.getConf)

val keyspace = "my_keyspace"

val table = "my_table"

// Create a StreamingContext

val ssc = new StreamingContext(sc, Seconds(1))

// Create a DStream from a Kafka topic (assumed) containing real-time data

val kafkaStream = KafkaUtils.createStream(ssc, "localhost:2181", "my-consumer-group", Map("my-topic" -> 1))

// Process the streaming data and store it in Cassandra

kafkaStream.foreachRDD { rdd =>

rdd.saveToCassandra(keyspace, table)

}

// Start the streaming context

ssc.start()

ssc.awaitTermination()
```

In this example, Apache Spark Streaming ingests real-time data from a Kafka topic and stores it in Apache Cassandra for further analysis.

In conclusion, integrating NoSQL databases with big data technologies offers organizations the flexibility to handle diverse data types, perform real-time analytics, and scale their data processing pipelines. It enables data-driven decision-making and empowers organizations to extract valuable insights from their data, whether it's structured, semi-structured, or unstructured. By choosing the right integration strategy and tools, organizations can build powerful and efficient data processing pipelines that meet their specific requirements.

5.5 Case Studies: NoSQL in Big Data Applications

Real-world case studies demonstrate how NoSQL databases have played pivotal roles in addressing the data challenges of large-scale and complex big data applications. In this section, we will explore several case studies where NoSQL databases have been successfully employed to solve real-world big data problems.

1. Airbnb: Scaling with Apache Cassandra

Airbnb[1] is a global online marketplace for lodging and travel experiences. With millions of users and hosts worldwide, Airbnb faced the challenge of managing a vast amount of data related to property listings, reservations, reviews, and user interactions.

Airbnb adopted Apache Cassandra, a distributed NoSQL database, to address their scalability needs. Cassandra allowed Airbnb to handle high write and read throughput while maintaining data availability and fault tolerance. By distributing data across multiple clusters, Airbnb ensured that their platform remained responsive even during peak booking times.

2. Netflix: Real-Time Analytics with Apache Kafka and Cassandra

Netflix[2] is a leading streaming platform, serving millions of subscribers worldwide. To provide a seamless streaming experience

1. https://www.airbnb.com/

and deliver personalized content recommendations, Netflix relies on real-time analytics.

Netflix combines Apache Kafka for real-time data ingestion and Apache Cassandra for data storage and retrieval. Kafka enables Netflix to collect and process real-time user interactions, such as video playback and searches. These events are then stored in Cassandra, allowing Netflix to analyze user behavior and make real-time content recommendations.

3. Uber: Managing Geospatial Data with Redis

Uber[3] relies heavily on geospatial data to match riders with drivers and optimize routes. Managing real-time geospatial data at Uber's scale is a complex task.

Uber uses Redis, an in-memory key-value store, to efficiently handle geospatial data. Redis supports geospatial indexing and querying, making it ideal for tracking drivers and riders in real-time. This allows Uber to calculate estimated arrival times accurately and match riders with nearby drivers quickly.

4. Twitter: Analyzing Social Media Trends with HBase

Twitter[4] processes an immense amount of data daily, including tweets, retweets, likes, and user interactions. To provide real-time trending topics and analytics, Twitter turned to HBase, a distributed column-family NoSQL database.

HBase enables Twitter to store and retrieve tweets and user interactions efficiently. Its scalability and low-latency access make it

2. https://www.netflix.com/

3. https://www.uber.com/

4. https://twitter.com/

suitable for serving real-time data to millions of users worldwide. Twitter uses HBase to power features like trending hashtags and personalized timelines.

5. Facebook: Handling Graph Data with Apache TinkerPop and Gremlin

Facebook[5] manages one of the largest social networks globally, with billions of users and intricate relationships between them. To handle the complex graph data representing social connections, Facebook uses Apache TinkerPop and Gremlin.

Apache TinkerPop is a graph computing framework, and Gremlin is its query language. They allow Facebook to navigate and analyze the vast social graph efficiently. This technology powers features like friend recommendations and the "People You May Know" functionality.

These case studies illustrate how NoSQL databases and related technologies have become integral components of big data applications in various domains. NoSQL databases provide the scalability, flexibility, and performance needed to manage and analyze vast amounts of data in real-time. Whether it's in the context of e-commerce, streaming services, ride-sharing, social media, or online marketplaces, NoSQL databases play a critical role in enabling data-driven decision-making and delivering a seamless user experience.

5. https://www.facebook.com/

Chapter 6: NoSQL and Scalability

6.1 Understanding Scalability in NoSQL

Scalability is a critical aspect of modern database systems, and NoSQL databases have gained popularity for their ability to scale horizontally and meet the demands of applications dealing with massive datasets and high traffic. In this section, we will delve into the concept of scalability in the context of NoSQL databases, exploring what it means, the types of scalability, and the challenges associated with it.

What is Scalability?

Scalability refers to a system's ability to handle an increasing amount of work or data as it grows, without sacrificing performance or availability. In the realm of NoSQL databases, scalability is essential because modern applications often deal with a growing user base, large volumes of data, and the need for real-time processing.

Types of Scalability

1. Horizontal Scalability

Horizontal scalability, also known as "scale-out," involves adding more machines or nodes to the database cluster to handle increased load. NoSQL databases excel in horizontal scalability because they can distribute data across multiple servers, balancing the workload and improving performance.

In horizontal scalability, each new node contributes to the overall capacity of the system, making it an effective solution for accommodating growing datasets and traffic. Popular NoSQL databases like Apache Cassandra and MongoDB are designed with horizontal scalability in mind.

2. Vertical Scalability

Vertical scalability, also known as "scale-up," involves upgrading the existing hardware of a single server to handle increased load. While NoSQL databases primarily focus on horizontal scalability, vertical scalability can be necessary in certain situations, such as when a single server needs more processing power or memory.

Vertical scalability can be achieved by upgrading CPU, RAM, or storage capacity on a server. However, there are limitations to how much a single server can be scaled vertically, making horizontal scalability a preferred choice for handling substantial growth.

Challenges in Scalability

While NoSQL databases offer impressive scalability capabilities, they come with their set of challenges:

1. Data Distribution

In a distributed NoSQL database, data is distributed across multiple nodes. Ensuring an even distribution of data and efficient data retrieval can be a complex task. Improper data distribution can lead to hotspots and performance bottlenecks.

2. Data Consistency

Maintaining data consistency across distributed nodes while allowing for high availability is a challenge. NoSQL databases often employ strategies like eventual consistency to strike a balance between availability and consistency.

3. Partition Tolerance

Partition tolerance is one of the components of the CAP theorem (Consistency, Availability, Partition Tolerance) and refers to a system's ability to continue functioning even if network partitions occur. Achieving partition tolerance without sacrificing consistency or availability is a significant challenge in distributed systems.

4. Load Balancing

Effective load balancing is crucial in a horizontally scalable NoSQL database. Distributing incoming requests evenly among nodes ensures optimal performance. Load balancing algorithms and strategies must be implemented effectively.

5. Data Sharding

Data sharding involves dividing a large dataset into smaller, manageable pieces called shards. While it can improve performance, sharding requires careful planning and maintenance to ensure data remains evenly distributed and queries are efficient.

In summary, scalability is a fundamental requirement for modern applications, and NoSQL databases offer valuable solutions to achieve it. Understanding the types of scalability and addressing associated challenges is essential for building robust, high-performance systems that can handle the demands of today's data-intensive applications. In the subsequent sections, we will explore horizontal vs. vertical scaling, auto-scaling capabilities, and real-world case studies showcasing successful scalability solutions in NoSQL databases.

6.2 Horizontal vs. Vertical Scaling

Horizontal and vertical scaling are two distinct approaches to achieving scalability in database systems. In this section, we will explore the differences between these two methods and when each is most appropriate.

Horizontal Scaling

Horizontal scaling, often referred to as "scale-out," involves adding more machines or nodes to a distributed system to accommodate increased load and demand. Each new node contributes additional processing power, storage capacity, and network bandwidth to the overall system.

Advantages of Horizontal Scaling:

1. **Cost-Effective:** Horizontal scaling typically involves using commodity hardware, which is cost-effective compared to upgrading a single, powerful server in vertical scaling.
2. **High Availability:** Distributed systems built for horizontal scaling can continue to operate even if some nodes fail, ensuring high availability.
3. **Easy to Add Resources:** Adding more nodes is straightforward. It allows systems to adapt to varying workloads quickly.
4. **Linear Scalability:** Horizontal scaling often exhibits linear scalability, where adding more nodes results in a proportional increase in system capacity.

Challenges of Horizontal Scaling:

1. **Data Distribution:** Distributing data evenly across nodes can be complex, and improper data distribution can lead to performance issues.
2. **Data Consistency:** Ensuring data consistency in a distributed system while maintaining high availability is challenging and may require trade-offs.
3. **Complexity:** Managing a distributed system with many nodes can be more complex than managing a single server.

Vertical Scaling

Vertical scaling, also known as "scale-up," involves upgrading the existing hardware resources of a single server to handle increased load and demand. This typically includes increasing CPU power, memory, or storage capacity.

Advantages of Vertical Scaling:

1. **Simplicity:** Upgrading a single server is simpler and requires less operational overhead than managing a distributed system with multiple nodes.
2. **Uniform Performance:** A single, powerful server can offer uniform performance, which can be advantageous for applications with specific performance requirements.
3. **Data Localization:** In some cases, having all data on a single server can simplify data access and reduce latency.

Challenges of Vertical Scaling:

1. **Limited Scalability:** Vertical scaling has inherent limits. A single server can only be upgraded to a certain extent, and

beyond that, it may not be feasible or cost-effective.

2. **Downtime:** Upgrading a server may require downtime, which can impact the availability of the application.
3. **Cost:** Vertical scaling can be costly, especially when using high-end server hardware.

Choosing Between Horizontal and Vertical Scaling

The choice between horizontal and vertical scaling depends on various factors, including the specific requirements of the application, budget constraints, and the expected growth in workload. In general, NoSQL databases are designed with horizontal scaling in mind, making them well-suited for applications with dynamic and unpredictable growth. However, there are situations where vertical scaling may be a better fit, such as applications with strict performance requirements and a relatively stable workload.

Ultimately, the decision should be based on a careful evaluation of the application's scalability needs, the available resources, and the trade-offs between the two approaches. In the next section, we will explore auto-scaling capabilities in NoSQL databases, which allow for dynamic resource allocation based on workload fluctuations.

6.3 Auto-Scaling Capabilities in NoSQL

Auto-scaling is a crucial feature in NoSQL databases, providing the ability to dynamically allocate and deallocate resources based on workload demands. In this section, we will explore the concept of auto-scaling in NoSQL databases, its benefits, and how it works.

What is Auto-Scaling?

Auto-scaling, also known as automatic scaling, is the process of automatically adjusting the computing resources (e.g., CPU, memory, storage, or database instances) allocated to an application or database system in response to changes in workload. The goal of auto-scaling is to ensure optimal performance and resource utilization while minimizing manual intervention.

Benefits of Auto-Scaling in NoSQL Databases:

1. **Cost Efficiency:** Auto-scaling allows resources to be provisioned only when needed, reducing operational costs during periods of low activity.
2. **Performance Optimization:** It ensures that the database can handle increased loads without performance degradation.
3. **High Availability:** Auto-scaling can enhance fault tolerance by distributing workloads across multiple instances or nodes, ensuring high availability.
4. **Resource Utilization:** It maximizes the efficient use of resources, preventing over-provisioning or under-provisioning.

How Auto-Scaling Works in NoSQL Databases:

Auto-scaling in NoSQL databases involves several key components and processes:

1. Monitoring Metrics:

Auto-scaling relies on continuous monitoring of various metrics, such as CPU utilization, memory usage, query response times, and the number of concurrent connections. These metrics provide insights into the database's performance and workload.

2. Scaling Triggers:

Scaling triggers are conditions or thresholds that, when met, trigger an auto-scaling action. For example, if CPU utilization exceeds a certain percentage for a specified duration, it may trigger a scaling event.

3. Scaling Actions:

Scaling actions are the responses to scaling triggers. They include adding or removing database nodes or adjusting resource allocations (e.g., increasing CPU cores or memory).

4. Auto-Scaling Policies:

Auto-scaling policies define the rules for how and when scaling actions should be taken. These policies specify the conditions that trigger scaling and the actions to be performed.

5. Dynamic Resource Allocation:

When a scaling event is triggered, auto-scaling systems dynamically allocate or deallocate resources as needed. For example, if the workload increases, additional database nodes may be added to distribute the load.

6. Load Balancing:

Auto-scaling often works in tandem with load balancing mechanisms to distribute incoming requests evenly across available database nodes. This ensures that the workload is balanced and resources are utilized efficiently.

7. Auto-Scaling Groups:

In cloud environments, auto-scaling groups are used to manage and scale instances automatically. These groups define the configuration and policies for a set of identical instances.

Considerations for Implementing Auto-Scaling:

Implementing auto-scaling in NoSQL databases requires careful planning and configuration:

1. **Selecting Scaling Metrics:** Choose the right metrics and thresholds to trigger scaling events based on your application's behavior and performance requirements.
2. **Testing and Validation:** Thoroughly test and validate auto-scaling policies to ensure they respond appropriately to workload changes.
3. **Resource Limits:** Set upper and lower resource limits to prevent over-provisioning or excessive scaling.
4. **Cost Management:** Consider the cost implications of auto-scaling, especially in cloud environments, and monitor resource costs to optimize spending.
5. **Security and Access Control:** Ensure that auto-scaling does not compromise security or access control policies.

Auto-scaling is a powerful feature that enables NoSQL databases to adapt to changing workloads automatically. When implemented correctly, it helps maintain performance, availability, and cost-efficiency for database-driven applications.

6.4 Scalability Challenges in NoSQL

While NoSQL databases offer scalability benefits, they also come with certain challenges that must be addressed to ensure effective scalability. In this section, we will explore some of the key scalability challenges in NoSQL databases and strategies to mitigate them.

1. Data Distribution and Sharding:

Challenge:

In distributed NoSQL databases, data must be distributed across multiple nodes or servers. Distributing data unevenly can lead to performance bottlenecks and data hotspots.

Mitigation:

- Use effective data partitioning and sharding strategies to evenly distribute data.

- Monitor data distribution regularly and rebalance data when necessary.

2. Data Consistency:

Challenge:

Maintaining data consistency in distributed systems, especially in the presence of failures or network issues, can be challenging. Achieving strong consistency may impact performance.

Mitigation:

- Choose an appropriate consistency model (e.g., eventual consistency, strong consistency) based on application requirements.
- Implement conflict resolution mechanisms to handle data conflicts in distributed environments.

3. Query Optimization:

Challenge:

As data grows, query performance can degrade. Complex queries or poorly optimized queries can strain the database.

Mitigation:

- Design efficient data models that minimize the need for complex joins or multiple queries.
- Use query optimization techniques provided by the NoSQL database, such as indexing and caching.

4. Network Latency:

Challenge:

Distributed databases often rely on network communication between nodes. High network latency can impact query response times.

Mitigation:

- Optimize network configurations and minimize data transfer over the network.

- Use distributed caching to reduce the need for frequent cross-node communication.

5. Load Balancing:

Challenge:

Balancing the workload evenly across nodes is critical for scalability. Uneven distribution can lead to overloading some nodes while underutilizing others.

Mitigation:

- Implement load balancing mechanisms to distribute incoming requests evenly.

- Use auto-scaling to add or remove nodes dynamically based on workload.

6. Data Backups and Recovery:

Challenge:

Ensuring data availability and recoverability in a distributed environment requires robust backup and recovery strategies.

Mitigation:

- Implement automated backup and recovery processes.
- Test backup and recovery procedures regularly to ensure they work as expected.

7. Resource Management:

Challenge:

Properly managing resources like CPU, memory, and storage in a distributed system is crucial for performance and cost-efficiency.

Mitigation:

- Use auto-scaling to allocate and deallocate resources dynamically based on workload.
- Monitor resource utilization and adjust resource allocations as needed.

8. Schema Evolution:

Challenge:

NoSQL databases often support flexible schema designs. However, evolving schemas can be challenging when dealing with existing data.

Mitigation:

- Plan for schema changes carefully and provide mechanisms for migrating existing data to new schemas.

- Consider schema versioning and backward compatibility.

9. Security:

Challenge:

Maintaining security across a distributed NoSQL database can be complex, especially when dealing with multiple nodes.

Mitigation:

- Implement robust access control and authentication mechanisms.
- Encrypt data in transit and at rest to protect sensitive information.

Addressing these scalability challenges requires careful planning, monitoring, and ongoing optimization. It's essential to select the right NoSQL database for your specific use case and design your database schema and application architecture with scalability in mind from the start. Additionally, regular performance testing and tuning are essential to ensure that your NoSQL database continues to scale effectively as your workload grows.

6.5 Case Studies: Scalability Solutions

In this section, we will explore real-world case studies that highlight successful scalability solutions implemented using NoSQL databases. These examples demonstrate how organizations have effectively addressed scalability challenges and achieved improved performance and reliability.

1. Netflix: Managing Massive Streaming Data

- **Challenge:** Netflix, the popular streaming service, faced the challenge of managing and serving a vast amount of streaming data to millions of users worldwide. Their existing relational databases couldn't handle the scale and real-time nature of streaming.

- **Solution:** Netflix adopted Apache Cassandra, a highly scalable NoSQL database. Cassandra allowed them to distribute data across multiple nodes, ensuring high availability and low latency. They use auto-scaling to add resources during peak usage hours.

- **Results:** With Cassandra, Netflix can seamlessly handle billions of requests per day, providing a smooth streaming experience to users globally.

2. Uber: Handling Real-Time Geospatial Data

- **Challenge:** Uber relies heavily on real-time geospatial data for matching riders with drivers and providing accurate ETAs. Managing and processing this data at scale was a significant challenge.

- **Solution:** Uber implemented a microservices architecture with Apache Kafka and Apache Cassandra. Kafka handles real-time data ingestion, while Cassandra stores and serves location data. They use auto-scaling to adapt to fluctuating demand.

- **Results:** Uber's system can process millions of location updates per second, ensuring that riders and drivers receive accurate information in real-time.

3. Instagram: Supporting Rapid Growth

- **Challenge:** Instagram experienced explosive user growth, leading to performance issues with their existing infrastructure. They needed a solution to handle the increasing volume of user-generated content.

- **Solution:** Instagram adopted sharded MongoDB clusters, distributing user data across multiple servers. They also implemented a caching layer using Redis to reduce database load. Auto-scaling helped them add new shards as needed.

- **Results:** Instagram's infrastructure can handle billions of photos and videos, ensuring a smooth user experience even during peak usage.

4. Amazon Web Services (AWS): Scaling for Cloud Services

- **Challenge:** AWS, a leading cloud services provider, needed a robust database solution to support their various cloud services and scale as their customer base grew.

- **Solution:** AWS developed Amazon DynamoDB, a highly scalable and fully managed NoSQL database service. DynamoDB uses auto-scaling to adjust read and write capacity based on traffic patterns.

- **Results:** DynamoDB has become a core component of AWS, serving millions of customers and handling trillions of requests daily.

5. Twitter: Handling Real-Time Tweets

- **Challenge:** Twitter needed a database solution that could manage the vast volume of real-time tweets, retweets, and user interactions.

- **Solution:** Twitter adopted Apache HBase, a distributed and scalable NoSQL database. HBase's horizontal scaling and strong consistency ensured high performance even during trending events.

- **Results:** Twitter can handle millions of tweets per minute, providing real-time updates to its users worldwide.

These case studies demonstrate the versatility and scalability of NoSQL databases in addressing the unique challenges of various organizations. By selecting the right NoSQL database and implementing effective scalability strategies, businesses can achieve the performance, availability, and reliability required to meet the demands of their applications and users.

Chapter 7: NoSQL and Security

7.1 Security Challenges in NoSQL Databases

In the world of NoSQL databases, security is a critical concern that organizations must address to protect their data and systems. While NoSQL databases offer flexibility and scalability, they also introduce unique security challenges. In this section, we will delve into some of the key security challenges associated with NoSQL databases.

1. Authentication and Authorization:

Challenge:

Managing user authentication and authorization in a NoSQL database can be complex. Ensuring that only authorized users have access to specific data is crucial for data security.

Mitigation:

- Implement robust authentication mechanisms, such as username/password authentication or integration with external identity providers.

- Define fine-grained access control policies to restrict access to specific database resources based on user roles and permissions.

2. Data Encryption:

Challenge:

Protecting data at rest and in transit is essential for preventing unauthorized access. NoSQL databases may store sensitive information that needs encryption.

Mitigation:

- Enable data encryption at rest and in transit using industry-standard encryption algorithms and protocols.
- Consider using encryption key management systems to securely manage encryption keys.

3. Injection Attacks:

Challenge:

NoSQL databases are susceptible to injection attacks if user input is not properly sanitized. Attackers may exploit vulnerabilities to manipulate database queries.

Mitigation:

- Use parameterized queries or prepared statements to prevent injection attacks.
- Implement input validation and sanitize user input to remove potentially harmful characters.

4. Data Exposure:

Challenge:

Misconfigured access controls or unintentional exposure of data can lead to data breaches. NoSQL databases often require careful configuration.

Mitigation:

- Regularly audit and review access control policies to identify and rectify misconfigurations.
- Implement proper data anonymization techniques to protect sensitive information.

5. Denial of Service (DoS) Attacks:

Challenge:

NoSQL databases can be vulnerable to DoS attacks that overload the system with requests, causing service disruption.

Mitigation:

- Implement rate limiting and request throttling to mitigate DoS attacks.
- Use load balancers and distributed architectures to distribute traffic and absorb malicious traffic.

6. Auditing and Compliance:

Challenge:

Maintaining audit logs and meeting compliance requirements, such as GDPR or HIPAA, can be challenging in a NoSQL environment.

Mitigation:

- Enable auditing features provided by the NoSQL database to log all access and modification activities.
- Establish procedures for regular compliance audits and ensure data retention policies comply with regulations.

7. Secure Configuration:

Challenge:

Securing a NoSQL database requires proper configuration. Inadequate configuration settings can lead to vulnerabilities.

Mitigation:

- Follow security best practices and guidelines provided by the database vendor.
- Periodically review and update the database configuration to address new security threats.

8. Third-Party Dependencies:

Challenge:

NoSQL databases often rely on third-party libraries and components. Vulnerabilities in these dependencies can impact database security.

Mitigation:

- Keep third-party dependencies up to date with security patches.
- Monitor security advisories related to the database and its dependencies.

9. Backup and Disaster Recovery:

Challenge:

Ensuring the security of backups and disaster recovery processes is essential to prevent data breaches during restore operations.

Mitigation:

- Encrypt backups and implement secure storage solutions for backup data.
- Test disaster recovery procedures to ensure data security during restoration.

Addressing these security challenges requires a proactive approach, including ongoing monitoring, security testing, and staff training.

Organizations must also stay informed about emerging threats and vulnerabilities in the NoSQL database ecosystem to adapt their security measures effectively. By implementing robust security practices, organizations can harness the benefits of NoSQL databases while safeguarding their data and systems.

7.2 Implementing Data Encryption

Data encryption is a fundamental security measure in NoSQL databases to protect sensitive information from unauthorized access. Encryption ensures that even if an attacker gains access to the underlying data files, they cannot decipher the data without the encryption keys. In this section, we will explore how to implement data encryption in NoSQL databases.

1. Encryption at Rest:

- **Challenge:** Protecting data stored on disk is crucial to prevent data breaches in case of physical theft or unauthorized access to storage devices.

- **Solution:** Most NoSQL databases offer encryption at rest as a feature. You can enable it by configuring encryption settings. For example, in MongoDB, you can enable encryption at rest by using WiredTiger encryption.

- **Code Example (MongoDB):**

```
storage:

wiredTiger:

encryption:
```

keyId: "myEncryptionKey"

name: "encryption"

• **Best Practices:** Rotate encryption keys regularly and securely manage encryption key storage to prevent unauthorized access.

2. Encryption in Transit:

• **Challenge:** Securing data as it travels between the client and the NoSQL database server is essential to prevent eavesdropping.

• **Solution:** Use secure communication protocols like SSL/TLS to encrypt data in transit. Most NoSQL databases provide options to enable SSL/TLS encryption for client-server communication.

• **Code Example (Cassandra):**

```
server_encryption_options:

internode_encryption: all

keystore: /path/to/keystore.jks

keystore_password: password123

client_encryption_options:

enabled: true

keystore: /path/to/keystore.jks
```

keystore_password: password123

• **Best Practices:** Regularly update SSL/TLS certificates and validate server certificates to prevent man-in-the-middle attacks.

3. Application-Level Encryption:

• **Challenge:** NoSQL databases may store sensitive data, but not all data in a database is necessarily sensitive. Implementing encryption at the application level allows you to selectively encrypt specific data.

• **Solution:** Implement encryption and decryption routines in your application code. Encrypt sensitive data before storing it in the database and decrypt it when retrieving it.

• **Code Example (Python using cryptography library):**

```
from cryptography.fernet import Fernet

# Generate a secret key

key = Fernet.generate_key()

cipher_suite = Fernet(key)

# Encrypt data

plaintext_data = "Sensitive information"

encrypted_data = cipher_suite.encrypt(plaintext_data.encode())
```

```
# Decrypt data

decrypted_data = cipher_suite.decrypt(encrypted_data).decode()
```

• **Best Practices:** Safely manage encryption keys and consider using key management solutions for better security.

4. Key Management:

• **Challenge:** Effectively managing encryption keys is crucial for data security. If encryption keys are compromised, the entire security of the encrypted data is at risk.

• **Solution:** Employ key management practices such as key rotation, secure storage of keys, and access control. Consider using Hardware Security Modules (HSMs) for enhanced key security.

• **Best Practices:** Regularly audit and review key management processes to identify and mitigate potential vulnerabilities.

5. Data Masking:

• **Challenge:** In some cases, you may want to protect sensitive data without encrypting it. Data masking allows you to hide sensitive information by replacing it with masked or pseudonymous data.

• **Solution:** Implement data masking at the application level. Define rules for how sensitive data should be masked before it is displayed to users or extracted for specific use cases.

- **Code Example (Java):**

```
String originalData = "Sensitive information";

String maskedData = originalData.replaceAll(".", "*"); // Masking all characters
```

- **Best Practices:** Ensure that data masking rules are consistent and compliant with privacy regulations.

Implementing data encryption in NoSQL databases is a critical step in securing your data. It helps protect sensitive information, maintains data integrity, and ensures compliance with data protection regulations. However, encryption is just one aspect of database security, and a comprehensive security strategy should also include access control, authentication, and monitoring to safeguard your NoSQL database effectively.

7.3 Access Control in NoSQL

Access control is a fundamental aspect of securing NoSQL databases, ensuring that only authorized users and applications can interact with the database and perform specific operations. In this section, we will explore various aspects of access control in NoSQL databases, including authentication, authorization, and role-based access control.

1. Authentication:

- **Authentication Challenge:** Verifying the identity of users or applications before granting access to the NoSQL database is essential for security.

- **Authentication Methods:** NoSQL databases support various authentication methods, such as username/ password, X.509 certificates, or integration with external identity providers like LDAP or OAuth.

- **Code Example (Couchbase):**

```
"saslauthdParams": "/var/run/saslauthd/mux",

"authentication": {

"saslauthdEnabled": true,

"saslauthdSocketPath": "/var/run/saslauthd/mux"

}
```

- **Best Practices:** Enforce strong password policies, use multi-factor authentication (MFA) where possible, and regularly audit and review authentication settings.

2. Authorization:

- **Authorization Challenge:** Once authenticated, users or applications should only have access to specific resources and perform authorized actions.

- **Role-Based Access Control (RBAC):** Implement RBAC to define roles, assign permissions to roles, and assign roles to users or applications. This allows fine-grained control over who can do what within the database.

- **Code Example (MongoDB):**

```
use admin

db.createRole(

{

role: "readWriteRole",

privileges: [

{ resource: { db: "mydb", collection: "" }, actions: ["find", "insert", "update", "remove"] }

],

roles: []

}

)
```

- **Best Practices:** Regularly review and update role assignments to ensure they align with the organization's security policies.

3. Access Tokens and API Keys:

- **Challenge:** Managing access for applications and services can be complex. NoSQL databases often provide access tokens or API keys for secure application access.

- **Solution:** Generate access tokens or API keys for applications and services. Use these tokens to authenticate and authorize access to the database.

- **Code Example (Redis):**

```
$ redis-cli

127.0.0.1:6379> AUTH my-api-key

OK
```

- **Best Practices:** Implement key rotation and regularly monitor the use of access tokens and API keys.

4. IP Whitelisting and Firewall Rules:

- **Challenge:** Restricting access to specific IP addresses or network ranges is crucial for protecting your NoSQL database from unauthorized access.

- **Solution:** Configure IP whitelisting or firewall rules to allow only trusted IP addresses to connect to the database.

- **Code Example (Cassandra):**

```
authorization: allow

datacenter: dc1
```

```
endpoint_snitch: GossipingPropertyFileSnitch

seeds: "127.0.0.1"

listen_address: localhost

rpc_address: 0.0.0.0

rpc_interface_prefer_ipv6: false

start_native_transport: true

native_transport_port_ssl: 9142
```

- **Best Practices:** Regularly review and update IP whitelists to accommodate changes in your organization's network infrastructure.

5. Audit Trails:

- **Challenge:** Maintaining an audit trail of database activities is essential for monitoring and identifying security incidents.

- **Solution:** Enable auditing features provided by the NoSQL database to log all access and modification activities. Store audit logs securely to prevent tampering.

- **Code Example (Elasticsearch):**

```
xpack.security.audit.enabled: true

xpack.security.audit.logfile.events:
["authentication_failed", "access_granted"]
```

xpack.security.audit.logfile.prefix: es-audit-log

- **Best Practices:** Implement a centralized log management system for audit logs and regularly review audit trails for suspicious activities.

6. Encryption and Secure Channels:

- **Challenge:** Ensuring that data remains confidential during transmission and that the communication channels are secure.

- **Solution:** Use encryption mechanisms like SSL/TLS for secure communication between clients and the database server. Encrypt sensitive data before storing it in the database.

- **Code Example (CouchDB):**

```
$ curl -X PUT https://admin:password@localhost:5984/mydb -H "Content-Type: application/json"
```

- **Best Practices:** Regularly update SSL/TLS certificates and validate server certificates to prevent man-in-the-middle attacks.

Implementing robust access control measures in your NoSQL database is vital to protect your data and ensure

7.4 Auditing and Compliance

Auditing and compliance are critical aspects of maintaining the security and integrity of NoSQL databases. In this section, we will explore the importance of auditing, compliance requirements, and best practices for implementing auditing in your NoSQL database.

1. Importance of Auditing:

- Auditing involves monitoring and recording all database activities, including access, modifications, and administrative actions.

- It plays a crucial role in identifying security breaches, tracking user actions, and ensuring data integrity.

- Auditing also helps organizations meet regulatory compliance requirements.

2. Compliance Requirements:

- Many industries and organizations have specific compliance requirements that mandate auditing for databases, including HIPAA, GDPR, PCI DSS, and more.

- Compliance standards often require auditing of user access, data changes, and administrative actions.

- Failing to comply with these standards can result in significant fines and legal consequences.

3. Auditing Features:

- NoSQL databases offer auditing features that allow you to capture and store audit logs.

• These logs typically include information such as user actions, timestamps, IP addresses, and the nature of the operation (read, write, delete).

• **Code Example (MongoDB):** Enabling auditing in MongoDB using the auditLog component:

```
security:

auditLog:

destination: file

format: JSON

path: /var/log/mongodb/auditLog.json
```

4. Audit Trail Analysis:

• Once audit logs are generated, they need to be regularly analyzed to identify security incidents or compliance violations.

• Automated tools and SIEM (Security Information and Event Management) systems can help in log analysis.

• Manual review by security personnel is also essential for detecting anomalies.

5. Data Retention Policies:

• Implement data retention policies to determine how long audit logs should be retained.

• Compliance standards often dictate specific retention periods.

• Regularly archive and securely store audit logs for future reference and compliance audits.

6. Access Control for Audit Logs:

• Ensure that only authorized personnel can access and modify audit logs.

• Implement strict access controls to prevent tampering or unauthorized deletions of audit data.

• **Code Example (Elasticsearch):** Setting up access control for Elasticsearch audit logs using role-based access control (RBAC):

```
xpack.security.enabled: true

xpack.security.authc.api_key.enabled: true

xpack.security.authc.realms.native.native1.order: 0

xpack.security.authc.realms.native.native1.size: 1000
```

7. Regular Auditing and Testing:

• Regularly review and test your auditing processes to ensure they are effective.

• Conduct audits of audit logs to verify that security policies and compliance requirements are being met.

• Address any identified issues promptly to maintain the security of your NoSQL database.

8. Documentation and Reporting:

• Maintain detailed documentation of auditing configurations, policies, and procedures.

• Generate audit reports and documentation for compliance audits to demonstrate adherence to regulatory standards.

• Ensure that audit reports are easily accessible to auditors when required.

9. Continuous Improvement:

• Continuously improve your auditing and compliance processes based on lessons learned, emerging threats, and changes in regulatory requirements.

• Stay up-to-date with industry best practices and incorporate them into your auditing strategy.

Implementing robust auditing and compliance measures in your NoSQL database is crucial for maintaining data security, ensuring data integrity, and meeting regulatory requirements. It's a proactive approach to identifying and addressing security threats and compliance violations.

7.5 Best Practices for NoSQL Security

In this section, we'll discuss best practices for enhancing the security of your NoSQL database systems. Security is a top priority in any database management system, and NoSQL databases are no exception. Adhering to these best practices helps protect your data and maintain the integrity of your database.

1. Role-Based Access Control (RBAC):

- Implement RBAC to control who can access the database and what actions they can perform.
- Assign roles with specific permissions to users and applications based on their responsibilities.
- Example (MongoDB): Define custom roles and assign them to users.

```
db.createRole({
role: "readWrite",
privileges: [
{ resource: { db: "mydb", collection: "" }, actions: ["find", "insert", "update", "remove"] }
],
roles: []
})
```

2. Data Encryption:

- Encrypt data at rest and in transit to protect it from unauthorized access.

• Use TLS/SSL for securing data in transit and encryption mechanisms provided by the database system for data at rest.

• Regularly update encryption keys and certificates.

3. Authentication Mechanisms:

• Enforce strong authentication methods, including multi-factor authentication (MFA), for database access.

• Use secure authentication mechanisms provided by the database system.

• Example (Cassandra): Enable PasswordAuthenticator and configure authenticator options.

authenticator: PasswordAuthenticator

4. Network Security:

• Isolate your database from public networks and use firewalls to restrict access to authorized IP addresses and ports.

• Employ Virtual Private Clouds (VPCs) or private network configurations to enhance network security.

• Implement network security groups or security rules to control inbound and outbound traffic.

5. Regular Patching and Updates:

• Keep your NoSQL database system and server operating systems up to date with the latest security patches and updates.

• Regularly review security bulletins and apply patches promptly to address vulnerabilities.

6. Backup and Disaster Recovery:

• Establish a robust backup and disaster recovery plan to ensure data availability in case of data loss or system failures.

• Store backups securely and regularly test the restore process to confirm its reliability.

7. Audit Logging:

• Enable audit logging to monitor and record database activities.

• Regularly review audit logs for suspicious activities or security breaches.

• Set up alerts for specific events or anomalies in the audit logs.

8. Data Minimization:

• Limit the amount of sensitive or confidential data stored in the database.

- Remove unnecessary data and periodically review the data retained in the database.

9. Incident Response Plan:

- Develop an incident response plan to handle security incidents effectively.

- Define roles and responsibilities for incident response team members.

- Conduct tabletop exercises to practice incident response procedures.

10. Security Awareness Training:

- Train your database administrators, developers, and users in security best practices.

- Create a culture of security awareness within your organization.

11. Third-Party Integrations:

- Carefully evaluate and secure third-party integrations, as they can introduce security risks.

- Review the security practices of third-party tools and libraries used in conjunction with your NoSQL database.

By implementing these best practices, you can significantly enhance the security of your NoSQL database systems. Security is an ongoing process, and it's essential to stay vigilant, adapt to new threats, and continuously improve your security measures.

Chapter 8: Performance Tuning in NoSQL

8.1 Analyzing NoSQL Performance

Performance tuning in NoSQL databases is a critical aspect of database management. It involves optimizing the database's efficiency and responsiveness to ensure that it can handle the workload efficiently. In this section, we'll discuss how to analyze the performance of your NoSQL database, identify bottlenecks, and implement optimizations.

Monitoring and Metrics:

- Start by monitoring your NoSQL database's performance using appropriate tools and metrics.

- Common performance metrics include throughput (requests per second), response time, CPU usage, memory consumption, and disk I/O.

- Use database-specific monitoring tools and third-party solutions to gather performance data.

Profiling Queries:

- Profiling allows you to examine the execution of individual queries to identify slow or inefficient operations.

- Most NoSQL databases provide profiling mechanisms to capture query execution details.

• Example (MongoDB): Enable profiling to record query execution information.

```
db.setProfilingLevel(1, { slowms: 100 })
```

Load Testing:

• Conduct load testing to simulate realistic workloads and identify performance bottlenecks.

• Adjust the load parameters to evaluate the system's behavior under different conditions.

• Use tools like Apache JMeter or custom scripts to perform load testing.

Query Optimization:

• Review and optimize queries to improve their efficiency.

• Utilize indexes to speed up query execution. Ensure that indexes are appropriately designed for the types of queries you run.

• Example (Cassandra): Create secondary indexes for frequently queried columns.

```
CREATE INDEX ON mytable (column_name);
```

Scaling:

• Consider horizontal scaling (adding more nodes) or vertical scaling (increasing the resources of existing nodes) to handle increased workloads.

• NoSQL databases often support automatic sharding and distribution, which can help distribute data and queries efficiently.

Caching:

• Implement caching mechanisms to reduce the need to query the database for frequently accessed data.

• Use in-memory caches like Redis or Memcached to store frequently requested data.

• Example (Redis): Store query results in a cache for quick retrieval.

```
cache.set("key", "value", expiration_time)
```

Regular Maintenance:

• Schedule regular maintenance tasks like compacting data, rebuilding indexes, and optimizing storage.

• Remove unnecessary data and perform data archiving to keep the database size manageable.

• Keep the database software and underlying infrastructure up to date.

Connection Pooling:

• Implement connection pooling to efficiently manage database connections.

• Connection pooling reduces the overhead of opening and closing connections for each request.

• Example (Node.js with MongoDB): Use a connection pool library like "mongodb" for connection management.

```
const { MongoClient } = require('mongodb');

const client = new MongoClient(uri, { poolSize: 10 });
```

Distributed Database Considerations:

• If you're using a distributed NoSQL database, monitor data distribution and ensure data is evenly balanced across nodes.

• Be mindful of data consistency and configure consistency levels based on your application's requirements.

• Example (Cassandra): Configure consistency levels for read and write operations.

```
consistency_level: LOCAL_QUORUM
```

By analyzing performance, monitoring metrics, and implementing optimizations, you can ensure that your NoSQL database performs efficiently, meets your application's requirements, and delivers a responsive user experience. Performance tuning is an ongoing process, so regularly review and fine-tune your database to accommodate changing workloads and data patterns.

8.2 Optimization Techniques

Optimization techniques play a crucial role in improving the performance of NoSQL databases. In this section, we'll explore various strategies and best practices for optimizing the performance of your NoSQL database.

Data Modeling:

- Effective data modeling is fundamental for database performance. Design your data schema to match your application's query patterns.

- Denormalization can be useful in NoSQL databases to reduce the need for complex joins and improve query speed.

- Utilize appropriate data types and structures for your data to minimize storage and improve retrieval efficiency.

Indexing:

- Indexes significantly enhance query performance by allowing the database to quickly locate relevant data.

- Choose the right columns to index based on your query patterns. Indexes come with an overhead in terms of storage and update performance.

- Periodically review and optimize indexes to ensure they are up-to-date and efficient.

Query Optimization:

- Craft efficient queries by utilizing query planning and optimization features provided by the database.

- Avoid using wildcards in queries, as they can lead to full table scans. Instead, use specific conditions and indexes.

• Use aggregation frameworks or equivalent tools to perform complex calculations on data within the database.

Sharding:

• Horizontal scaling through sharding can help distribute data and queries across multiple nodes.

• Choose an appropriate sharding strategy that evenly distributes data and queries to avoid hotspots.

• Be mindful of data partitioning to ensure data related to the same queries is stored together.

Load Balancing:

• Implement load balancing to evenly distribute incoming traffic across multiple database nodes.

• Use load balancers to route read and write requests to the appropriate nodes.

• Regularly monitor the load balancer's performance and adjust settings as needed.

Caching:

• Caching frequently accessed data in memory can significantly reduce the load on the database.

• Implement caching layers using tools like Redis or Memcached.

• Set cache expiration policies to ensure data consistency.

Connection Pooling:

- Connection pooling helps manage database connections efficiently by reusing existing connections.
- Configure appropriate connection pool settings based on your application's requirements.
- Monitor connection pool performance to prevent resource exhaustion.

Compression:

- Implement data compression techniques to reduce storage space and improve data transfer speeds.
- Many NoSQL databases support data compression out of the box.
- Be cautious about the trade-off between compression and CPU utilization.

Parallel Processing:

- Take advantage of parallel processing capabilities offered by your NoSQL database.
- Parallelism can improve query execution times by distributing tasks across multiple threads or nodes.
- Adjust parallelism settings based on the available resources and workload.

Regular Maintenance:

- Schedule routine maintenance tasks, such as data compaction, index rebuilding, and software updates.

- Regularly clean up outdated or unnecessary data to keep the database size manageable.

- Perform backup and recovery tests to ensure data integrity.

Optimizing the performance of your NoSQL database is an ongoing process that requires continuous monitoring and adjustment. The strategies mentioned here can serve as a starting point, but each database system may have its unique optimization options and considerations. By carefully designing your data model, employing effective indexing, optimizing queries, and implementing the right techniques, you can ensure that your NoSQL database performs efficiently and meets your application's requirements.

8.3 Caching Mechanisms

Caching mechanisms play a pivotal role in enhancing the performance of NoSQL databases. Caching involves storing frequently accessed data in memory, making it readily available for quick retrieval. In this section, we'll delve into the importance of caching in NoSQL databases and explore various caching strategies and tools.

The Significance of Caching:

Caching can substantially reduce the load on your NoSQL database by serving frequently requested data directly from memory. This results in faster response times and less strain on the database server.

Caching is especially beneficial for read-heavy workloads where the same data is queried repeatedly.

Types of Caching:

1. **In-Memory Caching:** This is the most common type of caching in NoSQL databases. Data is stored in memory, which offers low latency access. Popular in-memory caching solutions include Redis and Memcached.
2. **Page Caching:** Some databases, especially document-oriented databases, employ page caching to store entire database pages in memory. This technique can be effective for reducing disk I/O.
3. **Query Result Caching:** Caching the results of specific queries can be useful when dealing with complex or computationally intensive queries. It allows subsequent requests with the same query parameters to retrieve the cached result.

Strategies for Effective Caching:

1. **Cache Invalidation:** Implement mechanisms to automatically invalidate or refresh cached data when it becomes outdated. This can be achieved through time-based expiration or event-based invalidation.
2. **Cache Partitioning:** Divide your cache into multiple partitions to prevent cache contention. This is especially relevant in distributed systems where multiple cache nodes are involved.
3. **Cache Backing:** Decide what should be the source of truth when data is not found in the cache. It could be the database or a higher-level cache.
4. **Eviction Policies:** Implement cache eviction policies to

remove less frequently used or expired data from the cache to make room for new data.

Caching Tools:

1. **Redis:** Redis is an in-memory data store that supports various data structures. It is widely used for caching due to its speed and versatility.
2. **Memcached:** Memcached is another high-performance, distributed memory caching system. It is simple to use and effective for caching.
3. **Cache Libraries:** Many programming languages have cache libraries that simplify caching implementation. Examples include Guava Cache for Java and Django Cache for Python.

Sample Code (Using Redis in Python):

```
import redis

# Connect to Redis

redis_client = redis.StrictRedis(host='localhost', port=6379, db=0)

# Store data in the cache with a timeout of 3600 seconds (1 hour)

redis_client.set('my_key', 'my_value', ex=3600)

# Retrieve data from the cache

cached_data = redis_client.get('my_key')

if cached_data is not None:

print("Data from cache:", cached_data.decode('utf-8'))

else:
```

```
print("Data not found in cache. Query database and store in cache.")
# Query database and store the result in the cache
```

In summary, caching mechanisms are essential for optimizing NoSQL database performance, particularly in read-heavy scenarios. By implementing an effective caching strategy, you can reduce latency, improve response times, and lessen the burden on your database server. Understanding the types of caching, strategies for cache management, and utilizing appropriate caching tools are key steps in optimizing your NoSQL database system.

8.4 Balancing Read and Write Speeds

Balancing read and write speeds is a crucial aspect of optimizing the performance of NoSQL databases. In this section, we will explore strategies and considerations for achieving an equilibrium between read and write operations within your NoSQL database system.

The Read-Write Trade-off:

NoSQL databases come in various types, each with its strengths and weaknesses. One common trade-off in NoSQL databases is between read and write operations. Some NoSQL databases prioritize read performance, offering low latency and high throughput for retrieving data, while others prioritize write performance, ensuring efficient data ingestion and storage.

Strategies for Balancing Read and Write Speeds:

1. **Data Modeling:** The way you structure your data can significantly impact read and write performance. For read-heavy workloads, consider denormalizing data and optimizing it for query efficiency. For write-heavy

workloads, design your schema to minimize write conflicts and maximize write throughput.

2. **Partitioning:** Distributing your data across multiple partitions or shards can improve both read and write performance. By spreading the data load, you can parallelize operations, reducing contention.
3. **Caching:** As discussed in the previous section, caching read results can alleviate the load on the database and enhance read performance. Effective caching can help compensate for write-heavy workloads.
4. **Asynchronous Processing:** For write-heavy workloads, consider offloading time-consuming tasks to background processes or queues. This approach can speed up the response time of write operations while ensuring data consistency.
5. **Compression and Serialization:** Efficient data compression and serialization techniques can reduce the size of data being written or read, thus improving I/O performance.
6. **Indexing:** Carefully choose and optimize indexes to support frequently executed queries. Over-indexing can negatively impact write performance, so strike a balance between read and write requirements.

Sample Code (Python with MongoDB):

```
from pymongo import MongoClient

# Connect to MongoDB

client = MongoClient('localhost', 27017)

# Access the database and collection
```

```
db = client['mydb']

collection = db['mycollection']

# Insert a document (write operation)

data = {'name': 'John', 'age': 30}

collection.insert_one(data)

# Retrieve a document by name (read operation)

result = collection.find_one({'name': 'John'})

if result:

print("Found:", result)

else:

print("Not found")

# Close the MongoDB connection

client.close()
```

In conclusion, achieving a balance between read and write speeds in a NoSQL database requires careful consideration of your application's requirements and workload characteristics. By adopting appropriate data modeling, partitioning, caching, and optimization strategies, you can optimize the performance of your NoSQL database system to meet the specific needs of your application.

8.5 Monitoring and Maintenance

Monitoring and maintenance are essential aspects of managing a NoSQL database effectively. In this section, we will discuss the importance of monitoring and provide insights into best practices for maintaining the health and performance of your NoSQL database system.

Monitoring NoSQL Databases:

1. **Real-time Monitoring:** Implement real-time monitoring solutions that can provide you with insights into the current state of your NoSQL database. Tools like Prometheus, Grafana, or vendor-specific monitoring dashboards can help you track critical metrics such as read and write throughput, latency, error rates, and resource utilization.
2. **Alerting:** Set up proactive alerting mechanisms to notify you of potential issues or anomalies in your NoSQL database. Configure alerts for conditions like high query latency, low disk space, or increased error rates. Timely alerts can help you address problems before they impact users.
3. **Performance Metrics:** Monitor performance-related metrics to identify bottlenecks or areas that require optimization. This includes analyzing query execution plans, tracking index usage, and examining cache hit rates. Regularly reviewing these metrics can lead to informed performance improvements.

Maintenance Best Practices:

1. **Regular Backups:** Implement automated backup strategies to ensure data durability and recoverability. Regularly back up your NoSQL database to prevent data loss in case of failures or accidents.
2. **Data Compaction:** Depending on your NoSQL database

type, consider periodic data compaction to optimize storage and improve read and write performance. Compaction reduces fragmentation and disk space usage.

3. **Index Maintenance:** Maintain your database indexes by periodically rebuilding or optimizing them. Outdated or inefficient indexes can negatively impact query performance.
4. **Software Updates:** Stay up to date with the latest software releases and security patches for your NoSQL database system. Regularly applying updates helps protect your data from vulnerabilities and ensures compatibility with new features.
5. **Scaling Considerations:** Continuously monitor your workload and be prepared to scale your NoSQL database horizontally or vertically as needed. Scalability is crucial for accommodating growing data volumes and increasing user demands.
6. **Security Audits:** Perform regular security audits to identify and address potential vulnerabilities in your NoSQL database. Review access control policies, encryption mechanisms, and authentication protocols.

Sample Code (MongoDB Maintenance in Shell):

```
# Create a backup of the MongoDB database

mongodump—host localhost—port 27017—out /backup

# Restore data from a backup

mongorestore—host localhost—port 27017 /backup

# Check and repair a MongoDB database

mongod—repair
```

 # Update MongoDB to the latest version

sudo apt-get update

sudo apt-get install -y mongodb-org

 # Monitor MongoDB performance using the MongoDB shell

mongostat—host localhost:27017

 # Set up alerts and notifications in MongoDB Atlas (MongoDB's managed service)

 # Visit MongoDB Atlas dashboard for configuration options.

In summary, monitoring and maintenance are ongoing tasks that ensure the reliability, performance, and security of your NoSQL database. By adopting best practices and using appropriate monitoring tools, you can proactively address issues, optimize performance, and provide a seamless experience to your users.

Chapter 9: NoSQL in the Cloud

9.1 Cloud-Based NoSQL Services

The adoption of cloud computing has transformed the way organizations manage and operate their databases, including NoSQL databases. Cloud-based NoSQL services offer a range of benefits, from scalability and cost-efficiency to ease of management. In this section, we will explore the concept of cloud-based NoSQL services and delve into the advantages they bring.

Understanding Cloud-Based NoSQL Services:

Cloud-based NoSQL services, also known as Database as a Service (DBaaS), provide a managed environment for hosting and operating NoSQL databases in the cloud. These services abstract the underlying infrastructure complexities, allowing developers and businesses to focus on application development and data management rather than server provisioning and maintenance.

Key Characteristics of Cloud-Based NoSQL Services:

1. **Managed Infrastructure:** Cloud providers handle the provisioning, scaling, and maintenance of the underlying hardware and software infrastructure. This reduces the operational burden on organizations.
2. **Scalability:** Cloud-based NoSQL services offer seamless scalability, allowing you to adjust your database's capacity based on workload fluctuations. You can easily scale up or down as needed, ensuring optimal performance and cost-effectiveness.
3. **High Availability:** Cloud providers typically offer built-in

redundancy and failover mechanisms to ensure high availability of your NoSQL database. This minimizes downtime and data loss in case of hardware failures.

4. **Security and Compliance:** Cloud providers invest heavily in security measures and compliance certifications. They offer features like encryption, access controls, and auditing to help you secure your data and meet regulatory requirements.
5. **Automated Backups:** Most cloud-based NoSQL services offer automated backup and recovery options, simplifying data protection and disaster recovery planning.
6. **Pay-as-You-Go Pricing:** Cloud services often follow a pay-as-you-go pricing model, allowing you to pay only for the resources you consume. This cost-effective approach eliminates the need for upfront capital investments.

Advantages of Cloud-Based NoSQL Services:

1. **Rapid Deployment:** Cloud-based NoSQL services enable quick database setup and configuration, reducing the time to market for applications.
2. **Cost Savings:** Organizations can save on infrastructure costs, as they don't need to invest in physical servers, data centers, or hardware maintenance.
3. **Global Reach:** Cloud providers have data centers distributed worldwide, allowing you to deploy your NoSQL database in regions that best serve your user base.
4. **Automatic Updates:** Cloud services often handle software updates and patch management, ensuring that your NoSQL database is running the latest and most secure version.
5. **Elastic Scaling:** Easily accommodate traffic spikes or growth by scaling your NoSQL database resources up or

down as needed.

6. **Resource Optimization:** Cloud providers offer tools and recommendations for optimizing resource usage, helping you manage costs effectively.

Sample Code (Amazon DynamoDB - AWS SDK for Python):

```
import boto3

# Create a DynamoDB client

dynamodb = boto3.client('dynamodb')

# Create a DynamoDB table

table_name = 'MyTable'

key_schema = [

{

'AttributeName': 'UserID',

'KeyType': 'HASH'

},

{

'AttributeName': 'Timestamp',

'KeyType': 'RANGE'

}

]

attribute_definitions = [
```

```
{
'AttributeName': 'UserID',
'AttributeType': 'N'
},
{
'AttributeName': 'Timestamp',
'AttributeType': 'N'
}
]
provisioned_throughput = {
'ReadCapacityUnits': 5,
'WriteCapacityUnits': 5
}
dynamodb.create_table(
TableName=table_name,
KeySchema=key_schema,
AttributeDefinitions=attribute_definitions,
ProvisionedThroughput=provisioned_throughput
)
# Perform CRUD operations and queries on the DynamoDB table
```

 # (Code to interact with the table goes here)

In summary, cloud-based NoSQL services offer a convenient and cost-effective way to leverage the power of NoSQL databases without the complexities of infrastructure management. Whether you choose Amazon DynamoDB, Azure Cosmos DB, Google Cloud Firestore, or other cloud-based NoSQL solutions, the ability to focus on your applications and data rather than infrastructure can significantly boost your productivity and agility.

9.2 Benefits of NoSQL in the Cloud

Deploying NoSQL databases in the cloud offers a wide range of benefits that cater to the modern needs of businesses and developers. In this section, we will explore the advantages of leveraging NoSQL databases in a cloud environment.

1. Scalability and Flexibility:

One of the key advantages of using NoSQL databases in the cloud is the scalability they offer. Cloud providers allow you to easily scale your NoSQL database up or down based on your application's demands. This means you can handle sudden increases in traffic or data volume without worrying about infrastructure limitations. Whether you need to support a small application or a global-scale service, the cloud provides the flexibility to adapt to your requirements.

2. Cost-Efficiency:

Cloud-based NoSQL databases follow a pay-as-you-go pricing model. This means you only pay for the resources you use, making it cost-effective for both startups and large enterprises. You can avoid upfront capital expenditures on hardware and reduce operational costs related to maintenance and administration. Additionally, cloud providers offer tools to help optimize resource usage, ensuring you get the most value for your investment.

3. Global Availability:

Cloud providers operate data centers in multiple regions worldwide. This global presence allows you to deploy your NoSQL database close to your users, reducing latency and improving response times. Whether your application serves customers locally or globally, you can strategically place your database in regions that offer the best performance for your users.

4. High Availability and Disaster Recovery:

Cloud-based NoSQL databases come with built-in high availability features. Cloud providers replicate data across multiple data centers, ensuring data durability and availability even in the face of hardware failures or outages. This reduces the risk of data loss and minimizes downtime. Additionally, cloud services offer automated backup and recovery options, simplifying disaster recovery planning.

5. Security and Compliance:

Cloud providers invest heavily in security measures and compliance certifications. They offer features like encryption, access controls, and identity management to help you secure your NoSQL data. Cloud services also facilitate compliance with industry regulations by providing audit trails and compliance documentation. This is particularly important for businesses that handle sensitive or regulated data.

6. Automatic Updates and Maintenance:

Managing software updates and maintenance can be a time-consuming task. Cloud-based NoSQL services handle this burden for you. They automatically apply updates and patches to the database infrastructure, ensuring that your NoSQL database is running the latest and most secure version. This allows your team to focus on developing features and applications rather than managing infrastructure.

7. DevOps Integration:

Cloud environments are well-suited for DevOps practices. You can easily integrate cloud-based NoSQL databases with DevOps tools and practices, enabling automated provisioning, configuration management, and continuous delivery. This streamlines the development and deployment processes, increasing development team productivity.

8. Data Analytics and Machine Learning:

Cloud providers offer a wide range of analytics and machine learning services that can be seamlessly integrated with NoSQL databases. This allows you to derive valuable insights from your data, build predictive models, and improve decision-making processes. The combination of NoSQL and cloud-based analytics services can unlock new opportunities for innovation and business growth.

In conclusion, the benefits of using NoSQL databases in the cloud are compelling for businesses of all sizes. Whether you prioritize scalability, cost-efficiency, high availability, security, or ease of management, cloud-based NoSQL services provide a versatile and powerful solution to meet your database needs. When strategically utilized, they can enhance your application's performance, reduce operational overhead, and drive business success.

9.3 Choosing a Cloud Provider for NoSQL

When considering the deployment of NoSQL databases in the cloud, selecting the right cloud provider is a crucial decision. Each cloud provider offers its own set of services, pricing models, and features. In this section, we'll explore the factors to consider when choosing a cloud provider for your NoSQL databases.

1. Database Compatibility:

Start by evaluating the compatibility of the cloud provider's services with your chosen NoSQL database. Some cloud providers offer managed NoSQL database services that are specifically designed to work with popular NoSQL databases like MongoDB, Cassandra, or DynamoDB. This can simplify database setup and management.

2. Service Offerings:

Different cloud providers offer various NoSQL database services, each with its own set of features and capabilities. Consider your project requirements and the types of NoSQL databases you need. Look for features such as automatic scaling, high availability, and data replication that align with your application's needs.

3. Pricing:

Pricing is a critical factor when choosing a cloud provider. Compare the pricing models of different providers, including storage costs, data transfer fees, and operational costs. Pay attention to any hidden costs, and ensure that the pricing aligns with your budget and expected usage patterns.

4. Performance and Scalability:

Evaluate the performance and scalability options offered by the cloud provider. Consider factors like CPU, memory, and I/O performance. Ensure that the provider can handle your workload's performance requirements, especially if your application experiences rapid growth.

5. Geographic Reach:

Consider the geographic reach of the cloud provider's data centers. If your application serves a global audience, choose a provider with a wide range of data center locations to reduce latency and improve the user experience.

6. Security and Compliance:

Examine the security features and compliance certifications provided by the cloud provider. NoSQL databases often store sensitive data, so robust security measures are essential. Look for features like encryption at rest and in transit, access controls, and identity management.

7. Data Migration and Integration:

Consider how easy it is to migrate your existing NoSQL databases or data to the chosen cloud provider's platform. Additionally, assess the ease of integrating the cloud provider's services with your existing infrastructure and tools.

8. Vendor Lock-In:

Be aware of the potential vendor lock-in when choosing a cloud provider. Some providers offer proprietary services and tools that may make it challenging to migrate away in the future. Evaluate the long-term implications of vendor lock-in on your project.

9. Support and Documentation:

Check the availability of support options and the quality of documentation provided by the cloud provider. Access to timely support can be crucial in resolving issues and optimizing your NoSQL database deployments.

10. Ecosystem and Services:

Consider the broader ecosystem of services offered by the cloud provider. Many cloud providers offer additional services such as analytics, machine learning, and serverless computing that can complement your NoSQL databases and enhance your application capabilities.

11. Community and User Feedback:

Research the cloud provider's reputation and user feedback. Online communities and forums can provide insights into the experiences of other developers and organizations using the provider's services.

12. Trial and Testing:

Before making a final decision, take advantage of free trials or testing periods offered by cloud providers. This allows you to evaluate the provider's services in a real-world scenario and assess their suitability for your project.

In conclusion, selecting a cloud provider for your NoSQL databases is a critical decision that can significantly impact your project's success. By carefully evaluating factors such as database compatibility, service offerings, pricing, performance, security, and support, you can make an informed choice that aligns with your project's requirements and goals. Keep in mind that the right cloud provider can streamline database management, improve scalability, and enhance your application's performance.

9.4 Migration Strategies to Cloud NoSQL

Migrating your NoSQL databases to the cloud requires careful planning and execution. This section explores various migration strategies and best practices to ensure a smooth transition of your NoSQL databases to the cloud environment.

1. Assessment and Planning:

Before starting the migration process, perform a comprehensive assessment of your existing NoSQL databases. Identify the databases, data volumes, schemas, and dependencies. Assess the compatibility of your chosen NoSQL database with the cloud provider's services.

2. Data Modeling and Schema Design:

Review and optimize your data modeling and schema design. Consider any necessary adjustments to take advantage of cloud-specific features and optimizations. Ensure that your data models are suitable for the cloud environment.

3. Backup and Disaster Recovery:

Take complete backups of your NoSQL databases and establish a disaster recovery plan. This ensures that you can recover data in case of unexpected issues during migration. Store backups securely, preferably in a different geographic region.

4. Data Migration Tools:

Leverage data migration tools and services provided by the cloud provider. Many cloud platforms offer tools that simplify the migration process. These tools can help you move data efficiently while minimizing downtime.

5. Gradual Migration:

Consider a phased or gradual migration approach, especially for large or mission-critical databases. Start by migrating less critical data or non-production databases to the cloud. This allows you to test the migration process and identify potential challenges.

6. Data Transformation and Validation:

During migration, you may need to transform data to fit the cloud database's format or structure. Develop scripts or workflows for data transformation and validate the data integrity before and after migration.

7. Testing and Validation:

Thoroughly test the migrated databases in the cloud environment. Verify that data consistency, application functionality, and performance meet your expectations. Conduct comprehensive testing, including load testing and failover testing.

8. Rollback Plan:

Have a rollback plan in case the migration encounters critical issues. Ensure that you can revert to the on-premises environment without data loss or service interruption if necessary.

9. Monitoring and Optimization:

Implement monitoring and alerting for the cloud-based NoSQL databases. Continuously monitor performance, resource utilization, and security. Optimize database configurations based on real-world usage patterns.

10. Data Synchronization:

If you are running a hybrid setup with both on-premises and cloud databases during migration, establish data synchronization mechanisms to keep the databases in sync. This ensures data consistency between environments.

11. Security and Compliance:

Maintain a focus on security and compliance throughout the migration process. Encrypt data during transit and at rest. Ensure that access controls and security policies are configured correctly in the cloud environment.

12. Documentation:

Document the entire migration process, including configurations, scripts, and procedures. This documentation is valuable for reference, troubleshooting, and future migrations.

13. Training and Knowledge Transfer:

Train your team on the cloud-based NoSQL databases and the new cloud environment. Knowledge transfer is essential to ensure that your team can effectively manage and maintain the databases in the cloud.

14. Post-Migration Optimization:

After completing the migration, continue to optimize the cloud-based NoSQL databases. Adjust configurations, scale resources as needed, and implement best practices to ensure optimal performance and cost efficiency.

15. Continuous Improvement:

Use the experience gained from migration to the cloud to drive continuous improvement. Periodically review and optimize your cloud database deployments based on evolving requirements and technologies.

In summary, migrating NoSQL databases to the cloud is a strategic move that can offer benefits in terms of scalability, flexibility, and cost-effectiveness. However, it requires meticulous planning, careful execution, and ongoing management. By following these migration strategies and best practices, you can minimize risks, ensure data integrity, and maximize the advantages of the cloud for your NoSQL databases.

9.5 Managing NoSQL in Cloud Environments

Managing NoSQL databases in cloud environments presents unique challenges and opportunities. This section explores key considerations and best practices for effectively managing NoSQL databases in the cloud.

1. Cloud Provider Selection:

Choose a cloud provider that aligns with your organization's requirements and goals. Consider factors such as geographic presence, service offerings, pricing, and compliance certifications. Different providers may offer specialized NoSQL database services that cater to specific use cases.

2. Service Models:

Understand the various service models offered by cloud providers, including Infrastructure as a Service (IaaS), Platform as a Service (PaaS), and Database as a Service (DBaaS). Each model offers different levels of control and management responsibilities. Select the model that best suits your database management approach.

3. NoSQL Database as a Service:

Cloud providers often offer NoSQL database services as part of their DBaaS offerings. These managed services handle routine database tasks such as provisioning, patching, and backup. Utilizing such services can simplify database management and reduce operational overhead.

4. Scalability:

Leverage the scalability benefits of cloud environments. NoSQL databases can easily scale horizontally to accommodate growing workloads. Configure auto-scaling policies to adjust resources dynamically based on demand. Monitor performance metrics to ensure optimal scaling.

5. Backup and Recovery:

Implement robust backup and recovery strategies tailored to your cloud provider's offerings. Schedule regular backups and store them securely. Familiarize yourself with the process of restoring data from backups to minimize downtime in case of data loss or corruption.

6. High Availability:

Ensure high availability of your NoSQL databases by distributing them across multiple availability zones or regions provided by your cloud provider. Implement load balancing and failover mechanisms to maintain uninterrupted service.

7. Security:

Prioritize security measures in your cloud-based NoSQL deployments. Implement encryption at rest and in transit. Utilize identity and access management (IAM) to control who can access and manage the databases. Regularly audit and monitor for security threats.

8. Compliance:

Comply with industry-specific regulations and standards relevant to your organization. Cloud providers often offer compliance certifications for their services, which can streamline the process of meeting regulatory requirements.

9. Cost Optimization:

Monitor and optimize your cloud spending. Cloud resources can incur costs based on usage. Implement cost monitoring tools to track resource utilization and identify opportunities for cost savings through resource optimization.

10. Performance Monitoring:

Leverage cloud-specific monitoring and performance analysis tools to gain insights into the health and performance of your NoSQL databases. Set up alerts to notify you of performance anomalies or issues that require attention.

11. Automation:

Automate routine database management tasks using scripts or cloud-native automation tools. This reduces manual intervention and minimizes the risk of human errors. Common tasks to automate include scaling, backup scheduling, and resource provisioning.

12. Disaster Recovery:

Develop and test disaster recovery plans to ensure business continuity in the event of catastrophic failures or outages. Implement geo-replication or cross-region backups to safeguard data against data center failures.

13. Data Lifecycle Management:

Define data retention and archival policies to manage data lifecycle effectively. Identify which data should be retained, archived, or deleted based on business requirements and compliance regulations.

14. Training and Skill Development:

Invest in training and skill development for your database administrators and operations teams. Cloud environments and NoSQL databases may require specific knowledge and expertise, so ongoing training is essential.

15. Performance Optimization:

Regularly assess the performance of your NoSQL databases and optimize configurations as needed. Fine-tune indexes, query patterns, and resource allocation to ensure efficient operations.

16. Cost Visibility:

Maintain visibility into your cloud spending by using cost management tools provided by your cloud provider. Analyze cost reports, set budget alerts, and adjust resource allocations to control expenses effectively.

17. Vendor Lock-In:

Be mindful of potential vendor lock-in when using cloud-specific NoSQL database services. Consider the long-term implications and explore strategies for data portability and migration if necessary.

In conclusion, managing NoSQL databases in cloud environments offers scalability, flexibility, and cost-efficiency advantages. However, it also requires careful planning, ongoing monitoring, and adherence to best practices to ensure optimal performance, security, and cost control. By following these guidelines, organizations can effectively harness the power of NoSQL databases in the cloud while mitigating potential challenges.

Chapter 10: NoSQL for Mobile and Web Applications

10.1 NoSQL in Mobile App Development

Mobile app development has undergone a significant transformation with the adoption of NoSQL databases. This section explores the role of NoSQL databases in mobile app development and their impact on building scalable and feature-rich mobile applications.

1. Data Synchronization:

One of the primary challenges in mobile app development is data synchronization between devices and the server. NoSQL databases, particularly document-oriented databases like MongoDB and Couchbase, excel in handling data synchronization. They allow developers to model data in a way that aligns with the app's requirements, making it easier to synchronize data across devices and resolve conflicts.

2. Flexibility in Schema:

NoSQL databases provide schema flexibility, which is crucial for evolving mobile apps. As app requirements change over time, developers can make schema changes without disrupting existing data. This flexibility allows for rapid app iterations and feature enhancements.

3. Offline Data Access:

NoSQL databases support offline data access, a critical feature for mobile apps. Users can continue using the app even when they have limited or no connectivity. Data can be stored locally on the device and synchronized with the server when a connection is available.

4. Real-Time Data:

Many NoSQL databases offer real-time data capabilities through change streams and event-driven architectures. This is beneficial for mobile apps that require real-time updates, such as messaging apps, collaborative tools, and live tracking applications.

5. Scalability:

NoSQL databases are designed to scale horizontally, making them suitable for mobile apps with growing user bases. Cloud-based NoSQL services further simplify the scalability process by allowing developers to focus on app logic rather than infrastructure management.

6. Performance:

NoSQL databases are optimized for read-heavy workloads, which is common in mobile apps. They can efficiently retrieve and serve data to mobile clients, resulting in faster app performance and a smoother user experience.

7. Cross-Platform Development:

NoSQL databases can be used in cross-platform mobile app development frameworks like React Native and Flutter. This enables developers to write code once and deploy it on multiple platforms, reducing development time and effort.

8. Use Cases:

NoSQL databases are well-suited for various mobile app use cases, including:

- **Social Networking**: Storing user profiles, posts, and social interactions.

- **E-commerce**: Managing product catalogs, user preferences, and order histories.

- **Location-Based Services**: Tracking and serving location data efficiently.

- **Gaming**: Storing game states, scores, and player progress.

- **Content Management**: Handling user-generated content and multimedia.

9. Security:

Security is a critical aspect of mobile app development. NoSQL databases offer security features such as encryption at rest and in transit, access control, and auditing, helping developers protect sensitive user data.

10. Best Practices:

When using NoSQL databases in mobile app development, consider the following best practices:

- **Data Modeling**: Design data models that reflect the app's requirements and usage patterns.

- **Offline Handling**: Implement strategies for offline data access and synchronization.

- **Scalability Planning**: Anticipate app growth and plan for scalable database solutions.

- **Security Measures**: Apply appropriate security measures to safeguard user data.

- **Testing**: Thoroughly test the app's data access and synchronization features under different network conditions.

In summary, NoSQL databases play a pivotal role in modern mobile app development by addressing data synchronization challenges, offering schema flexibility, enabling offline access, and providing real-time data capabilities. Mobile app developers can leverage the scalability, performance, and security benefits of NoSQL databases to create robust and user-friendly applications.

10.2 Building Scalable Web Applications with NoSQL

Scalability is a critical consideration when building web applications, especially as they grow in terms of user base and data volume. NoSQL databases provide robust solutions for developing scalable web applications, and in this section, we'll explore how to leverage NoSQL for this purpose.

1. Data Distribution and Sharding:

One of the primary techniques for achieving scalability with NoSQL is data distribution through sharding. Sharding involves breaking down a database into smaller, more manageable partitions called shards. Each shard can be hosted on a separate server or cluster, allowing for parallel data access and reduced load on individual servers.

For example, in a document-oriented NoSQL database like MongoDB, data can be sharded based on a chosen shard key, such as a user's geographical location or a specific category. This ensures that related data is stored together and can be accessed efficiently.

2. Horizontal Scaling:

NoSQL databases are designed for horizontal scaling, which means you can easily add more servers or clusters to accommodate increasing workloads. This contrasts with traditional SQL databases, which often require vertical scaling (upgrading server hardware), which can be costly and less flexible.

Horizontal scaling is cost-effective and aligns with the elasticity of cloud computing platforms, making it a suitable choice for web applications that experience fluctuating traffic patterns.

3. Load Balancing:

To ensure even distribution of requests and efficient utilization of resources, load balancers are commonly used in conjunction with NoSQL databases. Load balancers distribute incoming requests across multiple database servers or clusters, preventing overloading of any single node.

Popular load balancing solutions, such as NGINX and HAProxy, can be configured to work seamlessly with NoSQL databases. They provide health checks, request routing, and session persistence features.

4. Caching:

Caching is another essential strategy for improving the performance and scalability of web applications. NoSQL databases often integrate with caching solutions like Redis and Memcached, allowing frequently accessed data to be stored in-memory for rapid retrieval.

By caching data at various layers of your application stack, you reduce the load on the database, resulting in faster response times and improved scalability. Additionally, caching helps mitigate the impact of database latency spikes.

5. Asynchronous Processing:

Web applications can benefit from asynchronous processing to offload time-consuming tasks and maintain responsiveness. NoSQL databases support asynchronous patterns by allowing data to be written or updated without immediate confirmation. Background processes can then handle data processing, validation, or aggregation.

Message brokers like RabbitMQ and Apache Kafka are commonly used for implementing asynchronous processing in web applications. They enable decoupling of components and the creation of resilient, distributed systems.

6. Event-Driven Architectures:

NoSQL databases, especially those offering change streams and event-driven capabilities, are well-suited for building event-driven architectures. Events can trigger actions and updates in real-time, making applications more responsive and capable of handling concurrent user interactions.

For example, when a user makes a reservation on a travel booking website, an event can be generated and processed to update availability, send confirmation emails, and notify relevant parties.

7. Microservices:

Microservices architecture is an approach where an application is divided into smaller, independent services that can be developed, deployed, and scaled individually. NoSQL databases support microservices by allowing each service to use its database, often referred to as a microservices database pattern.

Each microservice can choose the NoSQL database that best fits its data requirements. This flexibility enables teams to use the most suitable database technology for their specific service while benefiting from the scalability and performance advantages of NoSQL.

8. Serverless Computing:

Serverless computing platforms like AWS Lambda, Azure Functions, and Google Cloud Functions enable developers to run code in response to events without managing servers. NoSQL databases can be integrated seamlessly with serverless functions to build scalable and cost-effective web applications.

Serverless functions can interact with NoSQL databases to perform data retrieval, manipulation, and storage, allowing developers to focus on application logic while the underlying infrastructure is managed by the cloud provider.

9. Auto-Scaling:

Many cloud-based NoSQL database services offer auto-scaling capabilities. Auto-scaling automatically adjusts the database's capacity based on workload and resource utilization. This ensures that your web application can handle traffic spikes and maintain optimal performance without manual intervention.

10. Best Practices:

When building scalable web applications with NoSQL, consider the following best practices:

- **Data Modeling**: Design an effective data model that aligns with your application's access patterns.

- **Sharding Strategy**: Plan your sharding strategy carefully, considering data distribution and query performance.

- **Monitoring and Alerting**: Implement robust monitoring and alerting to detect performance bottlenecks and issues proactively.

- **Backup and Disaster Recovery**: Establish reliable backup and disaster recovery procedures to safeguard data.

- **Testing for Scalability**: Perform load testing and scalability tests to ensure your application can handle expected and unexpected traffic.

In conclusion, NoSQL databases offer a range of features and strategies for building scalable web applications. By leveraging data distribution, horizontal scaling, load balancing, caching, asynchronous processing, and event-driven architectures, developers can create web applications that are capable of handling large and dynamic workloads efficiently. Best practices in data modeling, sharding, monitoring, and testing are essential to ensure the scalability and reliability of these applications.

10.3 Real-Time Data Sync in NoSQL

Real-time data synchronization is a crucial requirement for many modern web applications. It ensures that data changes made by one user or system are quickly propagated to other users or components. NoSQL databases provide several mechanisms to achieve real-time data sync, enabling applications to deliver responsive and collaborative experiences.

1. Change Streams:

Many NoSQL databases offer a feature known as change streams or change data capture (CDC). Change streams allow applications to subscribe to real-time notifications about changes to the database. When data is inserted, updated, or deleted, the database triggers events that are pushed to subscribed clients or services.

For instance, MongoDB provides a change streams feature that allows developers to watch specific collections or documents. When changes occur, applications can react immediately, updating user interfaces, triggering notifications, or performing other actions.

2. WebSockets:

WebSockets are a widely used technology for enabling real-time communication between web clients (browsers) and servers. NoSQL databases can integrate with WebSocket libraries and frameworks to push data updates to connected clients.

For example, a chat application can use WebSockets to transmit new messages to all connected users in real time. When a user sends a message, it's stored in the NoSQL database, and the server broadcasts it to all connected clients using WebSockets.

3. Publish-Subscribe (Pub/Sub) Patterns:

NoSQL databases can implement publish-subscribe patterns to enable real-time data synchronization. In a pub/sub system, clients subscribe to specific channels or topics of interest. When new data is published to a channel, all subscribers receive the data in real time.

Redis, a popular NoSQL database, provides built-in support for pub/sub patterns. Applications can use Redis as a message broker to publish and subscribe to real-time updates. This is commonly used in applications like news feeds and notifications.

```
# Python code using Redis for publish-subscribe

import redis

# Initialize a Redis client

redis_client = redis.StrictRedis(host='localhost', port=6379, db=0)

# Subscribe to a channel

pubsub = redis_client.pubsub()

pubsub.subscribe('news_updates')

# Listen for messages

for message in pubsub.listen():

print(f"Received: {message['data']}")
```

4. Webhooks:

Webhooks are HTTP callbacks that allow external systems to be notified of specific events in real time. NoSQL databases can be configured to send webhook notifications when changes occur. External systems, such as third-party services or microservices, can then react to these events.

For example, an e-commerce application can send a webhook notification to a shipping service when an order is placed. The shipping service can then start processing the order immediately.

5. Event-Driven Architectures:

Event-driven architectures, which we discussed earlier, are closely related to real-time data synchronization. NoSQL databases that support event-driven capabilities enable applications to respond to events triggered by data changes.

In an event-driven architecture, events such as "user profile updated" or "new document created" can be captured and processed in real time. This allows applications to update user interfaces, notify users, or perform other actions as soon as data changes occur.

6. Conflict Resolution:

In collaborative applications, where multiple users can modify the same data concurrently, conflict resolution becomes crucial. NoSQL databases often provide mechanisms for resolving conflicts that may arise when multiple users attempt to update the same data simultaneously.

Conflict resolution strategies can include last-write-wins, versioning, or custom logic based on application-specific rules. It's essential to implement conflict resolution strategies that align with your application's requirements to maintain data consistency.

7. Scalability Considerations:

When implementing real-time data synchronization with NoSQL databases, consider the scalability of the system. As the number of clients or subscribers increases, the system should be able to handle the additional load. Load balancers, caching, and auto-scaling strategies are critical to ensuring the system's responsiveness and reliability.

In conclusion, real-time data synchronization is a fundamental requirement for many modern web applications, and NoSQL databases offer several mechanisms to achieve this goal. Change streams, WebSockets, pub/sub patterns, webhooks, event-driven architectures, and conflict resolution strategies are key components of building responsive and collaborative applications. Scalability considerations are essential to ensure that the real-time synchronization system can handle growing numbers of users and data changes.

10.4 Offline Data Handling

In modern mobile and web applications, users expect seamless experiences even when they are offline or have limited connectivity. Handling data offline is a critical aspect of building robust applications. NoSQL databases provide various strategies for managing data when the network is unreliable or unavailable.

1. Offline Data Storage:

One common approach to handling offline data is to store a local copy of data on the user's device. NoSQL databases can be used as local data stores, allowing users to interact with data even when they are offline. This local data can be synchronized with the remote database when connectivity is restored.

For example, a mobile note-taking app may use a NoSQL database to store user-generated notes locally. Users can create, read, update, and delete notes even without an internet connection. When the device is online again, the app can sync the local changes with the central database.

2. Conflict Resolution:

Offline data handling often involves conflict resolution. When multiple users or devices modify the same data independently while offline, conflicts can arise when attempting to sync changes with the central database.

NoSQL databases provide mechanisms for conflict resolution, such as timestamp-based conflict resolution or the use of vector clocks. These mechanisms help ensure that data consistency is maintained even when conflicts occur.

3. Offline-First Architectures:

The concept of "offline-first" design promotes building applications with offline capabilities as a primary consideration. In an offline-first architecture, the application is designed to work offline by default, with data synchronization happening in the background when connectivity is available.

NoSQL databases play a crucial role in offline-first architectures by providing tools and libraries for data synchronization. Developers can use these tools to design applications that minimize disruption when transitioning between online and offline modes.

4. Data Synchronization Strategies:

Data synchronization between the local and remote databases can follow different strategies. One common approach is to use a queuing system to capture changes made locally while offline. When the device regains connectivity, these changes are sent to the central database in the order they were made.

Some NoSQL databases offer built-in support for data synchronization, making it easier to implement offline data handling. For instance, Couchbase Mobile provides a solution for offline-first mobile applications, allowing developers to build applications that seamlessly sync data between devices and a central database.

5. Conflict-Free Replicated Data Types (CRDTs):

CRDTs are data structures designed to be merged automatically without conflicts, making them well-suited for offline data synchronization. NoSQL databases can incorporate CRDTs to handle data changes made independently by multiple users or devices.

CRDTs can be used for various purposes, such as collaborative document editing, real-time collaborative applications, and distributed databases. They ensure that data remains consistent and mergeable even in offline scenarios.

6. Progressive Web Apps (PWAs):

Progressive Web Apps are web applications that provide an app-like experience in web browsers. They are designed to work offline and can cache data locally using technologies like service workers and IndexedDB, which can be used to store data offline.

NoSQL databases can be integrated into PWAs to enable data storage and synchronization. This allows users to access web applications even when they are not connected to the internet, providing a seamless user experience.

In summary, handling offline data is crucial for delivering robust and responsive applications. NoSQL databases offer various strategies and tools to manage data offline, including local data storage, conflict resolution, offline-first architectures, data synchronization strategies, CRDTs, and support for Progressive Web Apps. By incorporating these techniques, developers can build applications that meet users' expectations for offline usability while maintaining data consistency and integrity.

10.5 Case Studies: Successful NoSQL Implementations

To gain a deeper understanding of how NoSQL databases are effectively used in real-world scenarios, let's explore some case studies of successful implementations across different domains.

1. E-commerce: Amazon DynamoDB

Amazon, one of the world's largest e-commerce companies, relies on Amazon DynamoDB, a managed NoSQL database service. DynamoDB helps Amazon handle massive amounts of data related to products, orders, customer profiles, and more. It provides low-latency access to product catalogs, supports high-traffic shopping events like Black Friday, and ensures data consistency across geographically distributed regions. DynamoDB's scalability and performance capabilities align with Amazon's need for a highly responsive and reliable e-commerce platform.

2. Social Media: Instagram's Cassandra

Instagram, a popular social media platform, employs Apache Cassandra, a wide-column store NoSQL database, to manage user data, media, and interactions. Cassandra's distributed architecture helps Instagram handle billions of photos and videos uploaded daily, along with user interactions like likes and comments. The decentralized nature of Cassandra allows Instagram to provide a seamless experience to its global user base.

3. Financial Services: Goldman Sachs' ScyllaDB

Goldman Sachs, a global investment banking firm, relies on ScyllaDB, a highly performant NoSQL database compatible with Apache Cassandra. ScyllaDB helps Goldman Sachs manage and analyze large volumes of financial data, execute complex queries, and ensure low-latency access for trading and risk assessment. The database's horizontal scalability and robust support for time-series data make it a valuable asset in the financial industry.

4. Healthcare: UnitedHealth Group's MongoDB

UnitedHealth Group, a healthcare provider and insurer, uses MongoDB as its NoSQL database of choice. MongoDB helps UnitedHealth Group manage electronic health records (EHRs), patient data, claims processing, and healthcare analytics. The flexibility of MongoDB's document model allows UnitedHealth Group to adapt to evolving healthcare standards and regulations while ensuring data security and privacy.

5. Gaming: Riot Games' Redis

Riot Games, the developer behind the popular online game League of Legends, utilizes Redis, an in-memory key-value store, for various aspects of game infrastructure. Redis helps Riot Games manage player profiles, leaderboards, and real-time game data, ensuring a smooth gaming experience for millions of players worldwide. The database's speed and simplicity make it an ideal choice for real-time gaming applications.

6. IoT: General Electric's InfluxDB

General Electric (GE) employs InfluxDB, a time-series database, to handle data generated by IoT devices in various industries, including manufacturing and energy. InfluxDB allows GE to store, analyze, and visualize sensor data from machines and equipment, enabling predictive maintenance and operational efficiency improvements. The database's focus on time-series data makes it well-suited for IoT applications.

7. Content Management: Adobe Experience Manager's MongoDB

Adobe Experience Manager, a content management solution, utilizes MongoDB to store and manage digital content for websites and applications. MongoDB's flexibility and scalability enable Adobe to handle content of all types, including text, images, videos, and metadata. It supports content personalization, versioning, and collaboration, enhancing the digital experiences delivered by Adobe's customers.

These case studies illustrate the versatility of NoSQL databases across diverse industries and use cases. Whether it's handling massive e-commerce data, supporting real-time social media interactions, managing sensitive healthcare records, powering online games, processing IoT sensor data, or enabling content management, NoSQL databases have proven their value in meeting the demands of modern applications and services. Successful implementations demonstrate the adaptability, scalability, and performance of NoSQL solutions in addressing unique business challenges and opportunities.

Chapter 11: Advanced Querying in NoSQL

Section 11.1: Complex Queries in NoSQL

In the world of NoSQL databases, complex queries often play a crucial role when you need to extract specific information from vast datasets or when you want to perform aggregations and calculations. Complex queries go beyond simple key-value lookups and can involve filtering, sorting, and combining data from various documents or rows within a database. Understanding how to create and optimize complex queries is essential for harnessing the full power of your NoSQL database.

Characteristics of Complex Queries

Complex queries in NoSQL databases can be characterized by the following aspects:

1. **Multiple Criteria:** They involve multiple conditions or criteria that must be met for the query to return the desired results. These criteria can include filtering by specific fields, comparing values, or even using regular expressions.
2. **Aggregation:** They often require aggregating data, such as calculating sums, averages, counts, or other statistical measures across a dataset. Aggregation queries are common in scenarios like analytics and reporting.
3. **Join Operations:** While NoSQL databases are designed for schema-less data, there are situations where you need to join data from multiple collections or tables, similar to

SQL joins. Handling these joins efficiently is essential for complex queries.

4. **Sorting:** Sorting results based on specific fields or criteria may be necessary for presenting data in a structured manner. Complex queries often involve sorting in ascending or descending order.

Query Languages and Tools

NoSQL databases use various query languages and tools to perform complex queries:

1. **MongoDB Aggregation Framework:** MongoDB, a popular document-oriented NoSQL database, provides an extensive Aggregation Framework that enables users to perform complex operations, including filtering, grouping, sorting, and projecting data. It supports a pipeline-based approach to building complex queries.
2. **Cassandra Query Language (CQL):** Cassandra, a wide-column store NoSQL database, uses CQL for querying data. CQL is similar to SQL in terms of syntax and supports complex queries like filtering, sorting, and aggregations.
3. **Gremlin for Graph Databases:** Graph databases like Apache TinkerPop-compliant databases use the Gremlin query language for traversing and querying graph structures. Gremlin allows you to create complex queries to navigate relationships and find patterns in graph data.

Optimization and Indexing

Efficiently executing complex queries often involves optimization techniques and the use of appropriate indexes. NoSQL databases provide indexing mechanisms to improve query performance. Understanding which fields to index and how to structure your data for efficient querying is a key consideration when working with complex queries.

Additionally, distributed NoSQL databases may require optimization for scalability and parallel query processing to handle complex queries on large datasets.

In the next sections of this chapter, we will delve deeper into the specifics of complex queries in different types of NoSQL databases, including examples and best practices to help you master this essential skill in NoSQL data management.

Section 11.2: Aggregation Frameworks

Aggregation frameworks are a powerful feature in NoSQL databases, particularly in document-oriented databases like MongoDB. They allow you to perform complex data transformations and aggregations within the database itself, rather than fetching large datasets and processing them in your application code. This can significantly improve query performance and reduce network overhead.

Key Concepts

Pipeline-Based Processing

Most NoSQL databases that support aggregation frameworks use a pipeline-based processing approach. You construct a sequence of stages, and each stage applies a specific operation to the data. Data passes through these stages sequentially, and at each stage, you can reshape, filter, group, and manipulate the data as needed.

Aggregation Operators

Aggregation frameworks provide a wide range of operators to perform operations like grouping, projecting specific fields, sorting, filtering, and calculating various metrics on your data. Some common aggregation operators include $match, $group, $project, $sort, $limit, and $unwind, among others.

Grouping and Summarizing

One of the primary use cases for aggregation frameworks is grouping and summarizing data. You can group documents by one or more fields and then calculate aggregate values for each group. For example, you can calculate the total sales amount for each product category in an e-commerce dataset.

Nested Aggregations

Aggregation frameworks often allow for nested aggregations, which means you can perform multiple aggregation operations within a single query. This is useful for more complex scenarios where you need to calculate multiple statistics or metrics in a single pass.

Example

Let's consider a simple example in MongoDB's aggregation framework. Suppose you have a collection of orders, and each document has the following structure:

```
{
"_id": 1,
"product": "Widget",
"quantity": 10,
"price": 25
}
```

You want to calculate the total revenue for each product category. You can achieve this with the following aggregation query:

```
db.orders.aggregate([
{
$group: {
_id: "$product",
totalRevenue: { $sum: { $multiply: ["$quantity", "$price"] } }
}
},
{
$sort: { totalRevenue: -1 }
```

```
}
])
```

In this query:

- The $group stage groups the documents by the "product" field and calculates the totalRevenue for each group by multiplying the "quantity" and "price" fields.
- The $sort stage then sorts the results in descending order of totalRevenue.

This is just a simple example, but aggregation frameworks allow you to perform much more complex operations, including joining data from multiple collections, handling nested arrays, and more.

Use Cases

Aggregation frameworks are invaluable for various use cases, including:

- Analytics and reporting: Calculating sums, averages, and other statistics.
- Data transformation: Reshaping data for different purposes.
- Real-time dashboards: Aggregating data for visualization.
- Event-driven processing: Processing streams of data in real-time.

- Complex data manipulations: Handling complex data structures.

In the next section, we'll explore more advanced aggregation scenarios and best practices for using aggregation frameworks effectively in NoSQL databases.

Section 11.3: MapReduce in NoSQL

MapReduce is a programming model and processing technique used in NoSQL databases to perform distributed and parallel data processing. It was popularized by Google and is widely used for large-scale data analysis and transformation tasks. In NoSQL databases, MapReduce can be a powerful tool for complex data processing when other query methods fall short.

Key Concepts

Map Function

The MapReduce process begins with the "map" phase. In this phase, a "map" function is applied to each document in a dataset. The purpose of the map function is to extract and emit key-value pairs from the input data. These emitted key-value pairs are then grouped by key in preparation for the "reduce" phase.

Shuffle and Sort

After the map phase, the framework performs a "shuffle and sort" operation. During this step, all emitted key-value pairs are grouped by key and sorted. This process ensures that all values associated with a particular key are grouped together and ready for reduction.

Reduce Function

In the "reduce" phase, a "reduce" function is applied to each group of key-value pairs with the same key. The reduce function takes this group of values and produces a single output value. The output from all reduce functions is then collected to produce the final result of the MapReduce operation.

Parallel Processing

One of the strengths of MapReduce is its ability to perform parallel processing. The map phase can be distributed across multiple nodes in a cluster, and the reduce phase can also be parallelized. This parallelism allows for efficient processing of large datasets.

Example

Let's consider a simple example of using MapReduce in MongoDB to calculate the average quantity of products sold for each product category in a collection of orders. Here's how you might implement this in MapReduce:

```
var mapFunction = function () {

emit(this.product, this.quantity);

};

var reduceFunction = function (key, values) {

var totalQuantity = Array.sum(values);

var averageQuantity = totalQuantity / values.length;

return averageQuantity;
```

```
};

db.orders.mapReduce(

mapFunction,

reduceFunction,

{ out: "averageQuantityByCategory" }

);
```

In this example:

- The map function extracts the product category as the key and emits the quantity as the value for each order document.
- The reduce function calculates the total quantity for each product category and then computes the average quantity.
- The result is stored in the "averageQuantityByCategory" collection.

Use Cases

MapReduce is suitable for various use cases in NoSQL databases, including:

- Complex data transformations: When you need to perform intricate data transformations that are challenging with traditional query methods.

- Large-scale data processing: MapReduce can handle massive datasets and distribute the processing load across a cluster.

- Aggregations: It can be used for advanced aggregations and calculations.

- Log analysis: Analyzing large volumes of log data to extract insights.

- Text analysis: Processing and analyzing unstructured text data for sentiment analysis or natural language processing.

While MapReduce is a powerful tool, it's essential to note that it often requires more developer effort to implement than standard query languages or aggregation frameworks. In some cases, newer technologies like Spark or Hadoop might be preferred for large-scale data processing tasks.

In the next section, we'll explore query optimization techniques in NoSQL databases, including ways to improve the performance of your database queries.

Section 11.4: Query Optimization Techniques

Query optimization is a critical aspect of database performance tuning in both SQL and NoSQL databases. In NoSQL databases, where data models can vary widely, query optimization techniques aim to improve the efficiency of data retrieval and manipulation. Let's explore some key query optimization techniques in the context of NoSQL databases.

Indexing

Just like in SQL databases, indexing is a fundamental technique in NoSQL databases for optimizing query performance. An index is a data structure that provides a fast lookup of records based on specific fields. By creating appropriate indexes on fields frequently used in queries, you can significantly speed up data retrieval.

In most NoSQL databases, you can define secondary indexes on fields of documents. For example, in MongoDB, you can create indexes using the createIndex method:

```
db.collection.createIndex({ fieldName: 1 }); // 1 for ascending, -1 for descending
```

Denormalization

Denormalization involves storing redundant data within documents to reduce the need for multiple queries and joins. While this can increase storage space requirements, it can significantly improve query performance by reducing the number of database operations required.

For example, in a social media application, you might denormalize user information into posts, so you don't need to perform additional queries to fetch user details when displaying posts.

Query Projection

Query projection involves specifying only the fields you need in the query result, rather than retrieving the entire document. By selecting only the necessary fields, you can reduce the amount of data transferred over the network and improve query response times.

In MongoDB, you can use the projection parameter to specify which fields to include or exclude in the query result:

```
db.collection.find({}, { _id: 0, fieldName: 1 }); // Exclude _id, include fieldName
```

Caching

Caching frequently accessed data in memory can significantly improve query performance. NoSQL databases like Redis and Memcached are designed for caching and can store frequently accessed data in memory for quick retrieval.

Caching is especially beneficial for read-heavy workloads, where the same data is repeatedly requested.

Query Planning and Profiling

Many NoSQL databases provide tools for query planning and profiling. Query planning involves the database system analyzing queries to determine the most efficient execution plan. Profiling allows you to analyze query performance and identify bottlenecks.

For example, MongoDB offers the explain method to retrieve execution plans and the ability to enable query profiling to capture query execution statistics.

```
db.collection.find({}).explain("executionStats");
```

Sharding

Sharding is a technique used in horizontally scalable NoSQL databases to distribute data across multiple servers or clusters. By dividing data into smaller partitions (shards), you can distribute the query load and improve query performance for large datasets.

For example, MongoDB's sharding allows you to partition data based on a shard key, ensuring that data is evenly distributed across shards.

Compression and Data Encoding

Some NoSQL databases offer data compression and encoding options to reduce storage space and improve query performance. Compressed data requires less disk space, and reading compressed data can be faster due to reduced I/O operations.

In summary, query optimization in NoSQL databases involves a combination of techniques such as indexing, denormalization, query projection, caching, query planning, sharding, and data compression. The specific optimization strategies you employ will depend on your application's requirements, data model, and workload characteristics. Profiling and monitoring query performance are essential to identifying areas for improvement and ensuring that your NoSQL database performs efficiently.

Section 11.5: Working with Unstructured Data

In the realm of NoSQL databases, one of the significant advantages is the ability to handle unstructured data effectively. Unstructured data refers to data that doesn't adhere to a predefined schema, unlike traditional relational databases. This section delves into how NoSQL databases are well-suited for working with unstructured data and the various ways in which they accommodate this data type.

What is Unstructured Data?

Unstructured data encompasses a wide range of data types, including text, images, audio, video, and more. It doesn't fit neatly into rows and columns, making it challenging to store and query within traditional relational databases. Examples of unstructured data include social media posts, email content, sensor data, and multimedia files.

NoSQL Databases and Unstructured Data

NoSQL databases excel at handling unstructured data due to their flexible data models. Here's how they manage unstructured data effectively:

1. **Schema Flexibility**: NoSQL databases, particularly document-oriented and key-value stores, allow you to insert data without a fixed schema. Each document or record can have varying fields and structures, making them ideal for storing unstructured data.
2. **BLOB (Binary Large Object) Support**: Some NoSQL databases offer support for storing binary data, such as images and videos, as BLOBs. These binary objects can be efficiently stored and retrieved.
3. **Text Search Capabilities**: Many NoSQL databases provide full-text search capabilities, allowing you to search for keywords or phrases within unstructured text data. Elasticsearch and Apache Solr are examples of NoSQL databases optimized for text search.
4. **Geospatial Data**: NoSQL databases like MongoDB can handle geospatial data, making them suitable for applications dealing with location-based unstructured data, such as mapping and geospatial analytics.
5. **Scalability for Large Files**: NoSQL databases with support for distributed file storage can efficiently manage large multimedia files and distribute them across multiple nodes for better performance.

Use Cases for Unstructured Data

Unstructured data is prevalent in various domains, and NoSQL databases find extensive use in these scenarios:

1. **Social Media Analytics**: NoSQL databases are employed to store and analyze social media data, which includes text posts, images, videos, and user-generated content.
2. **Content Management Systems (CMS)**: CMS platforms use NoSQL databases to manage web content, including articles, images, and multimedia.
3. **IoT Data**: The Internet of Things (IoT) generates vast amounts of unstructured sensor data, which NoSQL databases can efficiently store and process.
4. **Log and Event Data**: NoSQL databases are employed for log and event data storage and analysis, where logs may contain diverse unstructured data.
5. **Media and Entertainment**: In the media and entertainment industry, NoSQL databases are used to manage and serve multimedia content, including videos, music, and images.

Handling Unstructured Data in NoSQL Databases

When working with unstructured data in NoSQL databases, it's crucial to define appropriate data models and indexing strategies. Additionally, leveraging the right database features, such as full-text search, geospatial indexing, and distributed storage, can optimize the handling of unstructured data.

In conclusion, NoSQL databases offer a flexible and scalable solution for managing unstructured data effectively. Their ability to adapt to varying data structures and handle diverse data types makes them a valuable choice for applications dealing with the ever-growing volumes of unstructured data in today's digital landscape.

Chapter 12: NoSQL Data Replication and Distribution

Section 12.1: Principles of Data Replication

Data replication is a fundamental concept in database systems, and it plays a crucial role in ensuring data availability, fault tolerance, and scalability in NoSQL databases. This section explores the principles of data replication, its significance, and how it is implemented in the context of NoSQL databases.

What is Data Replication?

Data replication refers to the process of creating and maintaining multiple copies of the same data across different storage locations or nodes within a distributed system. The primary objective of data replication is to enhance data reliability, availability, and performance. In the context of NoSQL databases, data replication serves several essential purposes:

1. **Fault Tolerance**: Replicating data across multiple nodes ensures that if one node fails or becomes inaccessible due to hardware issues or network problems, the data remains accessible from other replicas. This enhances the system's fault tolerance.
2. **Load Balancing**: Replication allows for distributing read and write operations across multiple replicas, effectively balancing the load on the system. This improves overall system performance and responsiveness.
3. **Reduced Latency**: Replicating data closer to the point of access can reduce data retrieval latency. This is especially important for applications that require low-latency access

to data.

4. **Scalability**: Data replication is closely tied to the concept of horizontal scalability. As data and user load increase, additional replicas can be added to the system to handle the load efficiently.

Types of Data Replication

Data replication can take several forms, each offering specific advantages and trade-offs:

1. **Full Replication**: In full replication, every node in the system stores a complete copy of the entire dataset. This approach offers high fault tolerance and load balancing but can be resource-intensive as the dataset grows.
2. **Partial Replication**: Partial replication involves replicating only a subset of the data across nodes. This can be useful when certain data is accessed more frequently than others. However, it requires careful data partitioning and routing logic.
3. **Master-Slave Replication**: In this model, one node (the master) is responsible for handling write operations, while one or more other nodes (the slaves) replicate the writes from the master. Slave nodes are primarily used for read operations, improving read scalability.
4. **Multi-Master Replication**: In multi-master replication, multiple nodes can accept both read and write operations independently. This approach provides high write scalability but can introduce complexities related to data conflicts and consistency.

Data Consistency and Replication

One of the key challenges in data replication is maintaining data consistency across replicas. There are various consistency models that define how and when data changes are propagated to replicas. Two common models are:

1. **Strong Consistency**: In a strongly consistent system, all replicas are updated with the same data in the same order, ensuring that reads from any replica return the most recent write. Achieving strong consistency often comes at the cost of increased latency and reduced availability, as all replicas must agree before acknowledging a write.
2. **Eventual Consistency**: Eventual consistency relaxes the strict consistency requirements, allowing replicas to be temporarily out of sync. However, it guarantees that given enough time without new updates, all replicas will converge to the same state.

Implementation in NoSQL Databases

Different NoSQL databases implement data replication in their unique ways. For example:

- **Cassandra**: Cassandra uses a distributed architecture with tunable consistency levels, allowing developers to choose between strong and eventual consistency. It employs a masterless architecture, where all nodes are treated equally.

- **MongoDB**: MongoDB supports replica sets, where one node is designated as the primary (responsible for writes), and others are secondary nodes (replicating data from the primary). Failover and data consistency are managed automatically.

- **Redis**: Redis offers replication with high availability using a master-slave architecture. It also supports partitioning and clustering for horizontal scalability.

In conclusion, data replication is a fundamental strategy for enhancing data reliability, availability, and performance in NoSQL databases. Understanding the principles and trade-offs of data replication is crucial for designing and managing distributed database systems effectively. The choice of replication model and consistency level should align with the specific requirements and use cases of your application.

Section 12.2: Data Distribution Strategies

Data distribution strategies are a critical aspect of designing and managing NoSQL databases in a distributed environment. These strategies determine how data is divided and stored across multiple nodes or clusters, affecting data availability, performance, and scalability. In this section, we will explore various data distribution strategies commonly used in NoSQL databases.

1. Key-Range Partitioning

Key-range partitioning, also known as sharding, involves dividing the dataset into ranges or partitions based on the values of a specific key. Each partition is assigned to a separate node or server. This strategy is commonly used in distributed databases, where the key can be numeric, alphanumeric, or even date-based.

For example, consider a user database where data is partitioned based on user IDs. User IDs falling within a specific range (e.g., 1-1000,

1001-2000, and so on) are stored on different nodes. This approach ensures that data for different users is distributed across nodes, balancing the workload.

Pros:

- Effective load balancing, as data is evenly distributed based on key ranges.
- Straightforward to implement and manage.
- Well-suited for range-based queries (e.g., retrieving data within a specific date range).

Cons:

- May lead to hotspots if data distribution is uneven or if certain key ranges are more frequently accessed than others.
- Dynamically resizing partitions can be challenging and may require data migration.

2. Hash-Based Partitioning

Hash-based partitioning involves applying a hash function to a specific key attribute to determine the destination node for storing data. This strategy ensures that data is distributed uniformly across nodes, reducing hotspots and providing good load balancing.

In practice, a hash function takes the key as input and produces a numeric or alphanumeric value. The result is then used to determine which node should store the data. Hash-based partitioning is commonly used in NoSQL databases like Cassandra and DynamoDB.

Pros:

- Uniform distribution of data, minimizing hotspots.
- Scalable and efficient for large datasets.
- Well-suited for write-heavy workloads.

Cons:

- Limited support for range queries, as data is distributed randomly.
- Adding or removing nodes may require rehashing and data redistribution.

3. Directory-Based Partitioning

Directory-based partitioning is a strategy where a central directory or metadata service maintains information about the location of data. Instead of directly partitioning data across nodes, the directory service keeps track of which nodes store specific data ranges or partitions.

This approach offers flexibility and simplifies data distribution management. It allows for dynamic scaling, as data can be moved or replicated to different nodes without the need for complex partitioning algorithms. Some distributed databases use this strategy to combine the advantages of key-range and hash-based partitioning.

Pros:

- Flexibility in data distribution and node management.
- Efficient data migration and replication.

- Suitable for hybrid partitioning strategies.

Cons:

- Potential single point of failure if the directory service becomes unavailable.

- Requires additional network communication for data lookup.

4. Consistent Hashing

Consistent hashing is a technique that addresses the challenges of adding or removing nodes in a distributed system. It uses a hash function to map data and nodes onto a ring-like structure. Each node on the ring is responsible for a range of hash values, and data is stored on the node closest to its hash value on the ring.

The advantage of consistent hashing is that when a node is added or removed, only a fraction of the data needs to be redistributed. This minimizes data migration overhead and allows for seamless scaling and fault tolerance.

Pros:

- Efficient for dynamic node addition and removal.

- Minimizes data redistribution when nodes change.

- Suitable for fault-tolerant and highly available systems.

Cons:

- Complexity in implementation due to the use of hashing and ring structures.

- Limited support for range queries, as data distribution is random.

5. Geographical Data Distribution

In scenarios where data needs to be geographically distributed for low-latency access or compliance with data sovereignty regulations, geographical data distribution strategies are employed. Data is distributed to nodes located in different geographic regions or data centers.

For example, an e-commerce platform might store user data in data centers located in North America, Europe, and Asia to provide low-latency access to users in these regions. This approach helps reduce network latency and ensures data compliance with regional laws.

Pros:

- Low-latency access for geographically dispersed users.
- Compliance with data sovereignty regulations.
- Improved fault tolerance by distributing data across regions.

Cons:

- Increased complexity in data management and replication.
- Potential challenges in maintaining consistency across geographically distributed nodes.

In summary, selecting the appropriate data distribution strategy is crucial for optimizing the performance, availability, and scalability of NoSQL databases. The choice of strategy depends on factors like data access patterns, system requirements, and scalability needs. Combining multiple strategies or using advanced techniques like consistent hashing can further enhance the effectiveness of data distribution in distributed database systems.

Section 12.3: Handling Data Consistency

Data consistency is a fundamental concern in distributed NoSQL databases. In a distributed environment, where data is partitioned and stored across multiple nodes or clusters, ensuring that all copies of data remain consistent can be challenging. This section explores various strategies and techniques for handling data consistency in distributed NoSQL systems.

1. Eventual Consistency

Eventual consistency is a consistency model commonly used in distributed databases, including NoSQL databases. It allows for temporary inconsistencies between different replicas of the same data but guarantees that, given enough time and no further updates, all replicas will converge to a consistent state.

This approach is suitable for scenarios where low-latency and high availability are essential, and occasional temporary inconsistencies are tolerable. It is often used in systems where rapid data propagation and real-time access are critical, such as social media platforms or content delivery networks.

Eventual consistency is typically achieved through techniques like vector clocks, version vectors, or last-write-wins conflict resolution.

2. Strong Consistency

Strong consistency, on the other hand, enforces immediate consistency across all replicas of data. In a strongly consistent system, once a write operation is acknowledged, all subsequent read operations will return the updated data. This model guarantees that there are no temporary inconsistencies.

Achieving strong consistency often comes at the cost of higher latency and reduced availability, as systems need to ensure that all replicas are updated before confirming a write. Consensus algorithms like Paxos and Raft are commonly used to implement strong consistency in distributed databases.

Strong consistency is suitable for applications where data accuracy and integrity are critical, such as financial systems or healthcare databases.

3. Causal Consistency

Causal consistency is a middle-ground between eventual and strong consistency. It guarantees that if one operation causally depends on another, it will appear in the same order for all replicas. However, operations that are causally unrelated may be observed in different orders on different replicas.

This model allows for a balance between low-latency and data consistency. It is suitable for applications where preserving causal relationships between operations is essential, such as collaborative document editing or distributed gaming.

Implementing causal consistency often requires tracking dependencies between operations and using techniques like Lamport timestamps or vector clocks.

4. Read-Your-Write Consistency

Read-your-write consistency is a specific type of consistency model that ensures that once a client writes data to the database, any subsequent read operation by the same client will return the updated data. This provides a stronger guarantee of consistency for the client that initiated the write.

This model is essential for maintaining session consistency in applications where user sessions involve both read and write operations. It ensures that users see their own updates immediately after making changes.

Achieving read-your-write consistency may involve associating a unique client identifier with each write operation and using it to filter subsequent read requests from the same client.

5. Tunable Consistency Levels

Many NoSQL databases offer tunable consistency levels, allowing developers to choose the level of consistency that best suits their application's requirements. Common consistency levels include "strong," "eventual," "quorum," and "one."

By selecting an appropriate consistency level, developers can strike a balance between performance and data consistency. For example, they might choose strong consistency for critical transactions and eventual consistency for less critical data.

The implementation of tunable consistency levels varies between databases but often involves configuring replication factors, quorum sizes, and timeout settings.

In conclusion, handling data consistency in distributed NoSQL databases involves making trade-offs between consistency, availability, and partition tolerance. The choice of consistency model depends on the specific requirements of the application and the desired balance between these factors. Developers should carefully consider the implications of their consistency choices to ensure the system meets its operational and performance goals.

Section 12.4: Conflict Resolution in Distributed Databases

Conflict resolution is a crucial aspect of managing data consistency in distributed NoSQL databases. In a distributed environment, where data can be concurrently updated on different nodes or replicas, conflicts can arise when multiple updates conflict with each other. This section explores various conflict resolution strategies and techniques used to address such conflicts.

1. Last-Write-Wins (LWW)

The Last-Write-Wins strategy is one of the simplest conflict resolution methods. In this approach, when a conflict arises between two or more concurrent writes, the write with the latest timestamp is considered the winner, and its data becomes the authoritative version.

Here's a simplified example in pseudocode:

```
def resolve_conflict(existing_data, new_data):

if existing_data.timestamp < new_data.timestamp:

return new_data

else:

return existing_data
```

While LWW is straightforward to implement, it may not always produce the desired results, especially when it's essential to preserve causality or when timestamps are not synchronized across distributed nodes.

2. Vector Clocks

Vector clocks are a more sophisticated approach to conflict resolution that addresses some of the limitations of LWW. Each replica in the system maintains a vector clock, which is essentially a list of counters, one for each replica.

When a write operation occurs, the vector clock of the writing replica is incremented. During conflict resolution, the vector clocks of conflicting versions are compared to determine the causal relationship between updates.

This allows the system to differentiate between updates that are causally related and those that are not. The data with a vector clock that subsumes all other vector clocks is considered the authoritative version.

Vector clocks provide better causality preservation but require more complex implementation and increased metadata storage.

3. Dotted Version Vectors

Dotted Version Vectors are an extension of vector clocks that aim to simplify conflict resolution. Instead of maintaining a vector for each replica, each replica keeps a single version number. This version number is called a "dot."

During a write operation, the writing replica increments its dot. When conflicts arise, the version with the highest dot value wins.

If two versions have the same dot value, further resolution may be needed.

Dotted Version Vectors offer a balance between simplicity and causality preservation. They are more straightforward to implement than full vector clocks but still provide a good level of conflict resolution.

4. Custom Conflict Resolution Logic

In some cases, custom conflict resolution logic may be necessary, especially when the nature of data conflicts is specific to the application domain. Developers can implement custom rules to determine which version of data should prevail in a conflict.

Custom conflict resolution logic might involve considering additional metadata, such as user priorities, data types, or business rules, to make informed decisions during conflicts.

5. Automatic Conflict Resolution Policies

Certain distributed databases come with built-in conflict resolution policies that developers can configure. These policies can include rules for resolving conflicts based on various factors like timestamps, version numbers, or other metadata.

For example, a database might allow developers to configure a conflict resolution policy that prioritizes data from a specific replica or follows a first-write-wins strategy.

In conclusion, conflict resolution is a critical aspect of ensuring data consistency in distributed NoSQL databases. The choice of conflict resolution strategy depends on factors like the desired level of causality preservation, system complexity, and application-specific requirements. Implementing effective conflict resolution mechanisms is essential for maintaining data integrity and ensuring that the distributed database behaves as expected in the presence of concurrent updates.

Section 12.5: Geo-Distributed NoSQL Deployments

Geo-distributed NoSQL deployments involve the deployment of NoSQL databases across multiple geographical locations or data centers. This strategy is employed to enhance data availability, reduce latency for users in different regions, and ensure disaster recovery capabilities. In this section, we will explore the concepts and challenges associated with geo-distributed NoSQL deployments.

1. Benefits of Geo-Distributed Deployments

1.1 Improved Data Availability:

Geo-distribution increases data availability by replicating data across multiple regions or data centers. If one location experiences downtime or network issues, users can still access data from other replicas.

1.2 Reduced Latency:

By placing replicas closer to end-users, geo-distribution can significantly reduce data access latency. Users in different regions experience faster response times, leading to a better user experience.

1.3 Disaster Recovery:

In the event of a catastrophic failure or natural disaster in one region, geo-distributed deployments ensure that data remains accessible from other regions. This disaster recovery capability is crucial for business continuity.

2. Challenges of Geo-Distributed Deployments

2.1 Data Consistency:

Maintaining data consistency across geo-distributed replicas is one of the most significant challenges. As data is updated in one location, it must be propagated to other replicas while ensuring that conflicts and inconsistencies are appropriately resolved.

2.2 Network Latency and Bandwidth:

Geo-distribution relies on network connectivity between data centers. High network latency or limited bandwidth can impact the speed and efficiency of data synchronization between replicas.

2.3 Conflict Resolution:

Geo-distribution increases the likelihood of conflicts when multiple replicas receive concurrent updates. Implementing effective conflict resolution mechanisms is critical to maintaining data integrity.

3. Strategies for Geo-Distributed NoSQL Deployments

3.1 Multi-Master Replication:

Multi-master replication allows each replica to accept write operations independently. While this increases write availability and reduces latency, it also introduces the challenge of conflict resolution.

3.2 Consistency Models:

NoSQL databases often offer various consistency models, such as eventual consistency, strong consistency, or causal consistency. Choosing the right consistency model depends on the application's requirements and the trade-offs between data consistency and latency.

3.3 Data Partitioning:

Efficient data partitioning strategies can help distribute data evenly across replicas and reduce the impact of data synchronization on the network. Techniques like sharding can be employed to achieve this.

3.4 Global Load Balancing:

Global load balancing solutions can route user requests to the nearest data center or replica, optimizing response times. Content Delivery Networks (CDNs) and DNS-based load balancing are commonly used for this purpose.

3.5 Active-Active vs. Active-Passive:

In an active-active configuration, all replicas actively handle user requests and updates. In an active-passive setup, one replica is passive and serves as a backup. The choice between these configurations depends on the desired level of read and write availability.

4. Use Cases for Geo-Distributed Deployments

4.1 E-Commerce:

E-commerce platforms use geo-distribution to ensure fast and reliable access to product catalogs, shopping carts, and user profiles for customers worldwide.

4.2 Content Delivery:

Content delivery networks (CDNs) employ geo-distribution to cache and serve static content like images, videos, and web pages from edge locations, reducing load times for website visitors.

4.3 Financial Services:

Financial institutions leverage geo-distributed databases to provide real-time access to account information, trading data, and transaction history across global branches.

In conclusion, geo-distributed NoSQL deployments offer significant advantages in terms of data availability, reduced latency, and disaster recovery. However, they also introduce challenges related to data consistency, network performance, and conflict resolution. Choosing the right strategies and architectures for geo-distributed deployments depends on the specific requirements of the application and the trade-offs between data consistency and low-latency access.

Chapter 13: Transitioning from SQL to NoSQL

Section 13.1: Comparing SQL and NoSQL

In this section, we will explore the key differences between SQL (Relational) databases and NoSQL (Non-Relational) databases. Understanding these differences is crucial for organizations and developers considering a transition from SQL to NoSQL databases.

1. Data Models

1.1 SQL (Relational)

SQL databases use a tabular, structured data model. Data is organized into tables with rows and columns. Each row represents a record, and each column represents a specific attribute or field.

1.2 NoSQL (Non-Relational)

NoSQL databases offer various data models, including document-oriented, key-value, column-family, and graph databases. Each NoSQL type is optimized for specific use cases and data structures.

2. Schema

2.1 SQL (Relational)

SQL databases require a predefined schema that defines the structure of the data, including tables, columns, and data types. Changes to the schema can be complex and may require downtime.

2.2 NoSQL (Non-Relational)

NoSQL databases are schema-less or have flexible schemas. They allow dynamic and unstructured data, making it easier to adapt to evolving application requirements.

3. Query Language

3.1 SQL (Relational)

SQL databases use the Structured Query Language (SQL) for querying and manipulating data. SQL is a powerful language for complex queries and joins.

3.2 NoSQL (Non-Relational)

NoSQL databases often use query languages tailored to their data model. Examples include MongoDB's query language for document databases and Cassandra Query Language (CQL) for column-family stores.

4. Scalability

4.1 SQL (Relational)

SQL databases are traditionally scaled vertically (scale-up) by adding more resources to a single server. This approach has limits and can be costly.

4.2 NoSQL (Non-Relational)

NoSQL databases are designed for horizontal scalability (scale-out) by adding more servers or nodes to a cluster. This makes them well-suited for handling large volumes of data and high traffic.

5. Consistency

5.1 SQL (Relational)

SQL databases typically follow the ACID (Atomicity, Consistency, Isolation, Durability) properties, ensuring strong consistency. This makes them suitable for applications with strict data integrity requirements.

5.2 NoSQL (Non-Relational)

NoSQL databases may offer different consistency models, such as eventual consistency or strong consistency, allowing developers to choose the level of consistency that suits their application's needs.

6. Use Cases

6.1 SQL (Relational)

SQL databases excel in applications with complex relationships, well-defined schemas, and strict data integrity requirements. Examples include traditional business applications, financial systems, and e-commerce platforms.

6.2 NoSQL (Non-Relational)

NoSQL databases are preferred for applications that handle unstructured or semi-structured data, require horizontal scalability, and prioritize low-latency access. Use cases include social media platforms, content management systems, and real-time analytics.

7. Flexibility and Agility

7.1 SQL (Relational)

SQL databases can be rigid and require careful planning of schemas. Changes to the schema can be challenging and time-consuming.

7.2 NoSQL (Non-Relational)

NoSQL databases offer more flexibility and agility, allowing developers to adapt to changing requirements without significant schema modifications.

8. Cost

8.1 SQL (Relational)

SQL databases often involve higher licensing costs and infrastructure expenses, especially for vertical scaling.

8.2 NoSQL (Non-Relational)

NoSQL databases are typically more cost-effective for horizontal scaling due to the use of commodity hardware and open-source options.

In summary, transitioning from SQL to NoSQL involves understanding the fundamental differences in data models, schemas, query languages, scalability, consistency, use cases, flexibility, agility, and cost. The choice between SQL and NoSQL should align with the specific requirements of the application and its scalability, flexibility, and performance needs. Organizations should carefully evaluate these factors before making the transition.

Section 13.2: Decision Factors for Migrating

When considering a migration from SQL to NoSQL databases, organizations and developers must weigh various factors to make an informed decision. This section explores key decision factors that influence the migration process.

1. Data Model Compatibility

Before migrating, assess whether the data model of your existing SQL database aligns with the data model of the target NoSQL database. For example, if you have a complex relational schema with numerous joins, migrating to a document-oriented NoSQL database might require restructuring your data.

2. Scalability Requirements

Evaluate your scalability needs. If your application is experiencing rapid growth and requires horizontal scaling to handle increased traffic and data volume, NoSQL databases are well-suited for this purpose. They offer easier scaling options compared to traditional SQL databases.

3. Data Complexity and Structure

Consider the nature of your data. If your data is highly structured, well-defined, and adheres to a strict schema, a SQL database may be appropriate. NoSQL databases excel when dealing with unstructured or semi-structured data, making them suitable for scenarios like handling user-generated content or IoT sensor data.

4. Querying and Performance

Assess your application's querying requirements and performance expectations. SQL databases are known for their powerful query capabilities and support for complex joins. NoSQL databases optimize for specific query patterns, so if your application requires low-latency access to data or real-time analytics, NoSQL may be advantageous.

5. Consistency and Transactions

Examine your consistency and transactional requirements. SQL databases provide strong consistency through ACID properties, making them suitable for applications where data integrity is critical. NoSQL databases offer various consistency models, allowing you to choose an appropriate level of consistency based on your application's needs.

6. Development Flexibility

Consider the flexibility and agility required for your development process. NoSQL databases offer schema flexibility, enabling developers to make changes without extensive schema modifications. This can be advantageous in rapidly evolving applications.

7. Cost Considerations

Evaluate the cost implications of migrating to NoSQL. While NoSQL databases can be cost-effective for scaling out horizontally, there may be migration and training costs to consider. Additionally, licensing costs for SQL databases can vary significantly.

8. Existing Expertise

Assess the expertise and familiarity of your development team. Migrating to NoSQL may require learning new database technologies and query languages. Consider the learning curve and the availability of resources for NoSQL development.

9. Use Case Suitability

Ensure that the target NoSQL database aligns with your specific use case. For example, if your application involves storing and querying highly interconnected data, a graph database like Neo4j might be suitable.

10. Migration Planning

Develop a comprehensive migration plan that includes data migration, schema transformation, and testing procedures. This plan should address potential challenges and ensure a smooth transition from SQL to NoSQL.

In conclusion, the decision to migrate from SQL to NoSQL should be based on a thorough assessment of your application's requirements, data model compatibility, scalability needs, data complexity, querying and performance expectations, consistency and transactional requirements, development flexibility, cost considerations, existing expertise, use case suitability, and a well-defined migration plan. A carefully considered migration strategy can lead to improved performance, scalability, and agility in your application's database infrastructure.

Section 13.3: Migration Planning and Execution

The migration from SQL to NoSQL is a complex process that requires careful planning and execution. In this section, we'll explore the key steps involved in migration planning and provide insights into successfully transitioning your database.

1. Assessment and Inventory

Before beginning the migration, conduct a thorough assessment of your existing SQL database. Create an inventory of the database schema, data models, stored procedures, and queries. This inventory will serve as a reference throughout the migration process.

2. Selecting the NoSQL Database

Choose the appropriate NoSQL database that aligns with your application's requirements. Depending on factors like data structure, querying needs, and scalability, you may opt for a document store, key-value store, column-family store, or graph database.

3. Data Mapping and Schema Transformation

One of the most critical aspects of migration is mapping your SQL data to the NoSQL data model. This often involves denormalizing data, as NoSQL databases are schema-flexible and typically favor document-oriented or key-value data structures. Plan how your SQL tables and relationships will map to NoSQL collections or key-value pairs.

4. ETL (Extract, Transform, Load) Process

Develop an ETL process to extract data from your SQL database, transform it according to the new NoSQL schema, and load it into the target NoSQL database. Tools like Apache Nifi, Talend, or custom scripts can aid in this data migration process.

5. Query and Application Code Refactoring

Review and refactor your application code and queries to be compatible with the NoSQL database. SQL queries and joins will need to be adapted to the new data model and query language of the chosen NoSQL solution.

6. Testing and Validation

Thoroughly test the migration process and validate data integrity at each stage. Identify and rectify any data inconsistencies or discrepancies that may arise during migration. Consider using testing frameworks and tools for automated testing.

7. Performance Tuning

After migrating, monitor and fine-tune the performance of your NoSQL database. Optimize queries, indexing, and caching strategies to ensure your application meets performance expectations.

8. Backup and Rollback Strategy

Develop a robust backup and rollback strategy to mitigate risks during migration. In case of unexpected issues or data corruption, having a reliable backup ensures you can revert to the previous state.

9. Data Synchronization and Downtime Planning

Plan for data synchronization between the old SQL database and the new NoSQL database during the migration period. Minimize downtime by synchronizing changes made to the SQL database to the NoSQL database.

10. Training and Skill Development

Provide training to your development and operations teams to familiarize them with the new NoSQL technology. Ensure they understand the query language, data model, and best practices for managing the NoSQL database.

11. Monitoring and Post-Migration Support

Implement monitoring and alerting systems to track the health and performance of your NoSQL database. Be prepared to provide post-migration support to address any issues that may arise in the initial stages.

12. Documentation

Document the entire migration process, including decisions made, configurations, and lessons learned. This documentation will be valuable for future reference and for onboarding new team members.

13. User Communication

Communicate the migration plan and potential downtime to your end-users or stakeholders. Manage expectations and ensure they are informed about the transition.

14. Execution and Validation

Execute the migration plan according to the defined timeline. Validate the migrated data and the functionality of your application in the NoSQL environment. Be prepared to address any immediate issues.

15. Continuous Improvement

Continuously evaluate the performance and scalability of your NoSQL database. Iterate on your migration process and adapt to changing requirements as your application evolves.

In conclusion, migrating from SQL to NoSQL is a complex undertaking that requires careful planning, execution, and ongoing management. By following these steps and best practices, you can successfully transition your database to a NoSQL solution, unlocking the benefits of scalability, flexibility, and improved performance for your application.

Section 13.4: Handling Data Conversion Challenges

Data conversion is a critical aspect of migrating from SQL to NoSQL databases. It involves transforming data from one format to another, ensuring compatibility between the source SQL database and the target NoSQL database. In this section, we'll explore the common challenges associated with data conversion during migration and strategies to address them.

1. Data Type Mismatch

One of the primary challenges in data conversion is dealing with data type mismatches between SQL and NoSQL databases. SQL databases typically have strict data types, while NoSQL databases are more flexible. For example, converting SQL's numeric types to NoSQL's JSON or BSON formats can be challenging. Handling these mismatches requires careful mapping and data transformation.

```
# SQL to NoSQL data type mapping
SQL_INTEGER = 'INTEGER'
NoSQL_JSON = 'JSON'
# Data conversion example
if source_data_type == SQL_INTEGER:
# Convert to NoSQL JSON format
target_data = {target_field: int(source_data)}
```

2. Data Volume and Scale

Migrating large volumes of data from SQL to NoSQL databases can be time-consuming and resource-intensive. It's essential to optimize data transfer processes to minimize downtime and ensure a smooth migration. Techniques like parallel processing, batch processing, and data compression can help manage data scale.

```
# Example of batch processing for data migration
for batch in split_data_into_batches(source_data):
transformed_data = transform_data(batch)
load_data_into_NoSQL(transformed_data)
```

3. Data Consistency and Integrity

Maintaining data consistency and integrity during migration is crucial. Ensure that data transformations and conversions do not result in data loss or corruption. Implement validation checks and rollback mechanisms to handle issues that may arise during data conversion.

```
# Data consistency validation
if is_valid_data(source_data):
transformed_data = transform_data(source_data)
if is_valid_data(transformed_data):
load_data_into_NoSQL(transformed_data)
else:
# Handle data integrity issues
handle_data_integrity_error()
```

4. Complex Data Structures

SQL databases often use complex data structures, such as nested tables, arrays, or custom types. Converting these structures to NoSQL formats, which are primarily document-oriented or key-value-based, can be challenging. Plan and implement strategies for flattening or representing complex structures in a way that suits the NoSQL data model.

```
// Example of flattening nested SQL data into NoSQL format
{
```

```
"field1": "value1",

"field2": "value2",

"nestedField1": "nestedValue1",

"nestedField2": "nestedValue2"

}
```

5. Data Cleansing and Transformation Rules

Prepare a set of data cleansing and transformation rules to standardize data before migration. This may involve removing duplicates, handling missing values, and applying formatting rules. These rules ensure that data is consistent and ready for the NoSQL database.

```
# Data cleansing and transformation example

if source_data:

cleaned_data = apply_cleansing_rules(source_data)

transformed_data = transform_data(cleaned_data)

load_data_into_NoSQL(transformed_data)
```

6. Error Handling and Logging

Implement comprehensive error handling and logging mechanisms to capture issues encountered during data conversion. Logs should include details about data that failed to migrate, enabling efficient troubleshooting and resolution.

```
# Logging errors during data conversion

try:
```

```
transform_and_load_data()

except Exception as e:

log_error(e)

handle_error(e)
```

7. Testing and Validation

Perform extensive testing and validation of data conversion processes. Create test cases that cover various data scenarios and edge cases to ensure that data is accurately and consistently converted from SQL to NoSQL.

8. Data Mapping Documentation

Maintain detailed documentation of data mapping and transformation rules. This documentation serves as a reference for future migrations and helps onboard new team members.

Addressing data conversion challenges is crucial for a successful SQL to NoSQL migration. Thorough planning, testing, and adherence to best practices will ensure that your data remains accurate, consistent, and ready for use in the NoSQL environment.

Section 13.5: Post-Migration Evaluation

Once the migration from SQL to NoSQL is complete, it's essential to conduct a thorough post-migration evaluation to ensure that the transition was successful and that the NoSQL database is functioning optimally. This section outlines the key aspects to consider during the evaluation process.

1. Data Consistency and Completeness

Verify that all data has been successfully migrated from the SQL database to the NoSQL database. Conduct data consistency checks to ensure that no data was lost or corrupted during the migration process. This step is critical for data integrity.

```
# Check data consistency post-migration

if is_data_consistent():

print("Data consistency check passed.")

else:

print("Data consistency check failed. Investigate and resolve issues.")
```

2. Query Performance

Evaluate the query performance of the NoSQL database compared to the previous SQL database. Run a series of test queries to assess the speed and efficiency of data retrieval. Ensure that the NoSQL database meets the required performance benchmarks.

```
# Test query performance

query_execution_time = measure_query_performance()

if query_execution_time <= acceptable_threshold:

print("Query performance meets expectations.")

else:

print("Query performance falls below acceptable levels. Optimize queries if necessary.")
```

3. Scalability

Assess the scalability of the NoSQL database. Verify that it can handle increasing data volumes and concurrent requests without significant degradation in performance. If necessary, consider implementing auto-scaling mechanisms.

```
# Evaluate database scalability

if is_scalable():

print("Database scalability is satisfactory.")

else:

print("Database scalability needs improvement. Consider implementing auto-scaling.")
```

4. Data Validation

Perform data validation checks to ensure that the data stored in the NoSQL database is accurate and conforms to the expected format. Address any data validation issues that may arise.

```
# Data validation post-migration

if is_data_valid():

print("Data validation checks passed.")

else:

print("Data validation issues detected. Rectify data anomalies as needed.")
```

5. Security and Access Control

Review the security measures and access control policies implemented in the NoSQL database. Ensure that sensitive data is adequately protected, and access permissions are correctly configured.

```
# Security evaluation

if is_security_compliant():

print("Security measures are in compliance with requirements.")

else:

print("Security vulnerabilities detected. Enhance security configurations.")
```

6. Error Monitoring and Logging

Check the error monitoring and logging systems to ensure that they are actively capturing and reporting any issues or anomalies in the database. Evaluate the effectiveness of error handling mechanisms.

```
# Error monitoring and logging

if is_error_logging_effective():

print("Error monitoring and logging are effective.")

else:

print("Issues with error monitoring and logging. Address deficiencies.")
```

7. Backup and Recovery

Test the backup and recovery procedures to ensure that data can be restored in the event of data loss or system failures. Verify the integrity of backups and recovery mechanisms.

```
# Backup and recovery testing

if is_backup_and_recovery_robust():

print("Backup and recovery mechanisms are robust.")

else:

print("Backup and recovery procedures need improvement. Enhance data recovery capabilities.")
```

8. Documentation and Training

Review and update documentation related to the NoSQL database, including data mapping, migration procedures, and best practices. Provide training and resources to the team members who will be working with the NoSQL database.

9. Feedback and Optimization

Gather feedback from stakeholders, including developers and end-users, regarding their experience with the NoSQL database. Use this feedback to identify areas for optimization and improvement.

10. Future Planning

Consider long-term plans for the NoSQL database, including ongoing maintenance, performance tuning, and potential future migrations or upgrades.

A comprehensive post-migration evaluation ensures that the transition to a NoSQL database is successful and that the database is capable of meeting the organization's data storage and retrieval needs efficiently and securely. Address any issues or discrepancies promptly to ensure the continued reliability of the NoSQL database.

Chapter 14: NoSQL in Enterprise Applications

Section 14.1: Enterprise Needs and NoSQL Solutions

In the modern business landscape, enterprises face a growing challenge in managing and leveraging vast amounts of data for various purposes, including operations, decision-making, customer engagement, and analytics. Traditional relational databases, while suitable for certain tasks, may fall short when it comes to handling the scale, variety, and agility required by enterprises in today's digital age. This section explores the specific needs of enterprises and how NoSQL databases provide solutions to address these challenges effectively.

1. Scalability

Enterprises often deal with exponential data growth. NoSQL databases, designed for horizontal scalability, allow businesses to handle large datasets effortlessly. Whether it's e-commerce transaction data, customer records, or sensor data from IoT devices, NoSQL databases can scale out by adding more nodes or clusters, ensuring uninterrupted performance as data volumes increase.

2. Flexibility and Schema-less Data Models

In the enterprise environment, data schemas can evolve rapidly. NoSQL databases, particularly document-oriented and schema-less types, accommodate these changes seamlessly. Developers can insert new fields, structures, or data types without disrupting existing operations. This flexibility is valuable when dealing with changing business requirements.

3. High Throughput and Low Latency

Many enterprise applications, such as real-time analytics, recommendation engines, and financial trading platforms, require high throughput and low latency. NoSQL databases, especially key-value stores and in-memory databases, excel in delivering rapid data access and processing, ensuring that critical applications run smoothly.

4. Availability and Fault Tolerance

Downtime can be costly for enterprises. NoSQL databases are designed with built-in redundancy and fault tolerance mechanisms. They provide options for data replication and distribution across multiple nodes or data centers, minimizing the risk of data loss or service interruption.

```
# Configuring data replication in a NoSQL database
configure_replication()
```

5. Support for Unstructured and Semi-structured Data

Enterprises deal with a variety of data types, including text, images, videos, JSON documents, and more. NoSQL databases are well-suited for handling unstructured and semi-structured data, making them ideal for content management systems, media archives, and data lakes.

6. Real-time Analytics and Insights

Enterprises need to make data-driven decisions in real time. NoSQL databases, combined with analytics tools, enable organizations to extract valuable insights from data as it streams in. This capability is vital for personalization, fraud detection, and operational monitoring.

```
# Real-time analytics using NoSQL data

perform_real_time_analytics()
```

7. Cost-Efficiency

NoSQL databases often provide cost advantages over traditional relational databases, both in terms of licensing and hardware requirements. They allow enterprises to manage large datasets more economically, making them attractive options for organizations with budget constraints.

8. Integration with Modern Technologies

NoSQL databases easily integrate with other modern technologies, such as cloud computing, microservices architecture, and containerization. This compatibility facilitates the development of agile and scalable enterprise applications.

9. Multi-model Databases

Some NoSQL databases support multiple data models within a single database system. This versatility is beneficial for enterprises that need to manage different types of data, from structured to unstructured, using a unified platform.

In summary, NoSQL databases offer compelling solutions to the complex data management challenges faced by enterprises. Their scalability, flexibility, high performance, and ability to handle diverse data types make them valuable tools in modernizing and optimizing enterprise applications and infrastructure. Enterprises can leverage NoSQL databases to stay competitive, innovate faster, and harness the power of data for informed decision-making.

Section 14.2: Integrating NoSQL with Existing Systems

Enterprises typically have established IT infrastructures with legacy systems and relational databases. Integrating NoSQL databases into these existing systems can be a strategic move to modernize and enhance data management capabilities. This section explores the considerations and best practices for successfully integrating NoSQL with legacy and other systems in an enterprise environment.

1. Assessment and Planning

Before integrating NoSQL, it's essential to assess the current IT landscape and identify areas where NoSQL can provide the most significant benefits. Consider the types of data, performance requirements, and scalability needs. Develop a clear integration strategy and roadmap to ensure a smooth transition.

2. Data Migration

Migrating data from existing systems to NoSQL databases requires careful planning and execution. Choose migration tools and strategies that minimize downtime and data loss. It's crucial to maintain data integrity during the migration process.

 # Example of data migration from a relational database to NoSQL

```
execute_data_migration()
```

3. APIs and Connectors

NoSQL databases offer a variety of APIs and connectors that facilitate integration with popular programming languages, frameworks, and data processing tools. These APIs make it easier to interact with NoSQL data and incorporate it into existing applications.

4. Data Synchronization

In many cases, enterprises maintain both relational and NoSQL databases for different purposes. Implement data synchronization mechanisms to ensure that data remains consistent across these systems. Real-time data synchronization tools can help keep data up-to-date.

```
# Real-time data synchronization between relational and NoSQL databases

implement_data_synchronization()
```

5. Security and Access Control

Integrating NoSQL into existing systems should not compromise security. Ensure that access control measures are in place to protect sensitive data. NoSQL databases often provide authentication and authorization features to control who can access and modify data.

6. Testing and Validation

Thoroughly test the integration between NoSQL and existing systems. Verify that data flows correctly, applications perform as expected, and security measures are effective. Conduct load testing to assess scalability under various conditions.

7. Monitoring and Maintenance

After integration, establish robust monitoring and maintenance processes. Monitor the performance of both NoSQL and legacy systems to identify and address any issues promptly. Regularly update and maintain the integration components.

8. Documentation and Training

Document the integration process, configuration settings, and any custom code or scripts used. Provide training to IT staff and developers to ensure they are familiar with the new system and integration points.

9. Scalability and Future-Proofing

Consider future scalability needs when integrating NoSQL. As data volumes grow, the integration should be able to accommodate increased data loads without major disruptions. NoSQL's inherent scalability features can help future-proof the integration.

10. Performance Optimization

Optimize the performance of the integrated systems. This may involve fine-tuning NoSQL database settings, optimizing queries, and implementing caching mechanisms.

```
# Performance optimization in an integrated NoSQL system

optimize_integration_performance()
```

In summary, integrating NoSQL with existing enterprise systems is a strategic decision that can enhance data management capabilities, improve performance, and support scalability. Proper planning, data migration, security measures, and ongoing maintenance are crucial to the success of the integration. With careful consideration and execution, enterprises can leverage NoSQL to modernize their IT infrastructure and gain a competitive edge.

Section 14.3: NoSQL for Data Warehousing

Data warehousing plays a crucial role in large enterprises for aggregating and analyzing vast amounts of data from various sources. Traditionally, data warehouses have been associated with relational databases, but NoSQL databases are increasingly being considered as viable alternatives due to their scalability and flexibility. In this section, we explore the use of NoSQL databases for data warehousing purposes.

1. Challenges in Traditional Data Warehousing

Traditional data warehousing solutions often face challenges when dealing with the volume, variety, and velocity of data generated in today's digital age. Relational databases may struggle to handle unstructured or semi-structured data, such as social media posts, sensor data, and log files. Scaling relational databases can also be complex and costly.

2. NoSQL's Role in Data Warehousing

NoSQL databases offer several advantages for data warehousing:

- **Schema flexibility**: NoSQL databases can handle structured, semi-structured, and unstructured data, making them suitable for storing diverse data types in a single repository.

- **Horizontal scalability**: NoSQL databases are designed for horizontal scaling, allowing them to handle large datasets and high-velocity data streams more effectively.

- **Real-time analytics**: Some NoSQL databases support real-time analytics, enabling enterprises to make data-driven decisions more quickly.

- **Cost-effectiveness**: NoSQL databases can be more cost-effective than traditional relational databases, especially when dealing with massive data volumes.

3. Data Modeling in NoSQL Data Warehousing

When using NoSQL for data warehousing, it's essential to design an appropriate data model. Depending on the specific use case, you may choose from various NoSQL data models, such as document-oriented, column-family, or graph databases.

 # Example of data modeling in a document-oriented NoSQL data warehouse

define_data_model()

4. Data Ingestion and ETL

Ingesting data into a NoSQL data warehouse requires Extract, Transform, Load (ETL) processes. These processes are responsible for collecting data from source systems, transforming it into a suitable format, and loading it into the NoSQL database.

 # Example of ETL processes for NoSQL data warehousing

perform_etl()

5. Querying and Analytics

NoSQL data warehouses support a variety of querying and analytics tools. Depending on the chosen NoSQL database, you may use query languages, APIs, or analytics frameworks to extract insights from the data.

```
# Example of querying data from a NoSQL data warehouse

execute_query()
```

6. Data Security and Compliance

Data warehousing often involves sensitive or regulated data. Implement robust security measures in your NoSQL data warehouse to protect data at rest and in transit. Ensure compliance with relevant data protection regulations.

7. Performance Optimization

Optimizing the performance of a NoSQL data warehouse is critical for delivering timely insights. This may involve indexing, query optimization, and caching strategies.

```
# Performance optimization techniques for a NoSQL data warehouse

optimize_performance()
```

8. Scalability and Future-Proofing

NoSQL data warehouses are well-suited for scalability. As data volumes grow, you can scale out your NoSQL clusters to accommodate increasing data loads. Consider future growth when designing your data warehousing solution.

9. Monitoring and Maintenance

Establish monitoring and maintenance processes to ensure the health and performance of your NoSQL data warehouse. Regularly monitor system resources, query performance, and data consistency.

10. Use Cases and Case Studies

Explore real-world use cases and case studies of organizations that have successfully implemented NoSQL data warehousing solutions. Learn from their experiences and best practices.

In conclusion, NoSQL databases are increasingly being considered as viable options for data warehousing, particularly in scenarios where traditional relational databases may face limitations. When adopting NoSQL for data warehousing, careful consideration of data modeling, ETL processes, querying tools, security, and performance optimization is essential for success. NoSQL data warehousing can provide the scalability and flexibility needed to handle today's diverse and high-volume data sources.

Section 14.4: Handling Transactional Data

Transactional data, also known as operational data, represents the day-to-day interactions and transactions that occur within an organization. This data typically involves records of sales, purchases, customer interactions, inventory changes, and more. While NoSQL databases excel in handling large volumes of unstructured data, they are also capable of managing transactional data efficiently, provided the right design and considerations are in place.

1. Transactional Data in NoSQL

NoSQL databases, depending on their type, can handle transactional data in different ways:

- **Document-Oriented Databases**: These databases are well-suited for storing transactional data as documents. Each transaction can be represented as a JSON or BSON document, allowing for flexibility and easy retrieval.
- **Column-Family Stores**: Column-family databases can efficiently manage transactional data by using column families to group related transactions together. This can simplify queries for specific types of transactions.
- **Key-Value Stores**: Key-value stores can be used for transactional data, where each key represents a unique transaction identifier, and the associated value contains the transaction details.

2. Consistency in Transactional Data

Maintaining data consistency is crucial in transactional systems. NoSQL databases often follow the principles of eventual consistency, which means that data will eventually become consistent across all nodes in a distributed database. However, for transactional data, strong consistency may be required.

```
# Example of ensuring strong consistency in a NoSQL database

ensure_strong_consistency()
```

3. ACID Transactions

In the context of NoSQL databases, the term "ACID" stands for Atomicity, Consistency, Isolation, and Durability. ACID transactions ensure that database operations are reliable and maintain data integrity, even in the face of failures.

- **Atomicity**: Transactions are treated as a single, indivisible unit. Either all changes within a transaction are committed, or none are.

- **Consistency**: Transactions bring the database from one consistent state to another. This ensures that data is not left in an inconsistent state.

- **Isolation**: Transactions are isolated from each other, meaning that the changes made by one transaction are not visible to other transactions until the first transaction is complete.

- **Durability**: Once a transaction is committed, its changes are permanent and survive any system failures.

4. Implementing Transactions in NoSQL

Implementing ACID transactions in NoSQL databases varies depending on the database system. Some NoSQL databases offer native support for transactions, while others rely on application-level logic to maintain consistency.

 # Example of implementing transactions in a NoSQL database

implement_transactions()

5. Distributed Transactional Data

In distributed NoSQL databases, handling transactional data across multiple nodes can be challenging. Distributed transactions require coordination and consensus mechanisms to ensure data consistency.

```
# Example of handling distributed transactions in a NoSQL database

handle_distributed_transactions()
```

6. Use Cases for Transactional Data in NoSQL

Transactional data in NoSQL databases finds applications in various domains, including e-commerce, finance, healthcare, and more. Examples include processing customer orders, recording financial transactions, and managing patient records.

7. Considerations for NoSQL Transactional Data

When handling transactional data in NoSQL databases, consider factors such as data modeling, consistency requirements, transaction volume, and the database's native support for transactions. Choose the appropriate NoSQL database type that aligns with your specific transactional use cases.

In summary, NoSQL databases can effectively handle transactional data, provided that the right design, consistency mechanisms, and transaction management practices are in place. Whether you need to process financial transactions or manage operational data, NoSQL databases offer flexibility and scalability to meet the demands of transactional workloads in modern applications.

Section 14.5: Case Studies: Enterprise Success with NoSQL

In this section, we will explore real-world case studies of enterprises that have successfully leveraged NoSQL databases to address their specific business challenges and achieve notable success. These case studies demonstrate the versatility and effectiveness of NoSQL in a variety of industries and use cases.

1. Netflix: Personalized Content Recommendation

Netflix, the world's leading streaming entertainment service, relies heavily on NoSQL databases to power its recommendation engine. By analyzing user viewing habits, Netflix can provide highly personalized content recommendations to its subscribers. This level of personalization has played a crucial role in retaining and attracting new customers. Netflix utilizes NoSQL databases to efficiently store and process vast amounts of user data, ensuring a seamless and enjoyable streaming experience.

2. Uber: Real-Time Data Analysis

Uber, the ride-sharing giant, relies on NoSQL databases to handle the immense volume of real-time data generated by its platform. From tracking the locations of drivers and riders to calculating optimal routes, Uber's operations depend on rapid data processing and analysis. NoSQL databases enable Uber to store, retrieve, and analyze this data at scale, helping drivers and riders connect efficiently and safely.

3. Airbnb: Search and Booking Optimization

Airbnb, the global online marketplace for lodging and travel experiences, uses NoSQL databases to enhance its search and booking capabilities. With millions of listings worldwide, Airbnb needs to quickly match travelers with suitable accommodations. NoSQL databases assist Airbnb in storing and querying diverse property data efficiently. This enables users to find and book accommodations that meet their preferences and requirements.

4. Cassandra at Apple: Scalable Time-Series Data

Apple employs Apache Cassandra, a popular NoSQL database, to manage massive volumes of time-series data generated by its devices and services. Cassandra's ability to handle high write and read throughput, along with its scalability, makes it a suitable choice for Apple's needs. It allows Apple to collect, store, and analyze data from millions of devices, contributing to product improvements and customer satisfaction.

5. Walmart: Inventory Management

Walmart, one of the world's largest retail chains, relies on NoSQL databases to manage its extensive inventory. These databases help Walmart track product availability, inventory levels, and supply chain data in real-time. This level of visibility allows Walmart to optimize its inventory management, reduce costs, and ensure that products are readily available to customers.

6. LinkedIn: Graph Data Processing

LinkedIn, the professional networking platform, utilizes NoSQL graph databases to build and maintain its social graph. This graph connects millions of professionals and helps users discover meaningful connections and opportunities. NoSQL graph databases excel at efficiently traversing complex relationships, making them ideal for social networks like LinkedIn.

7. NASA: Data Storage for Space Missions

NASA employs NoSQL databases to store and manage data from space missions, satellite observations, and scientific experiments. The flexibility and scalability of NoSQL databases are crucial for handling the diverse and evolving data collected from the vast reaches of space. These databases enable NASA scientists to analyze and draw insights from astronomical data.

8. Financial Institutions: Fraud Detection

Financial institutions worldwide use NoSQL databases to enhance fraud detection and prevention. These databases analyze vast datasets of financial transactions in real-time to identify suspicious activities. By quickly spotting anomalies and patterns, financial institutions can take immediate action to protect their customers and prevent financial losses.

These case studies underscore the adaptability and scalability of NoSQL databases across various domains. Whether it's personalizing content recommendations, optimizing inventory management, or analyzing real-time data, NoSQL databases have proven to be invaluable tools for enterprises seeking to stay competitive and meet the demands of the digital age. As businesses continue to evolve and generate increasingly complex and diverse data, NoSQL databases will likely play an even more significant role in shaping the future of data management.

Chapter 15: NoSQL and the Internet of Things (IoT)

Section 15.1: IoT Data and NoSQL

The Internet of Things (IoT) represents a paradigm shift in how we collect, process, and utilize data. IoT encompasses a vast network of interconnected devices and sensors, such as smartphones, wearables, smart appliances, and industrial machines, all of which generate a continuous stream of data. This data is diverse, ranging from temperature readings and GPS coordinates to health metrics and environmental measurements.

Challenges in Handling IoT Data

IoT data presents several unique challenges that traditional relational databases struggle to address. These challenges include:

1. **Volume**: IoT devices generate enormous volumes of data, often in real-time. Storing and processing this data at scale can overwhelm traditional databases.
2. **Velocity**: IoT data is generated rapidly and continuously. Systems must handle high-speed data ingestion and real-time processing to derive valuable insights.
3. **Variety**: IoT data is diverse in format, including structured, semi-structured, and unstructured data. Traditional databases are ill-suited for handling this variety.
4. **Complexity**: IoT data often involves complex relationships between devices and events. Understanding these relationships is crucial for meaningful analysis.
5. **Geospatial Data**: Many IoT applications involve location data. Geospatial databases are essential for efficiently

managing and querying this data.

Why NoSQL for IoT

NoSQL databases are well-suited for addressing the challenges posed by IoT data:

1. **Scalability**: NoSQL databases can scale horizontally, accommodating the increasing volume of IoT data and the growing number of devices.
2. **Real-Time Processing**: NoSQL databases excel in real-time data processing, enabling quick responses to IoT events and insights extraction.
3. **Schema Flexibility**: NoSQL databases allow for flexible schema designs, accommodating the diverse and evolving data structures common in IoT.
4. **Geospatial Support**: Some NoSQL databases offer geospatial indexing and querying, making them suitable for location-based IoT applications.

Use Cases for NoSQL in IoT

NoSQL databases find applications in various IoT use cases:

1. **Smart Cities**: NoSQL databases help collect and analyze data from sensors embedded in urban infrastructure, optimizing services like traffic management, waste collection, and energy consumption.
2. **Healthcare**: IoT devices, such as wearable fitness trackers and medical sensors, generate patient data. NoSQL databases store and process this data for health monitoring and research.
3. **Industrial IoT (IIoT)**: Manufacturing facilities leverage IoT sensors to monitor machinery and processes. NoSQL

databases ensure real-time monitoring and predictive maintenance.

4. **Smart Agriculture**: IoT sensors collect data on soil conditions, weather, and crop health. NoSQL databases enable farmers to make data-driven decisions and improve yields.
5. **Energy Management**: IoT sensors in power grids and renewable energy sources provide real-time data. NoSQL databases help manage energy distribution efficiently.
6. **Home Automation**: Smart homes rely on IoT devices for security, energy efficiency, and convenience. NoSQL databases support real-time control and automation.

Choosing the Right NoSQL Database

Selecting the appropriate NoSQL database for an IoT project depends on specific requirements:

1. **Key-Value Stores**: Suitable for high-speed data ingestion and retrieval, ideal for scenarios where data structure is simple.
2. **Document Stores**: When data has a semi-structured format and flexible schemas, document-oriented NoSQL databases are a good choice.
3. **Time-Series Databases**: For IoT data with timestamped entries, time-series databases are designed to efficiently handle time-based queries.
4. **Graph Databases**: If the IoT application involves complex relationships between entities, graph databases can represent these connections effectively.
5. **Column-Family Stores**: When IoT data is predominantly write-heavy, column-family stores can handle massive write operations.

In this era of IoT, NoSQL databases have become indispensable tools for managing and deriving insights from the deluge of data generated by interconnected devices. Their ability to scale, handle diverse data types, and support real-time processing positions NoSQL databases as foundational components of IoT ecosystems, enabling innovations across industries.

Section 15.2: Real-Time Data Processing in IoT

Real-time data processing is a critical aspect of IoT applications, as it enables rapid decision-making and immediate responses to events. In the context of IoT, real-time processing involves ingesting, analyzing, and acting upon data as it is generated by devices and sensors. This section explores the importance of real-time data processing in IoT and how NoSQL databases play a pivotal role in achieving it.

The Need for Real-Time Data Processing

In IoT, many use cases demand real-time data processing, including:

1. **Security and Surveillance**: Instant detection of suspicious activities or breaches is crucial for security systems.
2. **Health Monitoring**: Continuous monitoring of vital signs or anomalies in patient data requires real-time alerts.
3. **Predictive Maintenance**: Identifying equipment failures or maintenance needs as soon as they occur helps prevent costly downtime.
4. **Environmental Monitoring**: Responding promptly to environmental changes such as pollution spikes or weather events.
5. **Traffic Management**: Managing traffic flow and congestion in real-time for efficient transportation.

Challenges in Real-Time Processing

Achieving real-time data processing in IoT presents several challenges:

1. **Latency**: IoT applications require low-latency processing to provide timely responses. Delays can have serious consequences in applications like autonomous vehicles or healthcare.
2. **Data Volume**: Handling the high volume of data generated by numerous devices simultaneously is a significant challenge. Scalability is key.
3. **Data Variety**: IoT data is diverse, including structured, semi-structured, and unstructured data. Processing this variety efficiently is essential.
4. **Data Quality**: Ensuring data accuracy and reliability is crucial for making informed decisions.

How NoSQL Databases Enable Real-Time Processing

NoSQL databases are well-suited for real-time data processing in IoT for several reasons:

1. **Scalability**: NoSQL databases can scale horizontally, allowing them to handle the growing volume of incoming data. They distribute data across multiple nodes, enabling parallel processing.
2. **Low-Latency Queries**: Some NoSQL databases, particularly key-value stores and in-memory databases, offer low-latency query responses, meeting the demands of real-time applications.
3. **Flexible Schema**: NoSQL databases support flexible schemas, accommodating the dynamic and evolving data

structures common in IoT. This agility is vital for real-time data ingestion.

4. **Event-Driven Architectures**: NoSQL databases can be integrated into event-driven architectures, where data is processed as events are generated. This approach aligns with the real-time nature of IoT.
5. **Caching**: Caching mechanisms in NoSQL databases can store frequently accessed data in memory, reducing query times and improving real-time responsiveness.

Real-Time IoT Use Cases with NoSQL

NoSQL databases power a range of real-time IoT use cases:

1. **Smart Grids**: NoSQL databases help manage power distribution by processing real-time data from smart meters and grid sensors.
2. **Fleet Management**: Tracking and optimizing the routes of delivery vehicles in real-time using IoT sensors and NoSQL databases.
3. **Environmental Monitoring**: Detecting environmental changes, such as air quality or pollution levels, and issuing immediate alerts.
4. **E-commerce**: Providing real-time product recommendations and personalized content based on user behavior and preferences.
5. **Smart Home Automation**: Responding instantly to user commands for lighting, climate control, and security in smart homes.
6. **IoT Analytics**: Real-time analysis of data from various IoT sources to derive insights and make informed decisions.

In summary, real-time data processing is essential for IoT applications to function effectively. NoSQL databases are instrumental in meeting the requirements of low latency, scalability, and flexibility, making them a fundamental technology for enabling real-time IoT solutions across various domains.

Section 15.3: NoSQL for Device Management and Monitoring in IoT

Effective device management and monitoring are crucial aspects of any IoT implementation. NoSQL databases play a significant role in handling the challenges associated with managing and monitoring IoT devices, ensuring their optimal performance and reliability. In this section, we will explore the key considerations and benefits of using NoSQL databases for device management and monitoring in IoT applications.

Challenges in IoT Device Management and Monitoring

IoT ecosystems typically involve a vast number of devices, each generating data and requiring management. Some of the challenges in this context include:

1. **Device Provisioning**: The process of onboarding and configuring devices needs to be automated and efficient.
2. **Device Health**: Monitoring device health in real-time, including detecting faults or malfunctions, is critical for maintaining the integrity of IoT solutions.
3. **Firmware Updates**: Managing and distributing firmware updates to devices securely and reliably is a complex task.
4. **Security and Access Control**: Ensuring that only authorized entities can access and control IoT devices is

essential for security.

5. **Scalability**: IoT ecosystems can quickly grow, making scalability a paramount concern.

How NoSQL Databases Address Device Management and Monitoring Challenges

NoSQL databases offer several advantages that make them well-suited for addressing the challenges of device management and monitoring in IoT:

1. **Schema Flexibility**: NoSQL databases allow for flexible data modeling, accommodating the evolving data structures and attributes associated with different types of IoT devices.
2. **High Write Throughput**: Many NoSQL databases are designed for high write throughput, enabling real-time ingestion of device data and updates.
3. **Scalability**: NoSQL databases can scale horizontally, distributing data across multiple nodes to handle a large number of devices and high data volumes.
4. **Low Latency**: Some NoSQL databases, particularly in-memory databases, provide low-latency query responses, ensuring real-time monitoring and control.
5. **Geo-Distribution**: NoSQL databases with geo-distribution capabilities can replicate data across multiple regions, enhancing fault tolerance and ensuring low-latency access.

Device Management and Monitoring Use Cases

NoSQL databases are applied to various device management and monitoring use cases in IoT:

1. **Remote Device Control**: IoT platforms use NoSQL databases to enable remote control and configuration of devices, such as adjusting settings or applying software updates.
2. **Real-Time Alerts**: Devices report their status and telemetry data to NoSQL databases in real-time, triggering alerts and notifications for immediate action in case of anomalies.
3. **Fleet Management**: IoT solutions for fleet tracking and management rely on NoSQL databases to monitor vehicle locations, fuel consumption, and engine health in real-time.
4. **Predictive Maintenance**: By analyzing historical data from IoT devices stored in NoSQL databases, predictive maintenance models can identify devices at risk of failure, allowing for proactive maintenance.
5. **Security and Compliance**: NoSQL databases help maintain audit logs, access control policies, and device authentication data to ensure the security and compliance of IoT systems.

Example of Device State Monitoring with NoSQL

```
# Python code snippet to illustrate device state monitoring using a NoSQL database

import pymongo

# Connect to a MongoDB NoSQL database

client = pymongo.MongoClient("mongodb://localhost:27017/")

db = client["iot_device_management"]

collection = db["device_states"]
```

```
# Simulate device state update

device_id = "device123"

state_data = {

"temperature": 25.5,

"humidity": 60.2,

"status": "operational",

}

# Insert the device state data into the NoSQL database

collection.insert_one({"device_id": device_id, "timestamp": datetime.now(), "state": state_data})

# Query the latest device state

latest_state = collection.find_one({"device_id": device_id}, sort=[("timestamp", pymongo.DESCENDING)])

print("Latest Device State:")

print(latest_state)
```

In this example, we use MongoDB, a popular NoSQL database, to store and query the state of an IoT device. The code demonstrates how device state updates can be efficiently managed and monitored using a NoSQL database.

In conclusion, NoSQL databases provide the scalability, flexibility, and low-latency capabilities necessary for effective device management and monitoring in IoT applications. They empower IoT platforms to efficiently handle device data, maintain device health, and ensure the seamless operation of IoT ecosystems.

Section 15.4: Data Storage and Retrieval Challenges in IoT

Effective data storage and retrieval are fundamental aspects of Internet of Things (IoT) systems. IoT applications generate vast amounts of data that need to be stored, managed, and retrieved efficiently. In this section, we will explore the challenges associated with data storage and retrieval in IoT and discuss strategies to address them.

Challenges in IoT Data Storage and Retrieval

IoT applications face several unique challenges when it comes to data storage and retrieval:

1. **Data Volume**: IoT devices generate large volumes of data, often in real-time, making it essential to have a scalable storage solution capable of handling massive data streams.
2. **Data Variety**: IoT data can be structured, semi-structured, or unstructured, and it may include sensor readings, images, videos, and more. Handling diverse data types efficiently is crucial.
3. **Data Velocity**: IoT data is often generated continuously and at high speeds, necessitating real-time or near-real-time storage and retrieval capabilities.
4. **Data Latency**: Some IoT applications require low-latency access to data for real-time decision-making or control, which can be challenging to achieve.
5. **Data Security**: IoT data may contain sensitive information, making data encryption, access control, and data privacy paramount concerns.
6. **Data Integrity**: Ensuring the integrity of IoT data,

especially during transmission and storage, is crucial to prevent data corruption.

Strategies for IoT Data Storage and Retrieval

To address these challenges, IoT systems employ various strategies and technologies:

1. **Distributed Databases**: IoT solutions often use distributed databases like Apache Cassandra or Amazon DynamoDB to achieve scalability and fault tolerance. These databases distribute data across multiple nodes, ensuring high availability and performance.
2. **Time-Series Databases**: For applications that rely on time-stamped data, time-series databases like InfluxDB and OpenTSDB are used. These databases are optimized for storing and querying time-series data efficiently.
3. **Edge Computing**: Edge computing brings data processing closer to IoT devices, reducing latency and enabling real-time decision-making. Edge databases and caching mechanisms are employed to store and retrieve data locally.
4. **Data Compression**: To reduce storage requirements and optimize data transmission, data compression techniques are applied, particularly for IoT deployments with limited bandwidth and storage capacity.
5. **Data Lifecycle Management**: Implementing data lifecycle policies helps manage data from creation to deletion efficiently. It involves archiving, purging, and migrating data as needed to optimize storage resources.
6. **Security Measures**: Robust encryption mechanisms, both in transit and at rest, are crucial for securing IoT data. Access control and authentication mechanisms ensure that only authorized entities can access the data.

Example of Efficient Data Retrieval in IoT

Consider an example of an IoT-based environmental monitoring system deployed in a smart city. This system collects data from various sensors placed throughout the city to monitor air quality. Citizens can access real-time air quality data through a mobile app. Efficient data retrieval is essential to provide up-to-date information.

```
# Python code snippet to retrieve real-time air quality data from an IoT database

import pymongo

# Connect to the MongoDB IoT database

client = pymongo.MongoClient("mongodb://localhost:27017/")

db = client["iot_data"]

collection = db["air_quality"]

# Query the latest air quality data

latest_data = collection.find_one(sort=[("timestamp", pymongo.DESCENDING)])

print("Latest Air Quality Data:")

print(latest_data)
```

In this example, we use MongoDB to store air quality data generated by IoT sensors. The code demonstrates how to efficiently retrieve the latest air quality data for presentation in a mobile app or dashboard.

Efficient data storage and retrieval are essential for the success of IoT applications, ensuring that valuable insights can be derived from the collected data in a timely manner. Employing the right database technologies and data management strategies helps IoT systems overcome the challenges posed by data volume, velocity, variety, and security.

Section 15.5: Case Studies: IoT Implementations Using NoSQL

In this section, we'll explore real-world case studies of Internet of Things (IoT) implementations that leverage NoSQL databases. These case studies demonstrate how NoSQL databases play a pivotal role in addressing the challenges and requirements of IoT applications.

Case Study 1: Smart Home Automation

Overview: A smart home automation company develops IoT solutions to enhance the convenience, security, and energy efficiency of residential properties. These solutions involve various IoT devices, such as smart thermostats, doorbell cameras, motion sensors, and lighting control.

Challenges: The company faced challenges related to handling real-time data from a large number of IoT devices, ensuring low-latency response times for user commands, and managing data security and privacy.

Solution: The company implemented a NoSQL database, such as Apache Cassandra, to store and manage data generated by IoT devices. Cassandra's distributed architecture allowed for seamless scalability to accommodate growing device counts and data volumes. It also offered the ability to store and retrieve data in real-time, enabling rapid response to user-initiated actions like adjusting thermostat settings or viewing camera feeds. Data security measures, including encryption and access control, were also implemented to protect user data.

Outcome: The use of NoSQL databases significantly improved the company's ability to handle the massive influx of IoT data. Users experienced minimal delays when interacting with their smart home systems. The company successfully addressed data privacy concerns, fostering trust among its customers.

Case Study 2: Industrial IoT (IIoT) Monitoring

Overview: An industrial equipment manufacturer adopted IoT technology to monitor and maintain its machinery deployed in factories worldwide. Sensors attached to the equipment collected real-time data on performance, temperature, and wear and tear.

Challenges: The manufacturer needed a data storage solution that could handle the high data velocity and provide predictive maintenance capabilities to reduce downtime. Data integrity and consistency were crucial for ensuring the safety of factory operations.

Solution: The company implemented a combination of NoSQL databases, including a time-series database like InfluxDB for storing sensor data and a distributed database like Apache HBase for managing equipment metadata. This hybrid approach allowed for efficient storage and retrieval of time-series data and enabled complex analytics for predictive maintenance. Data replication and distributed storage ensured data availability and fault tolerance.

Outcome: By leveraging NoSQL databases, the manufacturer achieved significant reductions in equipment downtime. Predictive maintenance algorithms detected potential issues early, allowing for proactive maintenance and minimizing production disruptions. The use of InfluxDB enabled efficient time-series data storage and retrieval for performance analysis.

Case Study 3: Environmental Monitoring in Agriculture

Overview: An agricultural technology company developed IoT solutions to monitor environmental conditions in farms, including soil moisture levels, weather patterns, and crop health. These solutions aimed to optimize irrigation, reduce water usage, and improve crop yields.

Challenges: Collecting and managing data from a network of remote agricultural sensors posed challenges in terms of data volume, data variety (including sensor readings, images, and GPS coordinates), and low-power, long-range communication requirements.

Solution: The company implemented a NoSQL database, such as MongoDB, to store and manage diverse IoT data types. MongoDB's flexibility in handling semi-structured and unstructured data allowed for the storage of sensor readings, images, and geospatial data. Additionally, lightweight IoT protocols like MQTT were used for efficient data transmission. Data aggregation and analytics were performed to provide actionable insights to farmers.

Outcome: Farmers using the IoT solutions observed significant improvements in crop yields and water savings due to precise irrigation control based on real-time data. MongoDB's flexibility and scalability accommodated the diverse data generated by agricultural sensors, enabling data-driven decision-making in farming operations.

These case studies exemplify the versatility and effectiveness of NoSQL databases in addressing the diverse requirements of IoT implementations. Whether it's in smart home automation, industrial IoT monitoring, or agricultural environmental monitoring, NoSQL databases have played a pivotal role in managing large volumes of data, ensuring real-time responsiveness, and enabling data-driven insights for decision-makers. These successes highlight the importance of choosing the right database technology to support IoT initiatives.

Chapter 16: Open Source NoSQL Databases

Section 16.1: Exploring Open Source Options

Open source NoSQL databases have gained popularity in recent years due to their flexibility, community support, and cost-effectiveness. In this section, we will explore some of the key open source NoSQL database options available for developers and organizations.

MongoDB

MongoDB is a widely used open source NoSQL database that falls into the category of document-oriented databases. It stores data in BSON (Binary JSON) format, which allows for flexible and schema-less data storage. MongoDB is known for its ease of use and scalability, making it a popular choice for a wide range of applications.

```
// Example MongoDB document

{

_id: 1,

name: "John Doe",

email: "john@example.com",

age: 30

}
```

Apache Cassandra

Apache Cassandra is an open source distributed NoSQL database that is designed for handling large amounts of data across multiple commodity servers. It is known for its high availability, fault tolerance, and linear scalability. Cassandra is particularly suitable for use cases involving time-series data, sensor data, and real-time analytics.

```
—Example Cassandra table creation

CREATE TABLE sensor_data (

sensor_id UUID PRIMARY KEY,

timestamp TIMESTAMP,

temperature DOUBLE

);
```

Redis

Redis is an open source, in-memory data store often referred to as a "data structure server." It is known for its exceptional performance and low latency, making it an ideal choice for caching, real-time analytics, and messaging systems. Redis supports a wide range of data structures, including strings, lists, sets, and more.

```
# Example Redis set operation

SET key1 "Hello, Redis!"
```

Apache CouchDB

Apache CouchDB is an open source document-oriented database that focuses on ease of replication and conflict resolution. It is designed for distributed environments and allows for seamless data synchronization between multiple nodes. CouchDB uses a schema-free JSON-based document format.

```
// Example CouchDB document

{

"_id": "1",

"name": "Alice",

"email": "alice@example.com"

}
```

Apache HBase

Apache HBase is an open source, distributed, and scalable NoSQL database modeled after Google Bigtable. It is designed for handling large volumes of sparse data and provides low-latency access to massive datasets. HBase is commonly used in conjunction with Apache Hadoop for big data processing.

```
// Example HBase table creation

create 'employee', 'personal', 'professional'
```

These are just a few examples of open source NoSQL databases available today. Each database has its own strengths and weaknesses, and the choice of database should be based on the specific requirements of your application. Open source NoSQL databases offer flexibility, community support, and cost savings, making them a compelling choice for many developers and organizations. In the following sections, we will dive deeper into each of these databases, exploring their features, use cases, and best practices for implementation.

Section 16.2: Community Support and Development

One of the key advantages of using open source NoSQL databases is the vibrant community support and active development that surrounds them. In this section, we'll delve into the importance of community support and the development ecosystem for open source NoSQL databases.

Community Support

Open source projects thrive on community involvement. The community includes developers, users, and enthusiasts who contribute to the project in various ways. Here are some aspects of community support in open source NoSQL databases:

1. **User Forums and Mailing Lists**: Most open source projects maintain user forums and mailing lists where users can ask questions, seek help, and share their experiences. These platforms are invaluable for troubleshooting issues and gaining insights from other users.
2. **Documentation and Tutorials**: The community often contributes to the documentation of open source projects, creating tutorials, guides, and best practices. This documentation helps new users get started and experienced users optimize their usage.
3. **Bug Reporting and Issue Tracking**: Users can report bugs and issues they encounter in the software. The community and project maintainers work together to resolve these issues promptly.

4. **Contributions and Code Development**: Developers from the community actively contribute code improvements, bug fixes, and new features to the project. This collaborative effort keeps the project evolving.

Active Development

The development of open source NoSQL databases is ongoing and dynamic. Here's why active development is crucial:

1. **Bug Fixes and Security Patches**: Active development ensures that critical bug fixes and security patches are released promptly. This helps maintain the reliability and security of the database.
2. **Feature Enhancements**: New features and functionalities are regularly added based on user needs and emerging trends in the database landscape. Active development keeps the database competitive and up-to-date.
3. **Compatibility Updates**: NoSQL databases often need to adapt to changes in the technology ecosystem, such as updates to programming languages and frameworks. Active development ensures compatibility with the latest software.
4. **Optimization**: Developers continually work on optimizing database performance, scalability, and resource utilization. This leads to improved efficiency and responsiveness.
5. **Community Feedback**: User feedback is a valuable source of information for developers. It helps them understand user requirements and pain points, guiding the direction of development.

When considering an open source NoSQL database for a project, it's essential to assess the level of community support and the activity of the development team. A thriving community and active development are indicators of a healthy and well-maintained database. It means you can rely on ongoing improvements, quick issue resolution, and a wealth of resources to support your implementation. However, it's also important to stay engaged with the community, contribute where you can, and keep up with updates and releases to make the most of the open source ecosystem.

Section 16.3: Customization and Extensibility

One of the significant advantages of open source NoSQL databases is their flexibility and extensibility. In this section, we'll explore how these databases can be customized and extended to meet specific requirements.

Custom Data Models

Open source NoSQL databases are known for their ability to accommodate various data models. Whether you need a document store, a key-value database, a column-family store, or a graph database, you can often customize the data model to fit your application's needs. Here are some ways you can achieve custom data models:

1. **Schemaless Design**: Many NoSQL databases are schemaless, meaning you can store data without a predefined schema. This flexibility allows you to adapt to changing data structures and requirements over time.
2. **Document Transformation**: In document-oriented databases like MongoDB, you can nest documents within

documents to create complex data structures. This is especially useful for representing hierarchical data.

3. **User-Defined Types**: Some NoSQL databases support user-defined types, allowing you to create custom data structures tailored to your application's requirements.

Extensible Querying

NoSQL databases typically offer query languages or APIs that allow you to retrieve and manipulate data. These query capabilities can often be extended to support custom querying needs:

1. **User-Defined Functions (UDFs)**: NoSQL databases like Couchbase and CouchDB allow you to define custom UDFs in JavaScript or other languages. This enables you to create custom query logic that can be applied to data.
2. **MapReduce**: Many NoSQL databases support MapReduce functions, which enable complex data transformations and aggregations. You can implement custom MapReduce functions to tailor your data processing.

Plug-ins and Add-ons

Open source NoSQL databases often provide mechanisms for adding plug-ins and extensions to enhance functionality:

1. **Storage Engines**: Some databases offer pluggable storage engines, allowing you to choose the most suitable engine for your use case. For example, RocksDB can be used as a storage engine for several NoSQL databases.
2. **Authentication and Authorization**: You can extend the security features of your NoSQL database by adding custom authentication and authorization modules.

3. **Replication and Sharding**: Custom replication and sharding strategies can be implemented through plug-ins, enabling you to optimize data distribution and redundancy.

Community Contributions

The open source nature of these databases means that the community often develops and shares custom extensions and plug-ins. You can leverage these contributions to enhance your database's functionality without starting from scratch.

When customizing and extending open source NoSQL databases, it's essential to strike a balance between meeting your specific needs and maintaining compatibility with the core database. Overly complex customizations can lead to challenges in terms of maintenance and upgrades. Therefore, it's crucial to thoroughly plan and document your customizations and keep an eye on updates and patches from the open source community to ensure your database remains robust and secure. Customization and extensibility are powerful features that can help you tailor your NoSQL database to your application's exact requirements, making it a versatile choice for various use cases.

Section 16.4: Pros and Cons of Open Source NoSQL Databases

Open source NoSQL databases offer many advantages, but they also come with their own set of challenges and limitations. In this section, we'll explore the pros and cons of using open source NoSQL databases.

Pros:

1. **Cost-Effective**: Open source NoSQL databases are typically free to use, making them a cost-effective choice for startups and small businesses with limited budgets.
2. **Community Support**: These databases often have active and vibrant user communities. You can benefit from community-contributed extensions, bug fixes, and support.
3. **Customization**: Open source databases are highly customizable and extensible. You can tailor them to your specific needs, from data models to query languages.
4. **Transparency**: With access to the source code, you have transparency into how the database works. This can be essential for security and troubleshooting.
5. **No Vendor Lock-In**: There's no vendor lock-in, which means you're not tied to a specific vendor's ecosystem. You have the freedom to switch providers or host the database on your infrastructure.
6. **Scalability**: Many open source NoSQL databases are designed for horizontal scalability, making them suitable for handling large amounts of data and high traffic.
7. **Security**: While security largely depends on your configuration, open source databases allow you to implement your security measures and audit the code for vulnerabilities.
8. **Community Contributions**: You can leverage community-contributed plug-ins, extensions, and optimizations to enhance your database's functionality.

Cons:

1. **Complexity**: Open source databases often require more technical expertise to set up, configure, and maintain

compared to managed database services.

2. **Limited Support**: While communities can be helpful, you may not have access to 24/7 professional support, which can be crucial for critical applications.
3. **Documentation Quality**: Documentation can vary in quality and completeness, leading to challenges when trying to implement specific features or troubleshoot issues.
4. **Security Risks**: The responsibility for securing your database largely falls on your shoulders. Without proper expertise, you may inadvertently expose your data to security risks.
5. **Maintenance Overhead**: You'll need to manage backups, updates, and patches yourself, which can be time-consuming and require a dedicated team.
6. **Integration Challenges**: Integrating open source databases with other services and tools may require custom development work, increasing project complexity.
7. **Lack of Enterprise Features**: Some enterprise-level features, like advanced monitoring and auditing, might be limited or absent in open source versions.
8. **Limited Vendor Ecosystem**: You won't have access to a vendor's ecosystem of services and tools that are integrated with their databases.

In summary, open source NoSQL databases offer cost savings, customization, and transparency, but they come with the responsibility of managing and maintaining the database infrastructure. Your choice between open source and managed databases should align with your organization's technical expertise, budget, and specific project requirements. Open source databases can be a powerful and flexible choice for organizations that have the necessary skills and resources to support them effectively.

Section 16.5: Popular Open Source NoSQL Databases

There are several popular open source NoSQL databases available, each with its own strengths and weaknesses. In this section, we'll introduce you to some of the well-known open source NoSQL databases, highlighting their key features and use cases.

1. MongoDB:

Key Features:

- Document-oriented database.
- Highly scalable and flexible.
- JSON-like documents with dynamic schemas.
- Rich query language.
- Support for geospatial data.
- Good for content management systems, catalogs, and IoT applications.

Use Cases: MongoDB is suitable for applications that require flexible and scalable data storage, such as e-commerce platforms, real-time analytics, and location-based services.

2. Cassandra:

Key Features:

- Distributed and highly available.
- Column-family data model.
- Excellent write performance.
- Tunable consistency.
- Automatic data partitioning.
- Good for time-series data and event logging.

Use Cases: Cassandra is ideal for handling large volumes of data across multiple data centers, making it a good choice for IoT, sensor data, and time-series data storage.

3. Couchbase:

Key Features:

- Document and key-value store.
- In-memory caching.
- High performance and scalability.
- Built-in full-text search.
- Multi-datacenter replication.
- Suitable for real-time applications and mobile synchronization.

Use Cases: Couchbase is well-suited for applications requiring low-latency data access, like gaming, ad tech, and user profile management.

4. Redis:

Key Features:

- In-memory data store.
- Support for various data structures (strings, lists, sets, etc.).
- Pub/sub messaging.
- High-throughput and low-latency.
- Ideal for caching and real-time analytics.

Use Cases: Redis is commonly used for caching frequently accessed data, real-time analytics, and message queuing in applications like gaming and social networking.

5. Neo4j:

Key Features:

- Graph database.
- Property graph model.
- Powerful querying with Cypher language.
- ACID compliance.
- Suitable for relationship-heavy data like social networks, recommendation engines, and fraud detection.

Use Cases: Neo4j excels in applications where relationships between data points are critical, such as recommendation systems and network analysis.

6. Elasticsearch:

Key Features:

- Distributed full-text search and analytics.
- Real-time indexing.
- RESTful API.
- Scalable and highly available.
- Excellent for log and event data analysis, as well as text search.

Use Cases: Elasticsearch is commonly used for log and event data analysis, text search in web applications, and monitoring and observability platforms.

7. HBase:

Key Features:

- Distributed and scalable.
- Column-family store.
- Strong consistency.
- Built on Hadoop Distributed File System (HDFS).
- Suitable for big data analytics and high-write workloads.

Use Cases: HBase is well-suited for applications that require storing and processing large volumes of data, such as social media analytics and recommendation engines.

These open source NoSQL databases offer a wide range of options to choose from, depending on your specific project requirements and use cases. Consider factors like data model, scalability, and performance when selecting the right database for your application.

Chapter 17: NoSQL and Artificial Intelligence

Section 17.1: AI Applications in NoSQL

Artificial Intelligence (AI) has become a transformative force in the world of technology and data management. NoSQL databases play a crucial role in enabling AI applications by providing the necessary infrastructure for handling and processing large volumes of diverse and unstructured data. In this section, we will explore the various AI applications where NoSQL databases are prominently used.

1. Machine Learning Data Management:

AI and machine learning (ML) heavily depend on data. NoSQL databases, with their ability to handle unstructured and semi-structured data, serve as an ideal storage solution for training data sets. They can store data in various formats, including text, images, audio, and video, making it easier to manage the data required for ML model training.

```
# Example of storing image data in a NoSQL database (MongoDB)

{

"_id": 1,

"image_data": Binary(image_bytes),

"label": "cat"

}
```

2. Predictive Analytics with NoSQL:

NoSQL databases are employed in predictive analytics to store and retrieve historical data efficiently. These databases can handle time-series data and log files, which are crucial for predictive modeling and forecasting. For instance, financial institutions use NoSQL databases to analyze transaction data and predict fraud.

```
// Querying time-series data in Cassandra

SELECT * FROM transaction_data WHERE transaction_date >
'2023-01-01';
```

3. Real-Time Decision Making:

In AI-driven applications, real-time decision making is vital. NoSQL databases excel in providing low-latency access to data, enabling AI algorithms to make decisions in real time. For example, recommendation engines use NoSQL databases to fetch and update user preferences on the fly.

```
// Real-time recommendation query in a NoSQL database
(Couchbase)

SELECT product_id, score FROM recommendations WHERE
user_id = '123' ORDER BY score DESC LIMIT 10;
```

4. Integrating AI Algorithms with NoSQL:

NoSQL databases support integration with AI and ML frameworks and libraries. By connecting these databases with AI tools like TensorFlow, PyTorch, or scikit-learn, organizations can leverage AI algorithms to gain insights from their data.

```
# Using TensorFlow with a NoSQL database (MongoDB)
```

```
import tensorflow as tf

# Load data from MongoDB for AI processing

data = load_data_from_mongodb()

# Build and train an AI model

model = tf.keras.Sequential([...])

# Train the model on the data

model.fit(data, ...)
```

5. Natural Language Processing (NLP):

NLP is a significant component of AI, and NoSQL databases are crucial for managing textual data. They are used to store large text corpora, linguistic resources, and text analytics results. NLP applications, such as chatbots and sentiment analysis, rely on NoSQL databases for data storage and retrieval.

```
# Storing and querying text data in a NoSQL database (Elasticsearch)

POST /my_index/_doc

{

"text": "NoSQL databases play a crucial role in enabling AI applications."

}

GET /my_index/_search

{

"query": {
```

```
"match": {
"text": "AI applications"
}
}
}
```

The synergy between NoSQL databases and AI technologies is evident in various domains, including healthcare, finance, e-commerce, and autonomous systems. Organizations harness the power of AI by utilizing NoSQL databases to store, manage, and analyze the diverse data required for AI-driven decision making and insights. As AI continues to advance, NoSQL databases will remain essential components of the AI ecosystem.

Section 17.2: Machine Learning Data Management

Machine learning (ML) has become an integral part of many applications and industries, from healthcare to finance to e-commerce. One of the critical aspects of successful machine learning projects is effective data management. NoSQL databases play a significant role in managing data for machine learning tasks, and in this section, we will explore their importance and use cases in machine learning data management.

1. Data Collection and Storage:

Machine learning models require large volumes of data for training and validation. NoSQL databases, with their ability to handle various data types, provide a flexible and scalable solution for storing diverse datasets. Whether it's structured data from databases, unstructured text, images, or sensor data, NoSQL databases can accommodate it all.

```
# Storing sensor data in a NoSQL database (MongoDB)

{

"_id": 1,

"timestamp": "2023-02-15T14:30:00",

"temperature": 25.5,

"humidity": 60.2,

"location": {

"latitude": 40.7128,

"longitude": -74.0060

}

}
```

2. Data Preprocessing:

Data preprocessing is a crucial step in machine learning. NoSQL databases allow you to perform various preprocessing tasks directly within the database. For instance, you can filter, aggregate, or transform data before feeding it into machine learning pipelines, reducing the need for complex ETL (Extract, Transform, Load) processes.

```
// Aggregating data in a NoSQL database (Cassandra)

SELECT date, AVG(temperature) AS avg_temp FROM sensor_data WHERE sensor_id = '123' GROUP BY date;
```

3. Data Versioning:

Versioning datasets is essential for reproducibility and tracking changes over time. NoSQL databases provide a way to manage and version datasets efficiently. You can store different versions of datasets or maintain historical records, ensuring that you can always trace back to the data used for a specific machine learning model.

```
# Versioning datasets in a NoSQL database (MongoDB)

{

"_id": 1,

"dataset_name": "sensor_data_v1",

"data": [...],

"timestamp": "2023-02-15T14:30:00"

}

{

"_id": 2,

"dataset_name": "sensor_data_v2",

"data": [...],

"timestamp": "2023-02-16T15:00:00"

}
```

4. Data Labeling and Annotation:

Supervised machine learning often requires labeled data for training. NoSQL databases can store both raw data and associated labels or annotations. This enables efficient data retrieval and management for tasks like image classification or natural language processing where labeled examples are vital.

// Storing labeled text data in a NoSQL database (Couchbase)

```
{
"document_id": "12345",
"text": "This is an example text.",
"label": "positive"
}
```

5. Scalability and Performance:

As machine learning projects grow, so does the data volume. NoSQL databases are known for their horizontal scalability, making it possible to handle large datasets and high-throughput workloads. This scalability ensures that your machine learning pipelines can handle increased data demands.

// Distributed data processing with a NoSQL database (Apache Cassandra)

```
SELECT * FROM sensor_data WHERE timestamp >= '2023-01-01' AND timestamp <= '2023-02-28';
```

Effective data management is a critical success factor for machine learning projects, and NoSQL databases offer the flexibility, scalability, and performance needed to handle the diverse and ever-growing data requirements of ML applications. Whether you're working on image recognition, natural language understanding, or predictive modeling, NoSQL databases are valuable tools for managing and processing your machine learning datasets.

Section 17.3: Predictive Analytics with NoSQL

Predictive analytics involves using historical data and statistical algorithms to make predictions about future events or trends. NoSQL databases play a vital role in predictive analytics by providing the flexibility to store and analyze large volumes of diverse data types. In this section, we'll explore how NoSQL databases are used for predictive analytics and the advantages they offer in this context.

1. Data Storage for Predictive Models:

To build predictive models, you need access to historical data. NoSQL databases excel in storing large datasets, including time-series data, logs, user interactions, and more. By efficiently storing this data, you can use it as the foundation for training and validating predictive models.

```
# Storing historical sales data for predictive demand forecasting (Cassandra)

{

"product_id": "12345",

"timestamp": "2023-02-15T14:30:00",

"sales_quantity": 100

}
```

2. Real-Time Data Ingestion:

Predictive analytics often require real-time data to make timely predictions. NoSQL databases are designed for high-speed data ingestion and processing. They can handle streams of data from various sources, ensuring that your predictive models are always up-to-date.

// Real-time data ingestion with a NoSQL database (Apache Kafka + Cassandra)

// Ingesting sensor data for anomaly detection

3. Scalable Model Training:

Training predictive models can be computationally intensive, especially when dealing with large datasets. NoSQL databases offer horizontal scalability, allowing you to distribute model training across multiple nodes or clusters. This ensures faster model training and the ability to handle growing data volumes.

// Distributed model training with a NoSQL database (Apache Spark + MongoDB)

// Training a machine learning model for recommendation based on user interactions

4. Integration with Machine Learning Frameworks:

NoSQL databases can seamlessly integrate with popular machine learning frameworks like TensorFlow, PyTorch, or scikit-learn. This integration simplifies data retrieval and preprocessing, making it easier to feed data into your predictive models.

 # Loading data from a NoSQL database into a TensorFlow model

```
import tensorflow as tf

import pymongo

# Connect to the MongoDB NoSQL database

client = pymongo.MongoClient("mongodb://localhost:27017/")

db = client["predictive_analytics_db"]

# Load training data

collection = db["training_data"]

training_data = list(collection.find({}))
```

5. Real-Time Predictions:

NoSQL databases enable real-time predictions by providing low-latency data access. This is crucial for applications such as fraud detection, recommendation systems, and predictive maintenance, where timely responses are essential.

```
// Real-time prediction using a NoSQL database (Couchbase)

// Recommending products to a user based on their browsing history
```

6. Handling Unstructured Data:

Predictive analytics often involve unstructured data sources like social media posts or customer reviews. NoSQL databases can store and process unstructured data efficiently, allowing you to extract valuable insights for your predictive models.

```
// Storing and analyzing unstructured text data for sentiment analysis (Elasticsearch)

{
```

"document_id": "98765",

"text": "This product is amazing! I love it."

}

In summary, NoSQL databases offer a robust foundation for predictive analytics by providing efficient data storage, real-time data ingestion, scalability, and integration with machine learning frameworks. Whether you're working on predicting sales, user behavior, or any other future event, NoSQL databases can empower your predictive analytics initiatives and help you derive valuable insights from your data.

Section 17.4: Real-Time Decision Making

Real-time decision making is a critical aspect of many applications, especially those that require instant responses to changing conditions or events. NoSQL databases play a pivotal role in enabling real-time decision making by providing fast and efficient data access and processing. In this section, we'll explore how NoSQL databases support real-time decision making and their significance in various use cases.

1. Low Latency Data Access:

One of the primary advantages of NoSQL databases in real-time decision making is their ability to provide low-latency data access. Traditional relational databases may struggle to handle the high read and write loads required for real-time applications. NoSQL databases, on the other hand, are designed for quick data retrieval, ensuring that decisions can be made promptly.

// Real-time data retrieval from a NoSQL database (MongoDB)

```
const MongoClient = require('mongodb').MongoClient;

// Connect to the MongoDB NoSQL database

MongoClient.connect("mongodb://localhost:27017/", (err, client) => {

if (err) throw err;

const db = client.db("realtime_decision_db");

// Query for real-time analytics

db.collection("sensor_data").find({}).toArray((err, result) => {

if (err) throw err;

// Make real-time decisions based on the retrieved data

console.log("Real-time analytics result:", result);

client.close();

});

});
```

2. Event-Driven Architectures:

Real-time decision making often relies on event-driven architectures, where events trigger actions or decisions. NoSQL databases are well-suited for storing and processing event data. They can efficiently handle event streams, enabling applications to respond to events as they occur.

```
# Event-driven real-time decision making with a NoSQL database (Apache Kafka + Cassandra)
```

 # Processing and reacting to user click events on a website

3. Complex Event Processing:

In some cases, real-time decision making involves complex event processing (CEP), which requires analyzing multiple events and patterns in real-time. NoSQL databases with built-in CEP capabilities or integrations with CEP engines can support such scenarios.

// Complex event processing with a NoSQL database (Apache Flink + Elasticsearch)

// Detecting anomalies in a production line by analyzing sensor data in real-time

4. Real-Time Alerts and Notifications:

Real-time decision making often leads to the generation of alerts or notifications. NoSQL databases can store and manage these alerts efficiently, ensuring that the right actions are taken promptly. This is crucial in applications like monitoring systems and cybersecurity.

// Sending real-time alerts using a NoSQL database (Redis)

// Notifying system administrators of critical events

5. Personalization and Recommendations:

Real-time decision making is vital in personalization and recommendation systems. NoSQL databases can quickly retrieve user profiles and historical data to provide personalized content or product recommendations in real-time.

 # Real-time personalized recommendations with a NoSQL database (Apache Cassandra)

 # Recommending movies to a user based on their viewing history

6. Internet of Things (IoT) Applications:

IoT devices generate a continuous stream of data that requires real-time processing and decision making. NoSQL databases are commonly used to store, analyze, and act upon IoT data, enabling applications like smart home automation and industrial monitoring.

// Real-time decision making in IoT using a NoSQL database (Amazon DynamoDB)

// Adjusting room temperature based on occupancy and temperature sensor data

In conclusion, NoSQL databases are instrumental in facilitating real-time decision making across a wide range of applications. Their low-latency data access, support for event-driven architectures, and ability to handle complex event processing make them a fundamental component of systems that require quick and informed decisions in response to changing conditions or events. Whether it's optimizing user experiences, ensuring system reliability, or enhancing IoT applications, NoSQL databases contribute significantly to real-time decision-making capabilities.

Section 17.5: Integrating AI Algorithms with NoSQL

The integration of artificial intelligence (AI) algorithms with NoSQL databases opens up a realm of possibilities for data-driven applications. In this section, we'll explore how AI and NoSQL can work together to enhance data management, analytics, and decision-making processes.

1. AI-Driven Data Processing:

NoSQL databases are well-suited for handling large volumes of data, but AI algorithms can extract valuable insights from this data. By integrating AI models with NoSQL databases, organizations can perform real-time data processing, sentiment analysis, image recognition, and natural language processing (NLP) on their stored data.

 # Integrating an AI sentiment analysis model with a NoSQL database (MongoDB + Python)

 # Analyzing customer reviews stored in a NoSQL database for sentiment analysis

2. Personalized Recommendations:

AI-powered recommendation engines can analyze user behavior and preferences. By integrating these engines with NoSQL databases, applications can provide personalized recommendations for products, content, or services in real-time. This enhances user engagement and satisfaction.

// Integrating a collaborative filtering recommendation system with a NoSQL database (Cassandra)

// Recommending music playlists to users based on their listening history

3. Predictive Analytics:

AI algorithms can make predictions based on historical data. When integrated with NoSQL databases, these models can analyze large datasets to make real-time predictions. This is particularly useful in industries like finance for fraud detection or in manufacturing for predictive maintenance.

// Integrating a machine learning model for predictive maintenance with a NoSQL database (Elasticsearch)

// Predicting equipment failures based on sensor data stored in a NoSQL database

4. Real-Time Decision Making:

AI algorithms can process data in real-time and trigger actions or decisions. By connecting AI models with NoSQL databases, applications can automate decisions based on changing data conditions. This is valuable in scenarios like autonomous vehicles or smart cities.

 # Integrating an AI-based traffic management system with a NoSQL database (Redis + Python)

 # Optimizing traffic signal timings based on real-time traffic data

5. Streamlining Data Management:

AI can assist in data cleaning, transformation, and enrichment. When AI tools are used alongside NoSQL databases, data quality can be improved automatically. This ensures that the data stored in NoSQL databases remains accurate and relevant.

 # Integrating AI data preprocessing tools with a NoSQL database (MongoDB + Python)

 # Automatically cleaning and enriching user-generated content before storage

6. Advanced Search and Recommendations:

NoSQL databases often power search functionalities in applications. AI-based search engines can provide more advanced and context-aware search and recommendation capabilities. By marrying these technologies, users can discover relevant content more easily.

// Integrating AI-powered search and recommendation algorithms with a NoSQL database (Elasticsearch)

// Enhancing e-commerce product search and recommendation features

In summary, the integration of AI algorithms with NoSQL databases empowers organizations to extract more value from their data. Whether it's delivering personalized user experiences, making real-time decisions, or improving data quality, the synergy between AI and NoSQL is transforming how businesses leverage their data assets. As AI continues to advance, the opportunities for enhancing NoSQL-based applications are boundless, making this integration a key aspect of modern data-driven solutions.

Chapter 18: NoSQL Database Administration

Section 18.1: Roles and Responsibilities of a NoSQL DBA

A NoSQL Database Administrator (DBA) plays a crucial role in ensuring the efficient operation, management, and optimization of NoSQL databases. In this section, we'll delve into the roles and responsibilities of a NoSQL DBA, highlighting the key tasks they perform to maintain database performance and reliability.

1. Database Deployment and Configuration:

One of the primary responsibilities of a NoSQL DBA is to deploy and configure NoSQL databases. This involves selecting the appropriate database type, setting up the required infrastructure, and configuring database parameters for optimal performance. For instance, in MongoDB, a DBA would define sharding and replication configurations.

2. Monitoring and Performance Tuning:

Continuous monitoring of database performance is essential. DBAs use monitoring tools to track metrics like query performance, resource utilization, and storage usage. They identify bottlenecks and tune the database for better efficiency, which may include creating indexes, optimizing queries, and adjusting hardware resources.

Example: Monitoring MongoDB performance using the 'mongostat' command

```
mongostat—host localhost—port 27017
```

3. Backup and Recovery Strategies:

DBAs are responsible for implementing robust backup and recovery strategies to safeguard data against loss or corruption. This involves regular backups of the database and defining recovery procedures in case of failures. In Apache Cassandra, for instance, DBAs manage snapshots and commit logs for backup and restore operations.

```
# Taking a snapshot backup in Cassandra

nodetool snapshot -t <snapshot_name> <keyspace_name> <table_name>
```

4. Security and Access Control:

NoSQL DBAs ensure that database security measures are in place. This includes setting up authentication mechanisms, role-based access control (RBAC), and encryption for data at rest and in transit. In Couchbase, DBAs manage users, roles, and permissions to control access to data.

```
// Example: Configuring RBAC in Couchbase

{

"name": "db_admin",

"roles": [

{

"role": "admin",

"bucket_name": "*",
```

```
"scope_name": "*",

"collection_name": "*"

}

],

"password": "password123"

}
```

5. Scaling and Clustering Management:

NoSQL databases often need to scale horizontally to handle increased loads. DBAs are responsible for managing cluster configurations, adding or removing nodes, and ensuring data distribution and load balancing. In Apache Cassandra, DBAs configure the replication factor to ensure data redundancy and availability.

```
# Altering the replication factor in Cassandra

ALTER KEYSPACE <keyspace_name> WITH REPLICATION = { 'class' : 'NetworkTopologyStrategy', 'datacenter1' : 3 };
```

6. Disaster Recovery Planning:

DBAs must develop disaster recovery plans to minimize downtime in the event of failures or disasters. This includes defining procedures for data restoration, failover mechanisms, and off-site backups. NoSQL DBAs also perform regular drills to test these plans.

7. Patch Management and Upgrades:

Keeping the NoSQL database software up-to-date is critical for security and performance. DBAs schedule and apply patches, updates, and version upgrades while ensuring minimal disruption to the production environment.

```
# Upgrading MongoDB to a new version

mongod—upgrade
```

8. Documentation and Training:

DBAs maintain documentation for database configurations, procedures, and best practices. They also provide training to developers and other team members on using the database effectively and adhering to best practices.

In summary, a NoSQL Database Administrator plays a pivotal role in managing and maintaining NoSQL databases, ensuring their availability, performance, and security. Their responsibilities span from initial deployment to ongoing monitoring, tuning, and disaster recovery planning. As organizations increasingly rely on NoSQL databases, the role of a skilled NoSQL DBA becomes indispensable in delivering reliable and efficient data solutions.

Section 18.2: Backup and Recovery Strategies

Backup and recovery are critical aspects of NoSQL database administration. In this section, we will explore the strategies and best practices that NoSQL Database Administrators (DBAs) employ to ensure data integrity and availability in the face of potential failures.

1. Regular Backups:

One of the fundamental tasks of a NoSQL DBA is to perform regular backups of the database. Depending on the database system, backups can be full, incremental, or differential. Regular backups create restore points, allowing DBAs to recover data to a previous state in case of data corruption or loss.

2. Snapshot Backups:

Some NoSQL databases, such as Apache Cassandra, provide snapshot-based backups. Snapshots are point-in-time copies of data files. DBAs can create snapshots manually or schedule them at regular intervals. Snapshots are space-efficient and can be used for both backups and disaster recovery.

3. Commit Logs:

Commit logs are essential for durability in databases like Apache Cassandra. DBAs must manage commit logs alongside backups. Commit logs capture all changes made to the database and are used during recovery to ensure data consistency. Proper commit log management is critical for data integrity.

4. Off-Site Backups:

To protect against site-wide disasters like fires or floods, DBAs often implement off-site backups. These backups are stored in geographically distant locations, ensuring that data can be restored even if the primary data center is inaccessible. Cloud storage solutions are commonly used for off-site backups.

5. Automated Backup Scheduling:

DBAs typically set up automated backup schedules to ensure that backups are performed regularly without manual intervention. Backup frequency may vary based on the database's update rate and criticality of data. Automation reduces the risk of human error.

6. Restore Testing:

Regularly testing the restoration process is essential to ensure that backups are viable and can be successfully restored. DBAs perform restoration tests in a controlled environment to verify the integrity of backups and to practice disaster recovery procedures.

7. Versioning Backups:

DBAs often maintain multiple versions of backups. This versioning allows for data recovery to a specific point in time, which can be useful when dealing with data corruption or unintended changes.

8. Monitoring and Alerts:

Monitoring tools are used to track the status of backups and to receive alerts in case of backup failures. DBAs proactively address any issues that may prevent successful backups.

Example: Monitoring backup status in MongoDB using 'mongodump'

mongodump—host <hostname>—port <port>—out <backup_directory>

9. Backup Encryption:

To ensure the security of backup data, DBAs may implement backup encryption. This protects sensitive information during transit and storage. Encryption keys must be securely managed.

10. Retention Policies:

DBAs define retention policies that determine how long backups are retained. These policies are based on regulatory requirements and business needs. Backups that are no longer needed are typically purged to free up storage space.

11. Backup Metadata and Catalogs:

Maintaining metadata and catalogs of backups is crucial. These catalogs provide information about the contents of each backup, making it easier to locate and restore specific data when needed.

In conclusion, backup and recovery strategies are fundamental aspects of NoSQL database administration. NoSQL DBAs must ensure that data is consistently backed up, securely stored, and readily available for recovery in case of data loss or corruption. These strategies are integral to maintaining data integrity and business continuity in organizations that rely on NoSQL databases.

Section 18.3: Performance Monitoring and Tuning

Performance monitoring and tuning are essential aspects of NoSQL database administration. In this section, we'll explore the key strategies and techniques that NoSQL Database Administrators (DBAs) employ to ensure optimal database performance.

1. Real-Time Monitoring:

DBAs use various monitoring tools and dashboards to keep an eye on the database's health in real-time. These tools provide insights into metrics such as query latency, throughput, CPU and memory utilization, disk I/O, and network activity. Real-time monitoring allows DBAs to identify performance bottlenecks and anomalies quickly.

2. Query Analysis:

Analyzing and optimizing database queries is a critical task. DBAs examine slow-running queries and identify opportunities for improvement. They may rewrite queries, add appropriate indexes, or adjust query parameters to enhance performance.

—Example: Adding an index in MongoDB

```
db.collection.createIndex({ field_name: 1 })
```

3. Indexing Strategies:

Proper indexing is crucial for efficient query execution. DBAs carefully choose which fields to index based on query patterns. They also monitor the size of indexes to avoid excessive storage consumption.

4. Query Caching:

Many NoSQL databases support query caching to store the results of frequently executed queries in memory. Caching reduces the need to recompute query results, leading to faster response times.

5. Load Balancing:

For distributed NoSQL databases, load balancing ensures that incoming requests are evenly distributed among nodes or shards. DBAs configure load balancers to prevent overloading specific nodes, thus maintaining overall system performance.

6. Scaling Strategies:

DBAs employ horizontal or vertical scaling strategies to accommodate increased workloads. Horizontal scaling involves adding more nodes to a cluster, while vertical scaling involves upgrading individual nodes with more resources (e.g., CPU, RAM).

7. Compaction and Cleanup:

Over time, NoSQL databases may accumulate deleted or outdated data. Compaction processes help reclaim storage space and improve query performance. DBAs schedule compaction tasks based on database usage patterns.

8. Monitoring Queries:

DBAs use tools to profile and monitor query execution plans. This allows them to identify inefficient query plans and make necessary adjustments.

```
# Example: Profiling queries in MongoDB

db.collection.find({}).explain("executionStats")
```

9. Resource Allocation:

DBAs allocate resources like CPU, memory, and disk space judiciously to ensure that the database has the necessary resources to meet performance requirements.

10. Replication Lag Monitoring:

In distributed NoSQL databases with replication, DBAs monitor replication lag to ensure data consistency across nodes. Reducing replication lag is crucial for maintaining real-time data access.

11. Disaster Recovery Planning:

DBAs also consider disaster recovery aspects in performance tuning. They ensure that backup and recovery processes are well-defined and that systems can be restored quickly in case of a catastrophic failure.

12. Query Throttling and Rate Limiting:

To prevent excessive resource utilization by certain queries or clients, DBAs may implement query throttling or rate limiting mechanisms. These controls help maintain overall system stability.

```
# Example: Rate limiting with Redis

redis-cli> CONFIG SET maxmemory-policy volatile-ttl
```

13. Regular Maintenance:

DBAs perform routine maintenance tasks, such as compacting databases, optimizing storage layouts, and applying software patches and updates to the database system.

14. Benchmarking and Testing:

DBAs conduct benchmarking tests to assess the database's performance under different loads and conditions. This information helps them make informed decisions regarding resource allocation and system architecture.

In conclusion, performance monitoring and tuning are ongoing responsibilities of NoSQL DBAs. By continuously assessing and optimizing database performance, DBAs ensure that NoSQL databases can meet the demands of modern, data-intensive applications while providing a seamless user experience.

Section 18.4: Scaling and Clustering Management

Scaling and clustering management are fundamental aspects of NoSQL database administration, especially for databases dealing with large volumes of data and high query loads. In this section, we'll delve into the strategies and considerations related to scaling and clustering in NoSQL databases.

1. Horizontal Scaling:

Horizontal scaling, also known as "scaling out," involves adding more machines or nodes to the database cluster. This approach distributes the workload across multiple servers, effectively increasing the database's capacity to handle more requests and store additional data. NoSQL databases like MongoDB, Cassandra, and Couchbase are designed to support horizontal scaling.

```
# Example: Adding a new node to a MongoDB replica set

rs.add("new_node.example.com:27017")
```

2. Vertical Scaling:

Vertical scaling, or "scaling up," involves upgrading individual nodes by increasing their computational power, memory, or storage capacity. While vertical scaling can provide immediate performance improvements, it may have limitations in terms of scalability compared to horizontal scaling.

3. Data Sharding:

Data sharding is a technique used to horizontally partition data across multiple nodes or shards. Each shard stores a subset of the dataset, and a shard key determines how data is distributed. Sharding helps distribute read and write operations evenly across nodes and is commonly used in distributed NoSQL databases like Apache Cassandra and MongoDB.

```
# Example: Sharding a MongoDB collection

sh.shardCollection("mydb.mycollection", { shard_key: 1 })
```

4. Automatic Sharding:

Some NoSQL databases, like MongoDB, offer automatic sharding capabilities. In this scenario, the database system manages the distribution of data across shards transparently, simplifying the administration of large datasets.

5. Load Balancing:

Load balancing is crucial in distributed NoSQL databases to ensure that requests are evenly distributed across nodes. Load balancers distribute incoming traffic based on predefined algorithms or policies, such as round-robin or least connections.

6. Replication and Failover:

Replication is essential for data redundancy and high availability. NoSQL databases often use replication to maintain multiple copies of data across nodes. In case of node failures, automatic failover mechanisms ensure that another healthy node takes over the responsibilities of the failed node.

```
# Example: Configuring replication in Redis

redis-cli> REPLICAOF <master_ip> <master_port>
```

7. Monitoring and Alerts:

DBAs implement monitoring solutions to keep track of the health and performance of database nodes. Alerts are set up to notify administrators of any issues, such as high resource utilization or node failures, so they can take prompt action.

8. Capacity Planning:

DBAs engage in capacity planning to estimate future resource requirements based on projected growth. This involves assessing factors like data volume, query patterns, and expected user load to determine when and how to scale the database.

9. Disaster Recovery Planning:

In a clustered environment, disaster recovery planning is essential. DBAs implement backup and recovery strategies to ensure that data can be restored in case of catastrophic events. Testing disaster recovery procedures is also part of this process.

10. Performance Testing:

Before deploying a scaled or clustered environment into production, DBAs conduct performance tests to validate that the new configuration meets performance requirements. These tests simulate various workloads to assess the system's stability and scalability.

11. Balancing Resources:

DBAs constantly balance resources among nodes to ensure that each node's load remains within acceptable limits. This may involve redistributing data, adjusting shard keys, or fine-tuning load balancing algorithms.

12. Rolling Upgrades:

When upgrading the database software or hardware, DBAs perform rolling upgrades to minimize downtime. This involves upgrading one node at a time while the others continue to serve requests.

In conclusion, scaling and clustering management are critical for maintaining NoSQL database performance, high availability, and scalability. These practices enable NoSQL databases to handle large workloads, provide fault tolerance, and ensure a seamless user experience even as data and query loads increase. Effective management of scaling and clustering is a key responsibility of NoSQL Database Administrators.

Section 18.5: Disaster Recovery Planning

Disaster recovery planning is an essential aspect of NoSQL database administration. It involves preparing for and mitigating the impact of catastrophic events that could lead to data loss or system downtime. In this section, we'll explore the key considerations and strategies for effective disaster recovery planning in the context of NoSQL databases.

1. Backup and Restore:

One of the fundamental components of disaster recovery planning is regular data backup. NoSQL databases provide mechanisms to create backups of the database, which can be used to restore data in case of data corruption, accidental deletion, or hardware failure. These backups should be automated and scheduled at regular intervals.

```
# Example: Creating a backup in MongoDB
```

mongodump—out /path/to/backup

2. Offsite Backups:

Storing backups offsite is crucial to ensure data recovery in the event of physical disasters, such as fires, floods, or earthquakes, that might affect the primary data center. Cloud storage services or remote data centers can be used to securely store offsite backups.

3. Redundancy and High Availability:

Implementing redundancy and high availability strategies within your NoSQL database cluster is essential. This includes maintaining multiple replicas of your data across different servers and geographic locations. In case of node failures, data can be seamlessly accessed from healthy replicas.

4. Disaster Recovery Testing:

Regularly testing disaster recovery procedures is vital to ensure they work as expected during an actual disaster. This testing should include not only data restoration but also failover scenarios, where a secondary data center takes over when the primary one becomes unavailable.

5. Data Archiving and Retention Policies:

Implement data archiving and retention policies to manage the lifecycle of data. This ensures that obsolete or less critical data is moved to lower-cost storage or archived to free up resources for active data.

6. Service Level Agreements (SLAs):

Define SLAs for disaster recovery, including Recovery Time Objectives (RTO) and Recovery Point Objectives (RPO). RTO specifies the maximum acceptable downtime, while RPO defines the maximum data loss allowed in case of a disaster.

7. Geographical Distribution:

For organizations with a global presence, consider geographically distributing database clusters. This strategy can help ensure that data remains accessible even if an entire region experiences a catastrophic event.

```
# Example: Deploying a globally distributed database in Cassandra

CREATE KEYSPACE my_keyspace WITH replication = {

'class': 'NetworkTopologyStrategy',

'us-east': 3,

'eu-west': 3,

'ap-southeast': 3

};
```

8. Disaster Recovery as a Service (DRaaS):

DRaaS providers offer cloud-based disaster recovery solutions that can simplify the process. These services often include automated failover, data replication, and backup management.

9. Documentation and Runbooks:

Maintain detailed documentation and runbooks that outline step-by-step procedures for disaster recovery. These documents should be easily accessible to the operations team and regularly updated.

10. Communication Plan:

Establish a communication plan that includes contact information for team members, third-party service providers, and stakeholders. Ensure everyone knows their role during a disaster and how to communicate effectively.

11. Regular Audits and Reviews:

Periodically review and audit your disaster recovery plan to identify and address any weaknesses or changes in your infrastructure. This proactive approach can help keep your disaster recovery strategy up to date and effective.

In summary, disaster recovery planning is a critical component of NoSQL database administration. By implementing robust backup and recovery processes, redundancy, and high availability strategies, as well as conducting regular testing and audits, you can minimize the impact of catastrophic events and ensure the integrity and availability of your data. A well-prepared disaster recovery plan is an insurance policy that can save your organization from costly data loss and downtime.

Chapter 19: Future Trends in NoSQL

Section 19.1: Emerging Technologies in NoSQL

In the rapidly evolving landscape of data management, NoSQL databases continue to play a pivotal role in addressing the growing demands of modern applications. As we look toward the future, it's essential to explore emerging technologies and trends that will shape the evolution of NoSQL databases. In this section, we'll delve into some of the key advancements and innovations on the horizon.

1. Multi-Model Databases:

One prominent trend is the emergence of multi-model databases. These databases support multiple data models within a single database system, allowing developers to work with structured, semi-structured, and unstructured data seamlessly. This flexibility simplifies data management for applications that require diverse data structures.

—Example of using a multi-model database to store JSON and graph data

```
INSERT INTO employees JSON '{ "name": "John", "age": 30 }';

CREATE GRAPH friends;

INSERT INTO friends VERTICES { (John) };
```

2. Serverless NoSQL:

Serverless computing is gaining traction across various cloud services. In the context of NoSQL databases, serverless offerings abstract infrastructure management, automatically scaling resources based on demand. Developers can focus on writing code rather than provisioning and managing database servers.

3. Edge Computing and NoSQL:

Edge computing, which involves processing data closer to its source (e.g., IoT devices), is driving the need for NoSQL databases at the edge. These databases enable efficient data storage and retrieval in low-latency, resource-constrained environments.

4. Time-Series Data:

The increasing importance of time-series data in applications like IoT, monitoring, and analytics is fueling the development of NoSQL databases tailored for time-series data storage and analysis. These databases offer optimized storage and retrieval for timestamped data points.

```
// Storing time-series data in a NoSQL database (e.g., InfluxDB)

measurement,tag1=tag1_value,tag2=tag2_value value=42 1588088726000000000
```

5. AI and NoSQL Integration:

The integration of artificial intelligence (AI) and machine learning (ML) capabilities within NoSQL databases is another promising trend. This enables real-time decision-making, predictive analytics, and automated data processing directly within the database.

```
// Using AI-powered functions in a NoSQL database to perform sentiment analysis

db.sentimentAnalysis("text", "This product is great!");
```

6. Blockchain and NoSQL:

Blockchain technology, known for its immutability and distributed ledger capabilities, is being explored in conjunction with NoSQL databases. Combining blockchain and NoSQL can provide enhanced data integrity and transparency in various applications, such as supply chain management and finance.

7. Quantum-Resistant Encryption:

With the emergence of quantum computing, concerns about the security of cryptographic algorithms have grown. NoSQL databases are exploring quantum-resistant encryption techniques to protect sensitive data from future quantum attacks.

8. Augmented Analytics:

Augmented analytics, which combines AI and analytics to automate data preparation, insight discovery, and sharing, is influencing NoSQL databases. These databases may incorporate augmented analytics features to assist users in deriving insights from their data.

In conclusion, the world of NoSQL databases is continuously evolving to meet the changing needs of modern applications. Emerging technologies, such as multi-model databases, serverless computing, and AI integration, are paving the way for more powerful and versatile data management solutions. Staying informed about these trends is crucial for organizations and developers looking to harness the full potential of NoSQL databases in the future.

Section 19.2: NoSQL and Blockchain

As we explore the future trends in NoSQL databases, it's essential to delve into the intersection of NoSQL and blockchain technology. Blockchain, best known for its role in cryptocurrencies like Bitcoin, has far-reaching implications beyond digital currencies. Its core features—immutability, decentralized architecture, and cryptographic security—make it a promising candidate for enhancing various aspects of NoSQL databases and data management.

Blockchain as an Immutable Data Store:

One of the primary advantages of blockchain technology is its immutability. Once data is recorded on a blockchain, it becomes nearly impossible to alter or delete it. This feature aligns with the principles of data integrity, ensuring that historical records in NoSQL databases remain tamper-proof. Organizations can use blockchain as a secondary layer to validate and secure critical data, such as financial transactions and audit logs.

```
# Example of appending data to a blockchain-like structure in Python

import hashlib

import json

def create_block(data, previous_hash):

block = {

'data': data,

'previous_hash': previous_hash,

}
```

```
block['hash'] = hashlib.sha256(json.dumps(block, sort_keys=True).encode()).hexdigest()

return block
```

Decentralization and NoSQL:

Blockchain's decentralized architecture, achieved through a network of nodes, offers advantages in terms of fault tolerance and data availability. NoSQL databases can leverage decentralized networks to distribute data across multiple nodes or servers, enhancing data redundancy and fault tolerance. This approach is particularly valuable in scenarios where high availability and data reliability are critical, such as IoT and mission-critical applications.

Enhanced Security through Blockchain:

Blockchain's cryptographic mechanisms provide an extra layer of security for NoSQL databases. Access control, authentication, and data encryption can benefit from blockchain-based authentication and authorization mechanisms. For example, blockchain can be used to securely manage access permissions for database resources.

```
// Implementing access control through a blockchain-based smart contract

pragma solidity ^0.8.0;

contract AccessControl {

address public owner;

mapping(address => bool) public authorizedUsers;

constructor() {
```

```
owner = msg.sender;

}

modifier onlyOwner() {

require(msg.sender == owner, "Only the owner can perform this action.");

_;

}

function grantAccess(address user) public onlyOwner {

authorizedUsers[user] = true;

}

function revokeAccess(address user) public onlyOwner {

authorizedUsers[user] = false;

}

}
```

Blockchain for Audit Trails:

Blockchain's transparent and immutable ledger is well-suited for maintaining audit trails and compliance records. NoSQL databases can incorporate blockchain to record every change made to the database, creating an unforgeable record of data modifications. This is invaluable for industries with strict regulatory requirements, such as healthcare and finance.

Smart Contracts and Data Interactions:

Smart contracts, programmable scripts executed on a blockchain, can facilitate automated interactions between NoSQL databases and external systems. For instance, when specific conditions are met in a NoSQL database, a smart contract can trigger actions on a blockchain or vice versa. This interoperability enables complex data workflows and automation.

```
// Example of a simple smart contract for data interaction

pragma solidity ^0.8.0;

contract DataOracle {

string public data;

function setData(string memory _data) public {

data = _data;

}

}
```

Challenges and Considerations:

While the integration of blockchain and NoSQL databases holds promise, it also presents challenges. These include scalability issues, as blockchain networks may have limitations in handling large volumes of data and transactions. Additionally, the cost of blockchain transactions and the choice of an appropriate blockchain platform need careful consideration.

In conclusion, the convergence of NoSQL databases and blockchain technology opens up new possibilities for data management, security, and integrity. Organizations exploring this synergy should carefully assess their specific use cases, ensuring that the benefits of blockchain align with their data management requirements and objectives. As the field continues to evolve, we can expect innovative solutions and best practices to emerge, further enhancing the synergy between NoSQL and blockchain.

Section 19.3: New Challenges and Opportunities

As NoSQL databases continue to evolve and adapt to emerging trends and technologies, they also face new challenges and opportunities. In this section, we'll explore some of the key factors that will shape the future of NoSQL databases.

Data Privacy and Compliance:

With the increasing focus on data privacy regulations such as GDPR and CCPA, NoSQL databases will need to provide robust features for data anonymization, encryption, and compliance reporting. Organizations will need to adopt NoSQL solutions that align with these regulations and prioritize user data protection.

Multi-Model Databases:

The demand for multi-model databases that can handle different types of data models within a single database system is on the rise. NoSQL databases are well-suited to meet this demand, as they often support a wide range of data models, including document, key-value, graph, and column-family. The ability to work with multiple data models simplifies data integration and reduces the need for complex data transformations.

Serverless and Event-Driven Architectures:

Serverless computing and event-driven architectures are gaining popularity due to their scalability and cost-effectiveness. NoSQL databases are a natural fit for these architectures, as they can seamlessly handle the variable workloads and data processing requirements of event-driven applications. Expect to see more integration between NoSQL databases and serverless platforms.

```
// Example of an AWS Lambda function using a NoSQL database

const AWS = require('aws-sdk');

const dynamoDB = new AWS.DynamoDB.DocumentClient();

exports.handler = async (event) => {

const params = {

TableName: 'MyTable',

Item: {

Key: 'Value',

},

};

await dynamoDB.put(params).promise();

const response = {

statusCode: 200,

body: JSON.stringify('Data added to NoSQL database'),

};
```

```
return response;

};
```

Edge Computing and NoSQL:

Edge computing, which involves processing data closer to the source of data generation, is driving the need for distributed and lightweight databases. NoSQL databases are well-suited for edge computing scenarios, as they can handle data from various sources and provide low-latency access. This trend is particularly relevant in IoT and real-time analytics applications.

AI and Machine Learning Integration:

The integration of AI and machine learning with NoSQL databases is expected to grow. NoSQL databases can store and process large volumes of unstructured and semi-structured data, making them ideal for training and deploying machine learning models. Expect to see more tools and libraries that facilitate this integration.

```
# Example of using a NoSQL database for machine learning data storage

import pymongo

client = pymongo.MongoClient("mongodb://localhost:27017/")

db = client["mydatabase"]

collection = db["mycollection"]

data = {

"features": [1.2, 2.3, 3.4, 4.5],
```

```
"label": "Category A",
}
collection.insert_one(data)
```

Data Governance and Metadata Management:

As data volumes grow, maintaining data governance and metadata management becomes crucial. NoSQL databases will need to provide features for data cataloging, lineage tracking, and data quality management. This is essential for ensuring that data remains reliable and well-documented.

Decentralized and Blockchain Integration:

As discussed in earlier sections, the integration of NoSQL databases with blockchain technology presents opportunities for enhancing data security and transparency. Organizations will explore how blockchain can be applied to NoSQL databases in a variety of use cases, including supply chain management, healthcare, and finance.

Hybrid and Multi-Cloud Deployments:

The flexibility of NoSQL databases makes them suitable for hybrid and multi-cloud deployments. Organizations will continue to adopt strategies that leverage multiple cloud providers and on-premises infrastructure. NoSQL databases will play a key role in ensuring data consistency and availability in these complex environments.

In summary, the future of NoSQL databases is characterized by adaptability and integration with emerging technologies. While challenges such as data privacy and compliance will need to be addressed, NoSQL databases are poised to play a central role in enabling modern data-driven applications and architectures. Organizations that leverage the strengths of NoSQL databases while staying attuned to these trends will be well-positioned for success in the evolving data landscape.

Section 19.4: Predictions for the Future of NoSQL

As we look ahead to the future of NoSQL databases, it's important to consider the trends and predictions that will shape the landscape of data management and storage. While we cannot predict the future with certainty, we can identify several key areas that are likely to influence the development and adoption of NoSQL databases.

1. Continued Diversification of NoSQL Databases:

The NoSQL ecosystem will likely continue to diversify, with the emergence of specialized databases tailored to specific use cases. We can expect to see databases optimized for time-series data, geospatial data, and more. This diversification will provide developers with more options for choosing the right database for their specific needs.

2. Integration with AI and Machine Learning:

As AI and machine learning become increasingly integral to business operations, NoSQL databases will evolve to better support these technologies. This includes improved integration with popular machine learning frameworks and enhanced capabilities for storing and processing large volumes of training data.

3. Enhanced Real-Time Data Processing:

Real-time data processing is a critical requirement for modern applications, particularly in sectors like finance, IoT, and e-commerce. NoSQL databases will continue to enhance their real-time data processing capabilities, enabling applications to react to events as they occur.

```
// Example of real-time data processing with a NoSQL database
const eventHandler = (event) => {
// Process the event data
// Update the database in real-time
// Trigger further actions or notifications
};
```

4. Improved Scalability and Performance:

Scalability will remain a key focus for NoSQL databases. As data volumes grow, databases will need to scale horizontally to handle increased workloads. Additionally, performance optimization will continue to be a priority, ensuring that NoSQL databases deliver low-latency responses even under heavy loads.

5. Integration with Cloud-Native Technologies:

NoSQL databases will increasingly integrate with cloud-native technologies such as Kubernetes, Docker, and serverless platforms. This will make it easier to deploy and manage NoSQL databases in cloud environments, further promoting the adoption of cloud-native architectures.

6. Enhanced Security Features:

With cybersecurity threats on the rise, NoSQL databases will invest in enhanced security features. This includes improvements in data encryption, access control, and auditing capabilities. Compliance with data protection regulations will also drive security enhancements.

7. Blockchain Integration for Data Integrity:

The use of blockchain technology to ensure data integrity and transparency will gain traction. NoSQL databases will explore ways to integrate blockchain for applications requiring immutable and auditable data storage.

8. Data Mesh and Federated Architectures:

Data mesh, a concept focused on decentralizing data ownership and access, will influence the design of NoSQL databases. We can expect to see databases that support federated architectures, enabling organizations to manage data across various domains.

9. Emphasis on Developer Productivity:

NoSQL databases will continue to prioritize developer-friendly features. This includes improved query languages, development tools, and documentation. The goal is to make it easier for developers to work with NoSQL databases and build applications quickly.

10. Increased Adoption in Regulated Industries:

Regulated industries such as healthcare and finance will increasingly adopt NoSQL databases as these databases enhance data security and compliance capabilities. NoSQL databases will need to cater to the unique requirements of these sectors.

In conclusion, the future of NoSQL databases is shaped by a combination of evolving technology trends and the ever-changing needs of businesses and developers. While NoSQL databases have already proven their value in addressing modern data challenges, their continued growth and adaptation to emerging technologies will ensure their relevance in the years to come. Organizations that stay informed about these trends and incorporate NoSQL databases into their data strategies will be well-positioned for success in the dynamic world of data management.

Section 19.5: Preparing for the Next Wave in Database Technology

As we near the conclusion of this book, it's important to reflect on the dynamic nature of the database technology landscape and how it continues to evolve. Preparing for the next wave in database technology involves staying informed, embracing change, and adopting strategies that ensure your organization remains agile and competitive in the digital era.

1. Continuous Learning and Skill Development:

The pace of technological change demands that IT professionals and data engineers invest in continuous learning. Whether you are a seasoned database administrator or a developer just starting in the field, keeping your skills up-to-date is essential. Attend industry conferences, enroll in online courses, and engage with communities to stay current.

2. Embrace Hybrid and Multi-Cloud Environments:

Hybrid and multi-cloud environments are becoming the norm for many organizations. Embrace these architectures as they offer flexibility, redundancy, and cost optimization. Consider strategies for data portability and interoperability between cloud providers to avoid vendor lock-in.

3. Evolve Data Governance and Compliance Practices:

Data governance and compliance will remain critical concerns. Stay informed about data protection regulations and implement robust data governance practices. Ensure your databases are compliant with GDPR, HIPAA, CCPA, or other relevant regulations depending on your industry and geographical reach.

4. Evaluate Emerging Technologies:

Keep a close eye on emerging database technologies, including those beyond NoSQL. Explore innovations like NewSQL databases, which aim to combine the best of both SQL and NoSQL worlds. Evaluate how these technologies can address your organization's specific requirements.

—Example of using a NewSQL database

SELECT customer_name, SUM(order_total)

FROM orders

GROUP BY customer_name

HAVING SUM(order_total) > 1000;

5. Foster Collaboration Between IT and Business Units:

Effective communication and collaboration between IT teams and business units are paramount. Understand the needs and objectives of various departments within your organization. IT should align its strategies with business goals to drive innovation and growth.

6. Invest in Data Security and Privacy:

Cybersecurity threats continue to evolve, making data security and privacy top priorities. Allocate resources to invest in robust cybersecurity measures, encryption, and access controls. Develop an incident response plan to mitigate data breaches effectively.

7. Embrace Automation and DevOps Practices:

Automation and DevOps practices streamline database management and application deployment. Implement automation for routine tasks, version control, and continuous integration/ continuous deployment (CI/CD) pipelines. This accelerates development and reduces errors.

 # Example of a CI/CD pipeline configuration for database deployments

stages:

- build

- test

- deploy

8. Foster a Culture of Innovation:

Encourage innovation within your organization. Create an environment where teams are encouraged to experiment with new technologies and approaches. Innovation often leads to breakthroughs in data management and application development.

9. Stay Customer-Centric:

Ultimately, the success of your database strategies depends on delivering value to customers. Continuously gather feedback, monitor user behavior, and iterate on your applications and databases to ensure they meet customer expectations.

10. Network and Collaborate:

Engage with the broader database and technology community. Attend meetups, webinars, and conferences. Collaborate with peers, share experiences, and learn from others in the field. Building a professional network can provide valuable insights and opportunities.

In conclusion, preparing for the next wave in database technology involves a combination of technical readiness, adaptability, and a forward-thinking approach. By staying informed about emerging trends, embracing change, and fostering a culture of innovation, you can position your organization for success in an ever-evolving digital landscape. The journey in database technology is ongoing, and those who approach it with curiosity and a willingness to evolve will thrive in the years to come.

Chapter 20: Conclusion and Further Resources

Section 20.1: Summarizing NoSQL Essentials

In this final chapter of our book, we wrap up our journey through the world of NoSQL databases. Throughout this comprehensive guide, we've explored various aspects of NoSQL, from its fundamentals to its applications in cutting-edge technologies. This section provides a summary of the key takeaways and insights gained from each chapter.

Chapter 1: Introduction to NoSQL

We began by introducing NoSQL databases and their role in modern data management. We discussed the key characteristics that differentiate NoSQL databases from traditional SQL databases and explored their advantages and use cases.

Chapter 2: NoSQL Database Types

In Chapter 2, we delved into the different types of NoSQL databases, including document-oriented databases, key-value stores, column-family stores, and graph databases. We also offered guidance on choosing the right type of NoSQL database for specific use cases.

Chapter 3: Core Concepts in NoSQL

Chapter 3 focused on core concepts in NoSQL, such as data modeling, schemas, indexing, and the CAP theorem. We explained how these concepts impact the design and functionality of NoSQL databases.

Chapter 4: Implementing NoSQL Solutions

In Chapter 4, we provided practical insights into setting up, performing CRUD operations, querying, and migrating data in NoSQL databases. Best practices for NoSQL implementation were also discussed.

Chapter 5: NoSQL and Big Data

We explored the intersection of NoSQL and big data in Chapter 5. Topics included handling large-scale data, real-time analytics, integration with big data technologies, and case studies showcasing NoSQL in big data applications.

Chapter 6: NoSQL and Scalability

Chapter 6 focused on scalability in NoSQL, explaining concepts like horizontal and vertical scaling, auto-scaling, and scalability challenges. We presented real-world case studies highlighting successful scalability solutions.

Chapter 7: NoSQL and Security

Security in NoSQL databases was the central theme of Chapter 7. We addressed security challenges, data encryption, access control, auditing, and best practices for securing NoSQL environments.

Chapter 8: Performance Tuning in NoSQL

Chapter 8 provided insights into performance analysis and optimization techniques for NoSQL databases. Topics covered included caching mechanisms, balancing read and write speeds, and monitoring and maintenance.

Chapter 9: NoSQL in the Cloud

We discussed the benefits and strategies of using NoSQL in the cloud in Chapter 9. This chapter covered cloud-based NoSQL services, choosing cloud providers, migration strategies, and managing NoSQL in cloud environments.

Chapter 10: NoSQL for Mobile and Web Applications

Chapter 10 focused on the application of NoSQL databases in mobile and web development. We explored real-time data synchronization, offline data handling, and presented case studies of successful NoSQL implementations.

Chapter 11: Advanced Querying in NoSQL

In Chapter 11, we delved into advanced querying techniques in NoSQL, including complex queries, aggregation frameworks, MapReduce, query optimization, and working with unstructured data.

Chapter 12: NoSQL Data Replication and Distribution

Chapter 12 discussed data replication principles, data distribution strategies, data consistency, conflict resolution, and geo-distributed NoSQL deployments.

Chapter 13: Transitioning from SQL to NoSQL

We compared SQL and NoSQL databases in Chapter 13, discussing decision factors for migration, migration planning, data conversion challenges, and post-migration evaluation.

Chapter 14: NoSQL in Enterprise Applications

Chapter 14 explored the role of NoSQL in enterprise applications. Topics included integrating NoSQL with existing systems, data warehousing, handling transactional data, and case studies of successful enterprise NoSQL implementations.

Chapter 15: NoSQL and the Internet of Things (IoT)

We examined the intersection of NoSQL and IoT in Chapter 15. Topics included real-time data processing, device management, data storage and retrieval challenges, and case studies of IoT implementations using NoSQL.

Chapter 16: Open Source NoSQL Databases

Chapter 16 introduced open-source NoSQL databases, including their benefits, community support, customization, and popular open-source options.

Chapter 17: NoSQL and Artificial Intelligence

In Chapter 17, we explored the applications of NoSQL in artificial intelligence, including machine learning data management, predictive analytics, and real-time decision-making.

Chapter 18: NoSQL Database Administration

Chapter 18 discussed the roles and responsibilities of NoSQL database administrators, backup and recovery strategies, performance monitoring and tuning, scaling and clustering management, and disaster recovery planning.

Chapter 19: Future Trends in NoSQL

We concluded our chapters with a look at future trends in NoSQL databases. Topics included emerging technologies, NoSQL's relationship with blockchain, new challenges and opportunities, predictions for the future, and preparing for the next wave in database technology.

Section 20.2: Lessons Learned and Key Takeaways

Our journey through the world of NoSQL has provided valuable insights and knowledge. Here are some key takeaways:

- NoSQL databases offer flexibility, scalability, and performance advantages for modern data management.

- Choosing the right type of NoSQL database depends on the specific requirements of your application.

- Data modeling, indexing, and schema design are essential for optimizing NoSQL database performance.

- NoSQL databases are well-suited for big data applications, real-time analytics, and IoT solutions.

- Security, data governance, and compliance are critical aspects of NoSQL database management.

- Continuous learning and adaptation are essential in the evolving field of database technology.

- Open-source NoSQL databases provide cost-effective and customizable solutions.

Section 20.3: Further Reading and Resources

For those eager to delve deeper into NoSQL databases and related technologies, we recommend the following resources:

- Books: Explore more specialized books on NoSQL databases, big data, cloud computing, and database administration.

- Online Courses: Enroll in online courses and certifications to enhance your skills in NoSQL and related fields.

- Conferences: Attend industry conferences and webinars to stay updated on the latest trends and technologies.

- Documentation: Refer to official documentation for specific NoSQL database systems for in-depth information.

- Community: Join online communities, forums, and discussion groups to connect with experts and peers.

Section 20.4: The Future Landscape of Databases

The database technology landscape continues to evolve rapidly. As we look to the future, we anticipate:

- Continued innovation in NoSQL databases, addressing new use cases and challenges.

- Integration of NoSQL with emerging technologies like AI, blockchain, and edge computing.

- Enhanced security and privacy features in response to evolving cybersecurity threats.

- Greater adoption of serverless computing and microservices architectures.

- A shift towards more sustainable and eco-friendly database solutions.

Section 20.5: Final Thoughts and Encouragement for Continued Learning

We conclude this book with the encouragement to embrace the dynamic world of database technology. Stay curious, keep learning, and adapt to the changes that lie ahead. As you explore NoSQL databases and their applications, remember that the journey is ongoing, and there are always new discoveries to be made in the ever-evolving landscape of data management.

Thank you for joining us on this journey through NoSQL, and we wish you continued success in your endeavors in the world of data and databases.

Section 20.2: Lessons Learned and Key Takeaways

Our exploration of NoSQL databases has provided valuable lessons and key takeaways for both beginners and experienced professionals in the field of data management. Let's summarize the most significant points we've covered in this book.

1. Flexibility and Scalability

One of the fundamental advantages of NoSQL databases is their flexibility. They allow you to store and manage a wide variety of data types, making them suitable for applications with evolving data requirements. Additionally, NoSQL databases offer excellent scalability, enabling you to handle growing amounts of data and traffic efficiently.

2. Choosing the Right NoSQL Database

Selecting the appropriate type of NoSQL database for your application is crucial. Document-oriented databases like MongoDB excel at handling semi-structured data, while key-value stores such as Redis are great for caching and fast data retrieval. Understanding the strengths and weaknesses of each type is essential to make an informed decision.

3. Data Modeling and Indexing

Proper data modeling and indexing are key to optimizing NoSQL database performance. Designing your data schema to match your query patterns and efficiently using indexes can significantly impact your application's responsiveness.

4. NoSQL in Big Data and IoT

NoSQL databases play a critical role in handling large-scale data in the era of big data and the Internet of Things (IoT). They can efficiently manage real-time data streams, making them suitable for applications that require instant insights from massive data volumes.

5. Security and Compliance

Securing your NoSQL databases is essential to protect sensitive data. Implement data encryption, access control, and auditing mechanisms to ensure data confidentiality and compliance with industry regulations.

6. Continuous Learning

The field of database technology is continually evolving. Staying updated with the latest trends, tools, and best practices is essential for database professionals. Embrace a culture of continuous learning to remain competitive in the industry.

7. Open Source Options

Open-source NoSQL databases provide cost-effective solutions with the flexibility to customize and extend their functionality. Many popular open-source NoSQL databases have active communities that contribute to their development and support.

These lessons and takeaways form a foundation for successfully working with NoSQL databases. As you apply these principles in your projects and adapt to the ever-changing landscape of database technology, you'll be well-equipped to harness the power of NoSQL for your data management needs.

Section 20.3: Further Reading and Resources

To deepen your knowledge of NoSQL databases and related topics, you can explore a wide range of resources, books, websites, and courses. Here, we provide some recommendations to help you continue your learning journey:

1. Books

- "NoSQL Distilled: A Brief Guide to the Emerging World of Polyglot Persistence" by Pramod J. Sadalage and Martin Fowler: This book provides a concise introduction to various NoSQL database types and their use cases.

- "MongoDB: The Definitive Guide" by Kristina Chodorow and Michael Dirolf: If you're interested in MongoDB, this comprehensive guide covers everything from basic concepts to advanced techniques.

- "Cassandra: The Definitive Guide" by Eben Hewitt: Learn about Apache Cassandra, a popular distributed NoSQL database, through this definitive guide.

2. Online Courses

- Coursera: Platforms like Coursera offer courses on NoSQL databases and related topics, often taught by experts from top universities.

- edX: Explore courses on database management systems, distributed systems, and big data technologies on edX.

3. Documentation and Official Websites

- MongoDB Official Documentation: The MongoDB website provides extensive documentation, tutorials, and resources for users of this popular document-oriented database.

- Cassandra Official Documentation: If you're working with Apache Cassandra, the official documentation is a valuable resource for understanding its features and best practices.

4. Community and Forums

- Stack Overflow: Join the NoSQL community on Stack Overflow to ask questions, share knowledge, and learn from experienced developers.

- Reddit NoSQL Subreddit: Reddit has a NoSQL subreddit where you can engage in discussions and find relevant news and resources.

5. Blogs and Websites

- Medium: Many professionals and experts share their insights on NoSQL databases and related topics through Medium articles.

- DZone: Explore the "NoSQL Zone" on DZone for articles, tutorials, and news about NoSQL databases and technologies.

6. Conferences and Meetups

- Attend industry conferences and meetups related to databases, big data, and NoSQL technologies to network and gain insights from experts.

7. Online Communities

- Join online communities and discussion groups focused on NoSQL databases, such as the NoSQL LinkedIn group, to connect with like-minded professionals.

Remember that the field of NoSQL databases is dynamic, with new technologies and techniques emerging regularly. Staying up-to-date with the latest trends and best practices is essential for successfully working with NoSQL databases and related technologies.

Section 20.4: Predictions for the Future of NoSQL

As we look ahead, it's clear that NoSQL databases will continue to play a significant role in the world of data management. Several trends and predictions shape the future of NoSQL:

1. Multi-Model Databases

One notable trend is the rise of multi-model databases. These databases allow developers to work with different data models (e.g., document, key-value, graph) within a single database system. This flexibility simplifies data management, enabling organizations to choose the most suitable data model for specific use cases while reducing data silos.

2. Serverless and Managed Services

The adoption of serverless computing and managed database services is expected to grow. Organizations will increasingly rely on cloud providers to manage their NoSQL databases, allowing them to focus on application development rather than database administration. This trend simplifies scaling, maintenance, and high availability.

3. Real-Time Data Processing

Real-time data processing will become even more crucial in various industries, such as IoT, finance, and e-commerce. NoSQL databases, with their ability to handle large volumes of data and provide low-latency access, will continue to be a foundational technology for real-time applications.

4. Advanced Analytics and Machine Learning Integration

NoSQL databases will integrate more closely with advanced analytics and machine learning frameworks. This will enable organizations to derive valuable insights from their data, automate decision-making processes, and build intelligent applications.

5. Security and Compliance

Security and compliance features will evolve to meet increasingly stringent requirements. NoSQL databases will continue to enhance data encryption, access control, and auditing capabilities to protect sensitive data and meet regulatory standards like GDPR and HIPAA.

6. Blockchain and NoSQL

The intersection of blockchain and NoSQL is an exciting area to watch. NoSQL databases can serve as the backend for blockchain applications, providing efficient data storage and retrieval. This synergy could lead to innovative solutions in various domains, including supply chain management and identity verification.

7. Graph Databases for Complex Relationships

Graph databases will gain prominence for modeling and querying complex relationships. They are well-suited for applications like social networks, fraud detection, and recommendation engines, where understanding intricate connections is critical.

8. Polyglot Persistence

Polyglot persistence, the practice of using multiple database technologies within a single application, will become more prevalent. Organizations will choose the best-suited databases for specific tasks, leading to a diverse database landscape.

9. Containerization and Orchestration

The use of containerization (e.g., Docker) and orchestration platforms (e.g., Kubernetes) will simplify the deployment and management of NoSQL databases, making it easier to scale and maintain distributed systems.

10. Edge Computing and NoSQL

Edge computing, which involves processing data closer to its source, will drive the demand for NoSQL databases at the edge. These databases will empower applications in remote and resource-constrained environments.

In conclusion, NoSQL databases will continue to evolve and adapt to the changing landscape of data management and application development. Staying informed about these trends and embracing new technologies will be crucial for organizations aiming to harness the full potential of NoSQL databases in the future.

Section 20.5: Final Thoughts and Encouragement for Continued Learning

As we conclude this journey through the world of NoSQL databases, it's essential to reflect on the key takeaways and encourage you to continue your learning and exploration in this ever-evolving field.

Embracing Flexibility

NoSQL databases offer a flexible and scalable approach to data management. They empower developers to design applications that can adapt to changing requirements and handle diverse data types. By embracing NoSQL, you've gained a valuable tool for addressing modern data challenges.

Diversity of Use Cases

Throughout this book, we've explored a wide range of use cases for NoSQL databases, from handling large volumes of unstructured data to powering real-time analytics and IoT applications. Remember that the choice of database should align with your specific application requirements.

Continuous Learning

The world of NoSQL databases is dynamic, with new technologies, features, and best practices emerging regularly. To stay competitive and make the most of NoSQL, commit to continuous learning. Engage with the community, attend conferences, read blogs, and explore hands-on projects.

Experimentation and Innovation

Don't be afraid to experiment with different NoSQL databases and data models. Innovation often comes from exploring new approaches and challenging the status quo. Try out graph databases for modeling relationships, document databases for flexibility, or key-value stores for simplicity.

Integration with Other Technologies

NoSQL databases are rarely used in isolation. They often form part of a broader technology stack, integrating with application frameworks, cloud services, and analytics platforms. Understand how NoSQL fits into your ecosystem and explore integration possibilities.

Data Privacy and Security

With data breaches becoming increasingly common, prioritize data privacy and security. Implement encryption, access controls, and auditing features to protect sensitive information. Compliance with regulations like GDPR and HIPAA is essential for many organizations.

Scalability and Performance

Scalability is a core strength of NoSQL databases. Learn how to scale horizontally to meet growing demands. Monitor performance regularly and optimize your database design and queries for efficiency.

Community and Collaboration

The NoSQL community is vibrant and collaborative. Engage with peers, join forums, and contribute to open-source projects if possible. Sharing knowledge and experiences benefits the entire community.

Diverse Career Opportunities

Proficiency in NoSQL databases opens doors to diverse career opportunities. Whether you're a developer, data engineer, database administrator, or data scientist, NoSQL skills are in demand across industries.

Inspiration from Success Stories

Throughout this book, we've highlighted case studies showcasing successful NoSQL implementations. Draw inspiration from these stories as you embark on your NoSQL journey.

In conclusion, the world of NoSQL databases offers exciting opportunities and challenges. It's a field where innovation is rewarded, and adaptability is essential. As technology continues to advance, NoSQL databases will play a pivotal role in shaping the future of data management and application development.

Remember that learning is a lifelong journey. Stay curious, stay passionate, and keep exploring the possibilities that NoSQL databases offer. Whether you're a seasoned professional or just starting, your commitment to mastering NoSQL will undoubtedly contribute to your success and the success of the projects you undertake. Happy learning!

www.ingramcontent.com/pod-product-compliance
Lightning Source LLC
LaVergne TN
LVHW090303210926
848480LV00001B/111
9798223209027